RECEPTION AND PERCEPTION OF EUROPEAN HORROR CINEMA

Patricia Allmer, Emily Brick and David Huxley

Horror fans tend to be treated differently from mainstream cinema audiences, or as Andrew Tudor puts it, 'a taste for horror is a taste for something seemingly abnormal and is therefore deemed to require special attention' (1997: 446). Matt Hills also argues that 'work on the pleasures of horror seems to have unwittingly adopted media discourses surrounding horror via its willingness to view horror's pleasures as a puzzle, conundrum or a "problem" which is in need for further study' (2005: 3). Approaches to the field of horror reception generally form four broad groups: psychoanalytic models of spectatorship, empirical audience studies, critical reaction (media and academic) and institutional surveillance for the purposes of censorship. Psychoanalytic models are, by their nature, ahistorical, and 'visual pleasure', whether conscious or unconscious, is not the same thing as socialised horror viewing. The significance of the nationality and location of the audience or even the nationality of the films being consumed is not something that has been foregrounded in studies of horror reception. In order to establish the importance of place, the essays in this section focus on the empirical audience, critical reception and institutional surveillance in examining the reception of European horror films and the consumption of horror by European audiences.

Peter Hutchings' chapter investigates the extent to which certain horror films, in particular *Resident Evil* (Paul W. S. Anderson, 2002) and *Suspiria* (Dario Argento, 1977), may be perceived by their audiences as being part of a European horror tradition, and thus addresses the complexities of defining European horror cinema. *Resident Evil* is a film not only co-produced by European companies, but also filmed in a Europe constructed in the film's *mise-en-scène* as a fictitious American city, so the film is perceived as an American product. Hutchings suggests, by proposing 'Eurohorror' as an umbrella term, that the fascination of European horror consists not in a cohesive totality, but precisely in the absence of this totality; European horror consists instead, he argues, of a variety of different practices with 'no geographical centre and no core identity'.

Resident Evil is a breed of horror film which also addresses the increasingly important market of video game players. Horror films now have a symbiotic relationship with video games, on the most obvious level through the adaptation of games such as *Resident Evil* but also at an aesthetic level through the development of CGI technology. European cinema has not embraced this aesthetic in the same way that American horror has, largely for reasons of cost. Increasingly, as different forms of media become more intertextual, film audiences cross over with video game players, and horror is the most prominent site of this intertext.[1] Video games also have similarities with horror film in being the subject of moral panics over violent content and the effects upon audiences.

Psychoanalytic models of spectatorship concerned with gender and sexuality have dominated studies of horror film spectators. Brigid Cherry has addressed the absence of a socialised audience and examined the tastes and viewing pleasures of actual horror audiences (1999; 2007). Her chapter here, 'Beyond *Suspiria*: The place of European Horror Cinema in the Fan Canon', is based on empirical study and discourse analysis, and examines the reception of European horror films within online fan communities. She focuses on the fan discourses and reception of *Suspiria* as the most popular European film among her subjects. For these audiences (primarily British and American) European films and directors have a particular status because of their 'exotic' national origins. A knowledge of, and liking for, European horror cinema marks fans as having more 'élite' tastes within an overall fan canon and the sub-groups of this fan culture.

Horror consumption and reception are also heavily influenced by horror production and distribution. The institutional gaze on horror, along with pornography, affects its aesthetics perhaps more than any other genre. Each country in Europe has different forms of censorship, and in a genre which can rely on explicit violence and sex, this produces a fragmented aesthetic. What is freely available for one audience within Europe may be banned for another, and state control over the production and consumption of texts was obviously particularly acute in Eastern Europe during the Communist era. Even within individual countries distribution and access is not equal. In the UK what may be shown in one council borough may be banned in another.

Russ Hunter and Ernest Mathijs's chapter on Belgian horror cinema looks at why Belgian film critics refuse to call horror films by that nomenclature although audiences outside Belgium will recognise these same texts as clearly belonging to the horror genre. The critical (rather than academic or fan) reception of a number of Belgian horror films discussed in this chapter highlights the fact that the notion of what constitutes a text as 'horror' is subjective and dependent on national and ideological constructions.

David Huxley's chapter on moral panics in relation to British and mainland European horror cinema examines how this institutional gaze affects the aesthetics of the films and the relationship between reception and critical reaction. He examines the ways in which this critical reaction has varied substantially between different sources, and also how the reaction has changed quite dramatically during a comparatively short period of time. This highlights the way in which the groundwork for the critical recuperation, both of studios such as Hammer and of European 'auteurs' such as Mario Bava, was already in place very soon after the height of their critical opprobrium.

Overall the essays in this section demonstrate problems of definition not only of horror itself but also of national and European cinemas in the post-war period. In doing so they also highlight the sheer breadth and complexity of the reception of the films under consideration.

NOTE

1   Although the design, production and distribution of the games is primarily Japanese and American, European landscape and history is used as the setting in many survival horror games: *Resident Evil 4* (2005, Capcom) is set in a Mediterranean village, *Resistance: Fall of Man* (1999, Insomniac Games) is set in Manchester Cathedral and the *mise-en-scène* of *Half Life 2* (2004, Valve Corporation) was inspired by old and new Eastern European architecture.

BIBLIOGRAPHY

Cherry, B. (2007) 'Subcultural Tastes, Genre Boundaries and Fan Canons', in M. Jancovich and L. Geraghty (eds) *Generic Canons: Genre, History, Memory*. Jefferson, NC: McFarland, pp. 201–15.

_____ (1999) 'Refusing to Refuse to Look: Female Viewers of the Horror Film', in R. Maltby and M. Stokes (eds) *Identifying Hollywood Audiences: Cultural Identity and the Movies*. London: British Film Institute, 187–203.

Hills, M. (2005) *The Pleasures of Horror*. London: Continuum.

Tudor, A. (1997) 'Why Horror?: The Peculiar Pleasures of a Popular Genre', *Cultural Studies*, 11: 3, 443–63.

RESIDENT EVIL?
THE LIMITS OF EUROPEAN HORROR: *RESIDENT EVIL* VERSUS *SUSPIRIA*

Peter Hutchings

What is a European horror film? The simple and obvious answer – simple and obvious to the point of banality – is that it is a horror film made in Europe. However, the reality of 'Eurohorror' as a distinct cinematic category turns out to be both more complex and more elusive than this apparently commonsensical definition might suggest.

Take *Resident Evil* (2002), for instance. This zombie-action thriller American-British-French-German co-production undoubtedly contained pronounced elements of horror and it was filmed mainly in Europe (in Germany to be precise, with a few scenes shot in Canada), and its cast and crew contained numerous Europeans. Yet it has not really been perceived or discussed as a European horror film by critics or by horror fans. For example, a recent article exploring the fan response to *Resident Evil* does not raise the film's potential 'European' identity at all (Lay 2007). This might have something to do with its setting (a fictitious American city) or its source material (a Japanese computer game), or the way in which it can in various ways be placed within an American horror idiom (with noted American horror director George Romero providing an early – if ultimately rejected – screenplay for the film). It might also be connected with the fact that many of the key

European creative figures involved in the film have international professional profiles. For example, Paul W. S. Anderson, *Resident Evil*'s writer-director, is British but associated mainly with Hollywood productions such as *Event Horizon* (1997), *Soldier* (1998) and *AVP: Alien versus Predator* (2004) (although, ironically, some of these had international financing and were shot partly or wholly in Europe). Bernd Eichinger, one of *Resident Evil*'s producers, has an extensive CV including both German- and English-language films, with the latter including what might appear to be the quintessentially American *Fantastic Four* (2005) and its sequel *Fantastic Four: Rise of the Silver Surfer* (2007), while Milla Jovovich, *Resident Evil*'s star, might be Ukrainian-born but, in career terms at least, is thoroughly international, with appearances in both American and European productions.

Perhaps more significant so far as *Resident Evil*'s apparent lack of Eurohorror credentials is concerned is its marked reliance on a type of narrative-driven cinema associated mainly with US genre product. (In this respect, the fact that *Resident Evil*'s two sequels were mainly filmed, respectively, in Canada and Mexico does seem to underline the original's apparent lack of connection with its European production context.) As one might expect, *Resident Evil* contains plenty of moments of generically motivated excess involving violence and/or gore along with some of the martial arts action that was internationally fashionable at the time of its production, but this is all wrapped up in a fast-moving narrative in which the main protagonists repeatedly and dynamically make life or death decisions and act upon these.

By contrast, *Suspiria* (1977), an Italian supernatural drama dealing with witchcraft in a sinister ballet school, is often seen as an exemplar of Eurohorror. Like *Resident Evil*, it is excessive but here the excess seems to entail a more forceful retardation of a narrative drive, to the extent that the narrative periodically ceases to exist. It is certainly the case that *Suspiria*'s narrative is considerably more attenuated than that of *Resident Evil* and its characterisations more perfunctory; instead the film is structured around a series of spectacular set pieces that combine displays of extreme terror and violence with some truly virtuoso stylistics. The fact that *Suspiria* was directed by Dario Argento further underlines its status as a classic Eurohorror inasmuch as Argento himself has often been presented, by critics and devoted fans, as a filmmaker whose entire career has offered a sustained commitment to, and excellence within, this particular area of European culture. (For a discussion of this, see Hutchings 2003.)

Having noted this, *Suspiria*, like *Resident Evil*, has an international dimension to it, manifested most obviously in the presence of an American actor, Jessica Harper, in the leading role. But the international elements so successfully integrated into a seamless whole in *Resident Evil* are in *Suspiria* visibly and roughly hewn together. The dubbing of certain actors is all too obvious – and presumably this would also have been the case for the Italian-language version where Jessica Harper would have been dubbed – and the use of music too eccentric and the diminution of narrative too obtrusive, thereby rendering a potential pandering to the American market awkward and unconvincing, just as Argento's career outside of his native Italy has exhibited an ungainly quality (although *Suspiria* did turn out to be the only one of Argento's films to be commercially successful in the United States).

It might seem from this that the identity of Eurohorror resides precisely in its visible difference from what is perceived as the American commercial mainstream. The more a film looks American (as *Resident Evil* might look American), the less value it has as an example of Eurohorror. Such a strategy for finding both a distinctiveness and positive cultural value in a perceived distance from a Hollywood aesthetic and ethos has, of course, been deployed in relation to other sectors of European film production as well, with such sectors figured as characteristically or even uniquely European or more specifically as part of a particular national cinema within Europe. However, these critically valorised areas of cinema tend to be culturally up-market – heritage films, for example, or 'art' films – while horror as a genre is generally positioned lower down the cultural hierarchy. It is perhaps not surprising then that 'Eurohorror' actually exists both as a critical and as a specialised subcultural category, knowledge and discussion of which circulates among a relatively small (although growing) band of critics and fans, and that often underpinning its use is an attachment to a particular set of attitudes about cultural value that has its own distinct history.

It can in fact be argued that when a small band of Eurohorrorphiles (and I include myself here) speak of European horror cinema, we are not just referring to a group of films but also, with varying degrees of explicitness, referring to a history of our own fascination with these films, a history that to all intents and purposes begins in the 1980s. A case can be made that 'European horror' as a meaningful cinematic category does not really exist before then. Of course, I do not mean by this that films we now think of as European horror were not being made before the 1980s. However, what are now perceived as Eurohorror classics – including films such *La maschera del demonio/The Mask of Satan* (Mario Bava, 1960), *Il mulino delle donne di pietra/Mill of the Stone Women* (Giorgio Ferroni, 1960), *Gritos en la noche/The Awful Dr. Orloff* (Jesus Franco, 1962), or, for that matter, *Suspiria* – were not generally marketed as European horror films nor generally perceived as such (critically at least); instead they were just horror films or, possibly, Italian (or Spanish or British or whatever) horror films. The idea implicit in the category 'European horror' that there is a group of films that in various ways share an identity that separates them out from Hollywood horror (and which also, incidentally, cuts across national borders within Europe) is constructed at a later date, and in its formation is shaped, and in part defined, by significant changes in the way that films circulated and were seen by audiences, changes that took place during the 1980s. As Rick Altman (1999) has noted, this kind of redesignation of films' identities is not some aberrant activity carried out on the margins of cinema but instead is an integral part of an ongoing process of genre formation, with the industry, critics and increasingly fans all contributing to this. In the case of horror, for example, a number of films not thought of as horror on their original release are now widely accepted as horror films (and other films initially marketed as horror are now thought of in different ways). There can be no doubt that this particular formation of 'European horror' has proved productive (although, as we will see, the nature of this productivity is sometimes surprising). Nevertheless, it is here, in this formation, that limitations and omissions are becoming increasingly apparent as the context within which it was evolved fades away, and other possibilities for thinking about the identity of European horror present themselves.

THE 'OLD' EUROHORROR

In order to pin down as precisely as possible the evolution of Eurohorror as a particular critical concept, it is helpful to go back to the 1980s and 1990s. One might go back further and find some 1970s cultish writings on Italian horror cinema that see it as special and different from the horror norm in a manner that anticipates the later 'Eurohorror' designation, or further back yet to some surrealist writings on film that offer comparable evaluations of low-cultural cinematic experiences. But the more organised and substantial discourses appear later, and in their formation they are inextricably bound up with the burgeoning popularity of home video technology during the 1980s, to the extent that the concept of European horror as we understand it today might be seen, in part at least, as a video-based concept. The impact of video on horror in the 1980s, in Britain and elsewhere, was significant. Three key features are worth mentioning here.

Firstly, the sudden availability during the early 1980s of horror videos (often of European films) that had not been readily available before, either because of the vagaries of film distribution or because of censorship constraints. Secondly, state attempts to control this new market; this was most notably manifested in Britain by the 1984 Video Recordings Act (which marked the culmination of the 'video nasties' scare). Thirdly, the emergence of fan cultures based around the obtaining, often nefariously, of banned, censored or just downright obscure horror videos. In Britain this kind of activity often involved anti-state posturings, but even in the United States, where the censorship restraints were less evident, subcultures of reception and interpretation based upon video emerged that, with varying degrees of explicitness, sought to critique or distance themselves from dominant cultures of consumption. (For a discussion of these, see Sconce 1995, Hawkins 2000 and Cherry, later in this volume).

Within such a context, European horrors (which did form a significant proportion of the banned or hard-to-see titles) acquired a special status. In effect, viewing uncut versions of these became the mark of how committed a horror fan you actually were. Not only did you in this way acquire a particular kind of subcultural or countercultural capital, you also got to thumb your nose at the repressive Thatcherite state – albeit from the relative safety of the private sphere opened up by video – while at the same time you distanced yourself from a popular entertainment market perceived as socially conformist and trivial, as opposed to the savage truth or wildness offered by video-based horror. Such a position sometimes led to an outright and rather crude rejection of social authority that had some decidedly adolescent qualities (unsurprisingly perhaps given the age of many of the fans involved) but it also facilitated an ambitious, and occasionally pretentious, reading strategy that sought to challenge what it perceived as normative standards and tastes.

One of the clearest expressions of such a strategy is provided by Cathal Tohill and Pete Tombs' book *Immoral Tales: Sex and Horror Cinema in Europe 1956–1984*, which was published in 1994 and which defines a European horror cinema that clearly has no place at all for a film like *Resident Evil*. *Immoral Tales* begins with a quote from Ado Kyrou's book *Le Surrealisme au Cinema*: 'I urge you: learn how to look at "bad" films, they are so often sublime', thus provocatively attaching ostensibly low-cultural products to an avant-garde tradition. The book's introduction continues,

> During the 1960s and 1970s, the European horror film went totally crazy. It began to go kinky – creating a new type of cinema that blended eroticism and terror. This heady fusion was highly successful, causing a tidal wave of celluloid weirdness that was destined to look even more shocking and irrational when it hit countries like England and the USA. (1994: 5)

Here one finds the expected distancing from American mainstream culture, along with a sense – again not uncommon in writings of this type – of the apparently awkward position of English cinema in the Eurohorror tradition, especially as the understanding of that tradition has been developed by English-speaking critics (with a recent collection of essays on European horror cinema not containing a single English film: see Schneider 2007).

As if to underline the exoticism of Eurohorror (for English speaking nations at least), Tohill and Tombs invoke the French term *'fantastique'* in a manner that clearly applies to *Suspiria* but probably not to *Resident Evil*. 'If it's *"fantastique"*, it has to be erotic, way out and fabulous. Linear narrative and logic are always ignored in a *"fantastique"* film. The pictorial, the excessive and the irrational are the privileged factors. If it does have a structure, it's the structure of a crazy dream' (ibid.). The authors go on to invoke surrealism and romanticism along with '20th century pulp-literature, filmed serials, creaky horror-movies and sexy comic-strips' as sources for the new erotic and fantastique Eurohorror films, which are then described as 'a curious hybrid, milking the dynamism of popular literature and comic books, combining it with the perverse romanticism of real Art' (ibid.). These are heady words; they conjure up a type of cinema embedded in broader European (or, to be more precise, continental Europe, with Great Britain excluded) cultural practices, a type of cinema that challenges established cultural distinctions and hierarchies, that is excessive and which – in true surrealist fashion – discovers its liberating power in the erotic. Significantly, Tohill and Tombs also point out that 'many of these films have resurfaced, uncut, on video' (ibid.). This reference to the uncut version is an important one, suggesting yet again a whole subculture devoted to tracking down the uncut version in the interests of truth, revelation and authenticity.

Interestingly, Tohill and Tombs do not make much of some of the major European horror auteurs, with Dario Argento, Mario Bava and Lucio Fulci, for example, only getting a few mentions in passing. However, other writers dealing with these directors have sometimes adopted a comparable terminology. Here is Stephen Thrower in *Beyond Terror: The Films of Lucio Fulci* on his first exposure to what came to be known as 'video nasties' in the early 1980s:

> This explosion of high gruesomeness, in a plethora of weird styles, was a welcome shock to the system. I would watch three or four films in a night (with friends at their VCR-equipped houses) before crashing into a brief hour or two's sleep. A line of speed, off to work, then out in the late afternoon to catch the next screening of whatever horror movie was being unspooled at the cinema. It was an exciting time to be a horror fan. (1999: 8)

And on seeing a double bill, at the cinema this time, of Fulci's *E tu vivrai nel terrore – L'aldilà/The Beyond* (1981) and Bava's *Schock/Shock* (1977): 'I had enough sense of the prevailing cultural norms to find these two Italian films immediately wild and disorientating' (ibid.).

What emerges from this is a compelling sense of a European horror cinema defined through marginality and resistance, defined precisely through its extreme difference from more readily available entertainments, as a space where the prevailing cultural norms were challenged or simply did not apply. This particular formation has subsequently inspired a good deal of academic work within what might be termed, for want of a better term, 'cult studies', an important aspect of which has sometimes been a self-reflexive interrogation of the uncertain and potentially transgressive position of this material and of the academic studying it within what are viewed as prevailing academic norms and institutions. Perhaps more interesting, for the purposes of this chapter at least, is the entrepreneurial activity undertaken in recent years in relation to this version of 'European horror'. One only has to look around the horror section in any largish DVD store or get on to Amazon to see that a market has now developed for the sort of material discussed by Tohill, Tombs, Thrower and other comparable fans/writers. Glossy, beautifully produced books – for example, the Thrower book on Fulci, published by FAB Press, one of several companies specialising in the distribution of cult material – are also available. And lest we think that this is just an exploitative industry crassly moving in on an area previously carved out by fans, it is worth noting that much of the entrepreneurship here is provided by horror fans themselves, people who have an informed knowledge of this area and of the market opportunities it presents. Everything, it seems, has changed.

In the 1980s, you had your third- or fourth-generation copy of an Argento film (with Dutch subtitles), and some grimy, badly photocopied fanzine – and the grainier the visual image and the grimier the written word the better because in itself this became an index of resistance, of a kind of authenticity. Now, by contrast, you have a sleekly packaged uncut and digitally remastered version of, say, *Suspiria* or *Tenebrae* (1982) on DVD – either purchased in your own country or easily imported from elsewhere – and some very well-informed and handsomely illustrated books on Argento provided by the likes of Alan Jones and Chris Gallant. In a manoeuvre that would have staggered many people in the 1980s, even the once demonic video nasty category appears to have been transformed into an object of nostalgia, with the phrase 'Previously banned' now a badge of honour in the marketing for numerous horror DVDs.

In a context within which 'Eurohorror' increasingly denotes a specialised market niche, one has to question how effective some of the initial critical constructions of Eurohorror still are, such is their dependence on notions of marginality and obscurity. In addition, the extent to which this kind of category can be sustained within the context of an increasingly sophisticated critical and academic understanding of the notions of the national and transnational within film culture also merits some consideration.

THE 'NEW' EUROHORROR

Let us now look at another horror film that was produced in Europe but, as much as *Resident Evil*, is not generally thought of as Eurohorror, namely the vampire film *Underworld* (Len Wiseman, 2003), which was filmed mainly in Budapest. These two films together are not offered here as in any way typical of a false or negative Eurohorror, but a closer study of them in all their apparent marginality and inauthenticity does suggest other ways of thinking about this particular area of European film culture.

So what might it be about *Underworld* that prevents its accession to European horrordom? For one thing, it is an apparently American-centred production that seems to use its East European production set-up for economic reasons (in the same way that other such films are filmed in Canada, Australia and Britain without necessarily sacrificing or attenuating their essential 'Hollywood-ness'). In this way it can be related in particular to other US horror films that just happen to be filmed in Hungary or, more frequently, in the Czech Republic, films of which Kim Newman recently commented:

> That rusting, apparently abandoned Slovak factory has become one of the key images of cheapskate cinema as similar locations throughout the former Warsaw Pact bloc, decommissioned from some state purpose, have served in direct-to-video or SciFi Channel 'original' films in which local actors commanded by a token downwardly mobile American name (Casper Van Dien, Dean Cain, Lance Henriksen) are pursued by CGI monsters through vast rooms full of leftover machine parts. (2006)

Underworld might be bigger-budgeted and more up-market than some of the low-budget films that Newman studiously avoids naming but, arguably, that makes it yet more American, with any East European names in its cast and crew featuring way down the list.

In an interview (included on the *Underworld* DVD), Len Wiseman indicates that one of the reasons that the film was based in Budapest was the availability of suitably atmospheric old buildings that could be used as settings along with some less salubrious disused buildings – notably an unfinished sports arena – that could cheaply and readily be adapted into sets. From this perspective, *Underworld*'s relation to Budapest itself seems to hover between tourism and exploitation, with the city's appeal involving both old-world architecture and the wreckage of defunct Communism. In terms both of its content and style, *Underworld* can also be seen as adopting American models and trends: the stylised body movement and computer generated imagery come out of *The Matrix* (Wachowski Brothers, 1999) and the mixing of horror and action conventions might also be seen as an American innovation, especially as evidenced in *The Mummy* (1999), *The Mummy Returns* (2001) and *Van Helsing* (2004), all directed by Stephen Sommers. In other words, *Underworld* does not seem in any meaningful way to be engaging with its European context; its being made in Europe is in itself of no particular significance. As noted above, something similar might be said of *Resident Evil*, which was shot largely in Germany and which benefited from German tax breaks but which does not seem, ostensibly at least, to be connecting with anything German.

However, a case can also be made for the European credentials of *Underworld* (and perhaps *Resident Evil* as well) – in terms of its content, for instance, or, more mundanely, its mere presence within Europe. Certainly its European, or more particularly its Hungarian, setting bestows upon the film a visual distinctiveness that, if filmed in the United States, it would lack. One might compare it in this respect with its sequel *Underworld: Evolution* (Len Wiseman, 2006), which – in terms of narrative – follows on directly from *Underworld* but which was filmed largely in Canada and which arguably looks quite different as a result. In other words, the setting of a film is not necessarily a neutral backdrop to the narrative but can inflect or permeate films in various ways, regardless of the ostensible nationality of the film in question. One should also note the Europeanness of the *Underworld* cast in this respect. Few of them are Hungarian but the English presence is substantial – with Kate Beckinsale, Bill Nighy and Sophia Myles featuring prominently among the vampires – while, with perhaps unintentional irony, the lycanthropic rebellion against arrogant (and implicitly English) vampire rule is led by a Welsh man, actor Michael Sheen. Of course, one could argue that casting the English as sinister aristocrats is pretty much par for the course as far as Hollywood is concerned. However, their presence here (and in *Resident Evil* as well) potentially provides grounds for a European framing or appropriation of an apparently American film. To give another example from a different historical period, the fact that many of the key cast and crew of the American horror classic *Bride of Frankenstein* (James Whale, 1935) were British has sometimes led to the film being seen as a kind of British horror film 'in exile' (for instance, see Barr 1986: 9–10).

The fact that *Underworld* is a vampire film might also be significant, inasmuch as the vampire mythos has pronounced European qualities. Of course, this does not mean that all vampire films are in some way 'European' (although such a claim might be made for most Dracula films). However, the sort of story told by *Underworld* does exhibit a fascination with 'old-world' customs and social structures that might conceivably be connected back to the United States' European origins. It is a story of bloodlines, of what in effect is a vampire aristocracy threatened by a proletariat werewolf rebellion. This fascination with pre-democratic social structures permeates a lot of US vampire fiction (including Anne Rice's bestselling vampire novels), and it is often associated with Europeanness. In the action-horror film *Blade* (Stephen Norrington, 1998), for example, the insurrectionary movement led by the American vampire played by Stephen Dorff confronts a vampire establishment led by German actor Udo Kier (who 25 years earlier had himself played Count Dracula in *Blood for Dracula*). And *Blade 2* (Guillermo del Toro, 2002) – which is equally obsessed with vampiric bloodlines and quasi-class rebellions – also features a German actor (Thomas Kretschmann) as its principal villain (and, for good measure, was filmed largely in the Czech Republic).

Contextualising films of this kind, or Eurohorror films in general, does not then involve simply addressing the question of whether such films are American or European, one thing or the other, but rather involves thinking about the often complex international relations in place within and around the films in question. Such an approach might also encompass the significant traffic between nations – both within Europe and across to the United States – so far as personnel and funding are concerned, with this in turn entailing a detailed and nuanced attention to specific sites of European horror production and to particular types and cycles of European horror rather than focussing on Eurohorror as a cohesive, pan-European phenomenon. To a certain extent, this is already happening, with accounts of various Eurohorror films and filmmakers elaborating upon national and international contexts of production and cultural significance, although what might be termed the romance of marginality and the gravitational pull exerted by the idea of some dramatic form of cultural transgression is often still evident, if only residually. Hence an unwillingness to recognise the likes of *Resident Evil* or *Underworld* as in any way European, as being just too 'mainstream' for that designation. In the face of this, it is worth pointing out what should be a self-evident truth, namely that this conceptualisation of the mainstream is an abstract one and that in actuality there is no such thing as the mainstream, at least in the singular and mono-dimensional sense offered up by some fan cultures, and that many of the Eurohorrors cited as classic examples of transgression are themselves 'mainstream' in some way or other, with their places in the market determined by specific production and distribution contexts. Moreover, this kind of sensitivity to the national and the international is arguably especially important for European horror films that are often international co-productions and/or designed to be released in more than one country.

The model of European horror that emerges from this is far from being a cohesive totality. Instead 'Eurohorror' becomes an umbrella term covering a variety of different practices, with no geographical centre and no core identity, and which is fractured, fragmented and dispersed unevenly across Europe. However, it still remains an eminently fascinating category, as fragmented as it is, because it is arguably in this fragmentation, in the interrelation of and influence between different national cinemas within Europe (and in certain instances outside Europe) that the distinctiveness of European horror cinema lies. This might not be a pure, unchanging and essential distinctiveness, something that separates it out completely from other areas of culture and entertainment, but, in all its nuance and detail, its constantly evolving shape continues to merit our attention.

BIBLIOGRAPHY

Altman, R. (1999) *Film/Genre*. London: British Film Institute.
Barr, C. (1986) 'Amnesia and Schizophrenia', in C. Barr (ed.) *All Our Yesterdays: 90 Years of British Cinema*. London: British Film Institute, 1–29.
Gallant, C. (ed.) (2001) *Art of Darkness: The Cinema of Dario Argento*. Guildford: FAB Press.
Hawkins, J. (2000) *Cutting Edge: Art-horror and the Horrific Avant-garde*. Minneapolis: University of Minnesota Press.
Hutchings, P. (2003) 'The Argento Effect', in M. Jancovich, A. Lazaro Reboll, J. Stringer and A. Willis (eds) *Defining Cult Movies: The Cultural Politics of Oppositional Taste*. Manchester: Manchester University Press, 127–43.
Jones, A. (2004) *Profondo Argento: The Man, The Myths and the Magic*. Guildford: FAB Press.
Lay, S. (2007) 'Audiences Across the Divide: Game to Film Adaptation and the case of Resident Evil', in *Participations*, 4: 2. On-line. Available HTTP: http://www.participations.org/Volume%204/

Issue%202/4_02_lay.htm (13 February 2008).
Newman, K. (2006) 'Torture Garden', in *Sight and Sound*, 16: 6, 28–31.
Schneider, S. (ed.) (2007) *100 European Horror Films*. London: British Film Institute.
Sconce, J. (1995) 'Trashing the Academy: Taste, Excess, and an Emerging Politics of Cinematic Style', in *Screen*, 36: 4, 371–93.
Thrower, S. (1999) *Beyond Terror: The Films of Lucio Fulci*. Guildford: FAB Press.
Tohill, C. and P. Tombs (1994) *Immoral Tales: Sex and Horror Cinema in Europe 1956–1984*. London: Primitive Press.

BEYOND *SUSPIRIA*?
THE PLACE OF EUROPEAN HORROR CINEMA IN THE FAN CANON

Brigid Cherry

On the rec.arts.horror.movies discussion list,[1] a male fan ('Loucyphre') asks about the films of Italian horror directors Dario Argento and Lucio Fulci: 'What are some of the titles of these two directors' best movies? I have *Suspiria* [Argento, 1977] and *Zombie* [aka *Zombi 2*, Fulci, 1979]. Point me in the gore and frightfest direction.' Such requests are commonplace amongst relatively new or young fans and established fans alike seeking to expand their experience of the genre and other fans with wider generic competencies are often happy to pass on their knowledge and recommend viewing according to their own tastes.

Fan cultures regularly present such opportunities for consumers with a specific set of tastes and preferences to come together, share their thoughts, and discuss the objects of their fandom. Ongoing debates between and amongst various groupings of fans tend to give precedence to a set of films that are held up as great examples of the genre across a wide spread of horror fandom. This chapter examines the positioning of European horror films within this fan canon of horror cinema. It explores the findings from an audience research project designed to identify a fan canon of horror cinema that reflects fan tastes across a wide demographic (see Cherry 2007: 204–5 for details). The findings presented here focus specifically on the place of European horror films in the fan canon and the discourses that circulate around European horror.

It is notable that *Suspiria* is the only non-British European title placed amongst the ten most frequently mentioned films when fans were asked what they regarded as the greatest examples of horror cinema[2] or would recommend to others. The significance of *Suspiria* is not only as a representative of a non-Anglophone national horror cinema, but of a very specific aesthetic of cinematic horror which is uniquely Italian and authorial. *Suspiria* is often held up as one of the key films of both Italian horror cinema and the work of Dario Argento, and is famed amongst fans for its graphic effects, music and use of saturated colour. Significantly, when fans speak of European horror, they are often thinking primarily (though not exclusively) of Italian horror.

The full list of significant films named by the respondents contains 88 titles and confirms that the fan canon as identified in this study is mainly centred around post-1960s American horror cinema, with key examples of significant films from earlier periods or horror cycles, and various national horror cinemas given prominent positions and significant circulating discourses. Of the total, 28 per cent of the most frequently named horror films are European,[3] with Italian horror well represented. *Opera* (1982) and *Tenebrae* (1987), two other Argento films, as well as *Suspiria* were all held in particularly high regard by the fans contributing to this study, as were films by Mario Bava. There is also recognition of British, French, German and Belgian cinema – though these are not generally accorded such high recognition as Italian horror and are often included because of their artistic (expressionism), authorial (Roman Polanski), sub-generic (vampire) or studio (Hammer) credentials.

As suggested by the comments of the fan who wants to be pointed in the direction of gore after watching *Suspiria* and *Zombi 2*, it is important to note that European horror and Italian horror are often conflated within fan discourse. The terms 'Eurohorror' and 'Eurogore' are used widely by the fans; both terms are frequently interpreted as referring specifically to Italian horror, and sometimes erroneously conflated, making it important to analyse the discourses surrounding these films. The significance of Italian horror and its importance to the fan canon is therefore considered here in terms of the cultural literacy or generic competencies operating within the fandom.

THE FAN AS CONNOISSEUR

The knowledge of and a taste for Eurohorror is regarded as a mark of the horror connoisseur-cum-film-buff; whilst a liking for Eurogore can sometimes be denigrated. A taste for Eurohorror marks the fan out as having somewhat more elite tastes within the fan culture. This is not to imply that the fans themselves divide horror cinema into 'lowbrow' and 'highbrow' forms, but rather that certain films and types of films are much harder to come by and thus lend the fan who has seen them an aura of authenticity (see Jancovich 2000: 30). An American male fan living away from a major centre on rec.arts.horror.movies ('Diablo') typifies this problem: 'Argento is hard to come by in my neck of the woods. Since I've been aware of him, precisely none of his films have made it to the cinema here and video copies are like hens' teeth.' Fans who wish to broaden their tastes within the genre, and increase their fan credentials, may thus have to actively seek out, often with financial or other costs, the more obscure but highly prized (amongst the older and more established fans) horror films.

Conversely, however, an uncritical liking for the gore film (although this can be central to patterns of taste amongst certain groups of fans, typically young male fans) can sometimes be positioned as the equivalent of having 'lowbrow' tastes by other fans – as is the case with Eurogore. Where such fans have mistakenly conflated Eurohorror and Eurogore, the fans who have a wide knowledge of European horror cinema can find themselves having to defend their tastes. This positioning of fans by other fans is used to demonstrate the presence or absence of cultural literacy (particularly here, generic competence), and can be a signifier, particularly amongst male fans, of an elite position within the fan hierarchy which is used to subordinate other fans.

A typical position is to use references to Eurohorror as a statement along the lines of expressing how knowledgeable the fan is about the films, and of having an (acquired) taste for these films, however obscure they may be; indeed the more obscure the better. For example, a taste for and knowledge of Eurohorror is employed as a signifier of the 'serious' or 'devoted' horror fan whose generic competencies extend beyond the American and other Anglophone horror cinemas. For example, on the Horror In Film and Literature list,[4] an American female fan ('Lynn') writes that:

> It was said that many people on the list are anti Eurogore, but it seems to me a lot of subscribers to the list have not seen many films at all. Once they deplete their limited source of mainstream splooge, they will come around looking for a good scare. I'm so sick of discussions on horror films that every 10 year old on my block has seen. I have not heard a discussion of a single horror film that I have not seen, and I was desperately hoping for some good recommendations. Because living in the United States tends to suck when it comes to the general population's taste, we don't get to see a lot of the stuff being made in Europe and Asia. I really want to know about it.

Such comments can and do create distinctions between fans, such as between the Horror in Film and Literature members and those on alt.horror.[5] Some fans – and this tends to be male and older fans (not necessarily in terms of age, but length of membership of the fan culture), though female fans can hold similar position as illustrated here – may use this discrimination to position themselves with respect to 'newbies' or younger and other fan demographics. Gender, despite the above example, can be a significant factor in this respect, with female fans generally not being as interested in acquiring deep knowledge of facts or trivia, or collecting in general, and thus sometimes lacking cultural currency – or having a different set of generic competencies on which their taste is defined.

Clear cases of what might be regarded as 'snobbery' – and indeed 'reverse snobbery' – can be identified in the fan discourses surrounding both Eurohorror and older (especially black-and-white) horror films. For example, newbies or younger fans are looked down on if they express dislike and/or ignorance of such films. This does, in some instances, lead to antipathy from the younger or more casual horror film viewers towards such indicators of cultural competence. Conversely, some fans can take up a superior position to other fans with respect to Eurogore, and where this is confused with European horror in its widest sense can lead to disputes between fans. In this case, the declaration of a taste for Eurogore (or for Eurohorror when there is a perception that Eurohorror and Eurogore are one and the same – this itself indicates a lack of generic literacy in one particular area) may be derided by others as a sign of a lack of intelligence or of bad taste.

As Kate Laity points out, Horror in Film and Literature attracts those who are 'drawn to the seriousness and focus of the discussion topics', whilst potentially turning away potential fans who are more 'appreciative of the anarchy of the web' (2004: 176). Nevertheless, even members of this group can have a taste for Eurogore amongst a wider set of preferences. As the male fan 'Reuven' states:

> Aside from the sometimes bad acting, I love the extremes that are explored. I don't know what it is but Italian gorefests intrigue me. ... [T]here are some real bad ones, but on the whole there is some talent involved with these productions: Argento, Bava, Fulci, D'Amato and Soavi. I think the great thing about these artists and their visions is that they do not hold anything back. Not all people will like it but there should be some kind of respect given to these artists. After all, isn't horror all about excess and shock.

If nothing else, this brings personal depth to the debate and an acknowledgement that tastes vary; luxuries that are not always available in the more chaotic spaces of alt-horror or rec.arts.horror.movies. Such discourses can lead to demarcations within the fan communities along lines of taste. However, this is not necessarily divisive (though it may well impact on overall conceptions of what demarcates the generic boundaries, as well as what is labelled 'good' and 'bad' taste). In practice such debates often lead to further and in-depth discussions of the films themselves.

In the above example of the discourses focused on distinctions between Eurohorror and Eurogore, there was additional discussion of key examples of Italian and other European horror films (including *Reazione a catena/Bay of Blood* [Mario Bava, 1971], *¿Quién puede matar a un niño?/Who Can Kill a Child?* [Narciso Ibáñez Serrador, 1976], *Dèmoni/Demons* [Mario Bava, 1985] and *Dellamorte Dellamore/Cemetery Man* [Michele Soavi, 1994]). The fans also went on to discuss the Americanised names of Italian directors. 'I made a huge list of Italian directors and all the pseudonyms they hide behind,' says 'Eric' – who now seems to be undermining his own dismissal of Eurohorror fans by revealing his own cultural currency of detailed and intimate knowledge of the filmmakers. 'Why didn't you say so earlier?' 'Reuven' replies, continuing with: 'We can compare notes. I'll get my list from home over the weekend and send you what I can add to your list' (before going on to discuss the various alternatives, as well as the mistakes made by 'Eric', in some depth).

Such fans also discuss the availability of various films (with European fans offering to make copies for their US counterparts), the differences between various cuts or versions of the film (original versus US or British cuts, for example) and the influence of Eurohorror on the American forms of the genre. Of *Bay of Blood* (in reference to a complaint about the film's slow pacing), 'Reuven' says: 'It starts slow, but you get into it after a while. The plot is really quirky, and it has influenced American horror films. Try comparing it to *Friday II*.' 'Reuven' is also typical of the fan who takes pride in having seen or possessing copies of obscure titles; of the Spanish film *Who Can Kill a Child?*, he says: 'The copy I have seems to have been distributed in Israel by accident, and may well be the only copy of that edition left.' Whilst there are obscure American films that fans may well be collectors of, there does seem to be greater prestige in owning or having seen obscure Eurohorror titles (as the previous comment made by 'Lynn' also demonstrates). In one further example of how Eurohorror has become established in the fan canon and the cultural economy, *Suspiria* is often used as a benchmark against which other horror films are judged. As, for example, when another fan ('Michael') discusses the Japanese film *Tetsuo* (Shinya Tsukamoto, 1989): 'Not unlike *Suspiria* in its dreamlike qualities but far more nightmarish.'

As the nuances of this discussion suggest, and as Steven Schneider has emphasised with respect to aesthetics (2004: 146), horror aesthetics and modes of emotional affect play a significant part in the position not just of Italian horror, but other examples of European cinema of artistic or authorial merit, in the fan canon. So why, in particular, is *Suspiria* given such prominence? An American fan ('Colin') when discussing the reasons for his choices of great horror cinema states that '*Suspiria* has the scariest, most effective murder I have ever seen in a film.' Another ('Tony') says that Argento's films are 'ultrastylish, very creepy at times, slightly gory at times, derivative but in the good sense.' Comments such as these suggest that Italian and other examples of Eurohorror offer an idealised combination of aesthetics and modes of affect.

The following quotes illustrate the main appeals of Eurohorror for these fans; the first is from a female respondent ('Peggy') and makes reference to *Suspiria* in particular:

> *Suspiria* is a genuine masterpiece ... I don't think any murder-on-film, either preceding or following *Suspiria*, has equalled the first double killing in this movie. The slowly building sense of terror/unknown, the overwhelming effect of the crashing *Goblin* music, the knife repeatedly stabbing the beating heart ... the violent colours reflecting the violent actions being depicted, and the camera slowly panning down the hanging body, then upwards until it unexpectedly comes to rest on a second, bloody body severed by falling glass shards. [It is] a horror lover's nirvana.

The loving detail with which this fan embroiders her answer, of both the aesthetics and affects of the film, are a clear demonstration of knowledge and thus underscore her fan credentials. Similar expressions of enjoyment are also expressed by fans coming new to Eurohorror. An American student ('Brian') writes on rec.arts.horror.movies:

> I just checked out *Suspiria* this past weekend. Pretty good. [Argento] is easily one of the most stylized horror directors around ... There is a quote somewhere that has him pegged as the 'Italian Hitchcock'. I think that this comment isn't totally off-base, [it] just underlines this guy's overall potential. Anyway, are there any Argento experts here that can give me more recommendations? I guess *Suspiria* is his most famous work, but is it his best? Anyone dare to come up with an Argento top five list? (http://groups.google.com.my/group/rec.arts.horror.movies/topics)

The journey that the fan is taking here in the accumulation of cultural currency is clear, with the viewing of the film being accompanied by additional background reading and the request for future viewing recommendations, together with the challenge thrown out to other fans to come up with a top five. Discussion of such lists (from personal favourites to the most nauseating films) are frequent in all the fan groups studied, and are a major factor in the development of fan canons.

There is also recognition in both these statements that the films themselves may not be perfect, and that they may be accused of having flaws, but that the other aspects make up for these or that they so match the individual fan's ideal, that these aspects are elided – a 'good taste of bad taste', to borrow from Susan Sontag (1999). The horror film that is 'so bad it's good' is a common topic in these groups, and fans accept that horror can be entertaining even where it fails in its attempted affects. In this way, the fan canon does not always reflect the cream of horror cinema, but can include disputed titles such as those representative of

Eurogore. There is also a celebration of cinematic horror, not only in the form of gore and gruesome special effects, but in the tension and suspense built through narrative, *mise-en-scène* and incidental music. Both fans quoted here align their tastes with graphic forms of horror cinema, and further acknowledge the specifics of central horror aesthetics and the way these work on them individually, drawing clear links between aesthetics and responses to horror.

FAN AFFILIATIONS

Identity group affiliation correlates strongly with responses, and thus tastes and preferences. Fan tastes are frequently divided along lines of gender, for example. This has implications for debates on the fan canon, since feminine forms of culture are often devalued and the opinions or contributions of women sometimes ignored. Nonetheless, feminine tastes do influence the fan canon and the case of *Suspiria* highlights the tensions that can emerge between different identity groups within the fan community. Half of the canonical films listed are liked equally by male and female fans, though *Hellraiser* (Clive Barker, 1987) is deemed to be an important film almost exclusively by female fans, whilst *The Thing* (John Carpenter, 1982) is named almost entirely by male fans. Slightly more male fans named *Suspiria*, whilst twice as many males as females named *Opera* and no females named *Tenebrae*, though more female fans did also cite Mario Bava's *La maschera del demonio/Black Sunday* (aka *Mask of the Demon* and *The Mask of Satan*, 1960). This gendered hierarchy of Argento/Italian horror films reflects a feminine aesthetic of horror that is epitomised by *Hellraiser*. In an earlier study of the tastes of female horror fans, *Hellraiser* was the most frequently named favourite film amongst the respondents (see Cherry 1999: 194). The feminine aesthetic epitomised by *Hellraiser* is defined (amongst other elements) by representations of

Dario Argento's distinctive aesthetic in *Suspiria* (1977) epitomises Eurohorror

strong femininity and female sexuality (see Cherry 2005). Barbara Steele's dual role in *Black Sunday*, for example, and the dominance of female characters in *Suspiria*, with the focus on Jessica Harper's role as an early example of the 'final girl' (as contrasted with the more male-orientated *Tenebrae*'s and *Opera*'s murders and torture of female characters) may be key to the different weight the male and female fans give to the Argento canon.[6]

Although some fans differentiate between Eurogore as a dominant subcategory and Eurohorror in general (and many male fans do privilege gore, though not all by any means), and some actively select or prefer one over the other, this is not always the case. Many fans do enjoy both forms, and even where they profess a preference for one this does not lead to outright rejection of all films in the other category. The aforementioned *Hellraiser*, for example, with its strong feminine aesthetic and female following is easily categorised as a 'splatterpunk' or gore film containing several graphic 'numbers' (Freeland 2000: 256). In general, however, male fans are more likely and female fans somewhat less likely to profess a taste (often acquired once the fan has become immersed in the fan culture, as seen in the quote which opened this chapter) for Italian horror – and the male fans often hold these films up as 'superior' examples of gore.

As with *Hellraiser*, however, a gore film which appeals to female fans is more likely to also include significant elements (including imagery and plot developments) of strong femininity, sexuality or the Gothic. A number of female fans love *Suspiria*. 'Peggy' makes a comment which is typical of the female fans, praising the female performances, and saying that:

> Jessica Harper's work in *Suspiria* should be listed in the top-ten all-time female genre performances. Also, Joan Bennett (from *Dark Shadows* [aka *House of Dark Shadows*, Dan Curtis, 1970]) was just perfect, but so was Alida Valli as the dark, stern female. She was a much-heralded exotic leading lady in films of the late '40s and early '50s, like Hitchcock's *The Paradine Case* [1947]) with Gregory Peck and also, I think, *Eyes Without a Face* [aka *Les yeux sans visage*, Georges Franju, 1960].

This fan's addition of detail from Bennet's and Valli's biography suggests that her cultural competencies are focused – at least in part – on female stars of the genre, and moreover around older, established female stars who are not the usual focus of the discussion (and coverage in the horror magazines) of the 'scream queens'. More significantly, it is the feminine and perhaps Gothic elements of the film that allow the female fans to elide any perceived misogynistic themes in Argento's work. The appeal of such films (*Hellraiser*, *Suspiria*) to female fans means that they have far greater significance in the fan canon.

AUDIENCE SEGMENTATION

Clear differences in tastes and preferences can be identified between the subcultural (fan) audience and the mainstream (teen) audience. Very few members of the teen audience who contributed to a control group[7] list any but the most recent examples of horror cinema, and where they do name older films, these are the post-1970s well known classics such as *Halloween* (John Carpenter, 1978) and *Alien* (Ridley Scott, 1979). They name no European horror films with the exception of the recent British horror film *Dog Soldiers* (Neil Marshall, 2002). In terms of world cinema, their tastes are limited to recent Japanese horror such as *Ringu* (Hideo Nakata, 1998) and *The Grudge* (Takashi Shimizu, 2003), again reflecting recent box office successes. Though the control group sample size was small (and it is therefore not possible to confidently extrapolate to the wider audience for horror), there were again divisions between those who prefer the original J-horrors and those who asserted the Hollywood remakes were superior or more likely had only seen the Hollywood versions. This suggests discrimination and an emerging distinction of taste and cultural accumulation here too, with the cultural economy of horror fandom being paralleled in that some members of the general audience seem content with the mainstream Hollywood films with a wide distribution, whilst others move beyond these to seek out older, subtitled or original versions. Just as the more knowledgeable fan audience exhibits cultural competencies far wider than the acknowledged teen audience, within the teen audience we perhaps begin to see 'fans' emerging from the followers of the genre.

In conclusion then, as is the nature of any subcultural taste, the tastes of the fans are extremely diverse, but these diversities are reflected in the fan canon. The significance of European cinema to different segments of the fan audience is clear, and whilst there are tensions, a taste for Eurohorror cuts across gender and national identity. Italian horror cinema is, in general, given precedence mainly by male and older or longer established fans, whereas female fans and new or potential fans are more selective about individual films which contain specific appeals (such as stronger elements of a feminine aesthetic for female fans, for example) or particular national cinemas making an appearance in more localised fan canons, as with British Hammer films being included by dint of their (nostalgic) appeal to British fans. This raises questions of gendered and national narratives and aesthetics, and how differences in style (reflecting national origin and period) might lead to quite different modes of horror that appeal to different identity groups within the audience. Furthermore, with the inclusion of Polanski films or examples of Expressionist cinema, the importance of various European horror (and avant-garde) cinemas beyond the widely regarded Italian examples is acknowledged due to the input of older and more widely-informed fans. The fan canon does then reflect a wide range of tastes and preferences, and European horror does hold a significant (even when in a minority) place in the fan canon.

NOTES

1. http://groups.google.com.my/group/rec.arts.horror.movies/topics
2. In order, from most popular first, these were *Alien, The Exorcist, The Thing, Dawn of the Dead, Halloween, Hellraiser, Suspiria, The Haunting, The Evil Dead* and *Evil Dead 2*. This list cannot be claimed as definitive, but provides an indication of the types of films – historical moments, sub-genres and styles, affects or national cinemas – given prominence in the fan canon.
3. These are, with most popular first, *Alien, Hellraiser, Suspiria, Shaun of the Dead, Opera, The Wicker Man, Nosferatu, Dracula, Frankenstein Must Be Destroyed, Nightbreed, Night of the Demon, Quatermass and the Pit, Tenebrae, Underworld, The Abominable Dr Phibes, The Beyond, Black Sunday, Daughters of Darkness, Dellamorte Dellamore, Demons, Dracula, Prince of Darkness, Gothic, The Tenant* and *Eyes Without a Face*.
4. http://mypage.iu.edu/~mlperkin/horror_about.html
5. http://groups.google.com/group/alt.horror/topics
6. Female fans do not necessarily reject gore and other forms of graphic horror out of hand, though they do exhibit a preference for this to be supplemented by intelligent plotting, a gothic or romantic aesthetic and sympathetic or erotic monsters (Cherry 2005: 11).
7. Eight regular horror film viewers aged between 15 and 20 who do not participate in fan culture.

BIBLIOGRAPHY

Cherry, B. (1999) 'Refusing to Refuse to Look: Female Viewers of the Horror Film', in R. Maltby and M. Stokes Identifying Hollywood Audiences: Cultural Identity and the Movies, London: BFI, 187-203.

_____ (2005) 'Broken Homes, Tortured Flesh: *Hellraiser* and the Feminine Aesthetic of Horror Cinema', *Film International*, 3: 17, 10–21.

_____ (2007) 'Subcultural Tastes, Genre Boundaries and Fan Canons', in M. Jancovich and L. Geraghty (eds) *The Shifting Definitions of Genre: Essays on Labelling Films, Television Shows and Media*. Jefferson, NC: McFarland, 201–15.

Fiske, J. (1992) 'A Cultural Economy of Fandom', in L. A. Lewis The Adoring Audience: Fan Culture and Popular Media. London: Routledge, 30-49.

Freeland C. (2000) *The Naked and the Undead: Evil and the Appeal of Horror*. Boulder, CO: Westview Press.

Jancovich, M. (2000) '"A Real Shocker": Authenticity, Genre and the Struggle for Distinction', in *Continuum: Journal of Media and Cultural Studies*, 14: 1, 23–35.

Laity, K. A. (2004) 'From SBIGs to Mildred's Inverse Law of Trailers: Skewing the Narrative of Horror Fan Consumption', in S. Hantke (ed.) *Horror Film: Creating and Marketing Fear*. Jackson, MI: University Press of Mississippi, 173–90.

Schneider, S. J. (2004) 'Toward an Aesthetics of Cinematic Horror', in S. Prince (ed.) *The Horror Film*. New Brunswick, NJ: Rutgers University Press, 131–49.

Sontag, S. (1999) 'Notes on "Camp"', in F. Cleto (ed.) *Camp: Queer Aesthetics and the Performing Subject: A Reader*. Ann Arbor: University of Michigan Press, 53–65.

REFUSING TO LOOK AT RAPE:
THE RECEPTION OF BELGIAN HORROR CINEMA

Ernest Mathijs and Russ Hunter

*'I shout your name
but can you hear me?'*

– Siglo XX, *Into the Dark* (1984)

Belgian horror cinema has a curious reputation. Local patrons and critics shun it, yet it fares extremely well in the global market. While Belgian critics fail to construct arguments on how their nation's horror movies address local cultural concerns, international observers have no qualms making links to local cultural excesses, with controversial cases of sexual abuse as symptomatic evidence.

In line with Ernest Mathijs' earlier research on the reception of Belgian cinema and building on Barbara Klinger's (1994) work on how socio-historical and intertextual contexts channel all kinds of receptions at any given moment, this chapter argues that local and international distributors, reviewers and audiences approach the key tropes of sexuality and religion in Belgian horror narratives differently. As a case in point, this chapter analyses the local and European prefigurations and receptions of *Les lêvres rouges/Daughters of Darkness* (Harry Kümel, 1971),

Au service du diable/The Devil's Nightmare (Jean Brismée, 1972), *C'est arrivé près de chez vous/Man Bites Dog* (Rémy Belvaux, André Bonzel, Benoît Poelvoorde, 1992), and *Calvaire/The Ordeal* (Fabrice Du Welz, 2004).[1] Based on the analysis of publicity materials and reviews, we assess these films' national and international receptions, demonstrating how sexuality and violence have become differently coded references for Belgian horror.

BELGIAN FILM CRITICISM

The federal structure of the Belgian state, with its three language groups (Dutch/Flemish, French, German) and five local governments (Flemish, Walloon, Brussels, German and federal), has traditionally meant Belgian cultural representations have been seen in terms of uncertainty and as being beset by a continuous search for identity. In the Belgian case, the necessity of consociational politics has led to the development of a peaceful anarchism, surrealist tendencies, hedonism and cultural particularism. A schizophrenic duality of national consciousness has evolved, never manifesting itself in violent disagreement with 'the Other' but unsure and undecided in relation to its own status (see Van de Craen 2002; Labio 2003).

Film criticism, however, is one area where Belgian cultural commentators seem to be in accord over 'the rules of the game'. Together with other forms of cultural discourse it compensates (and occasionally substitutes) for the lack of national unilateral consciousness by promoting a decided attitude towards, and pride in, the discerning appreciation of art and culture, with a quest for 'quality' at its core – Belgians may not know who they are and distrust those who claim they do, but they do believe they can tell the difference between good and bad art, good and bad popular culture, anytime and anywhere. As remarked elsewhere, this insistence has given Belgian cinephilia a rarely-equalled sophistication (some say pretension) in the appreciation of cinema (see Mathijs 2007a; 2007b).

Over time, several guiding notions regarding critical appraisal have developed, most notable amongst which is the conviction that film should be constructed as an art form and therefore films are to be judged in relation to their closeness to creative and artistic imperatives (see Biltereyst and Van Bauwel 2004; 2007a; 2007b). This position amounts to what David Bordwell (1989) would call an 'invisible college' of critical orthodoxy: an overarching evaluative framework developed that imposed a strict dichotomy between films with aesthetic qualities (to be admired) and those made for commercial purposes (to be dismissed as ephemeral 'trash'). The implication of this is that films have therefore tended to be slotted into either one of these two categories. Ready dismissals of the formulaic nature of any given genre movie, and forced comparisons with only the greatest of horror works (*Nosferatu* [1922] and *Psycho* [1960] has meant Belgian horror cinema has necessarily fared badly at the hands of domestic critics, often dismissed as 'not quite

Hitchcock or Murnau'. As a result horror has not traditionally been considered an important part of Belgian film culture, either as a stylistically innovative genre or a politically and thematically intrinsic part of its cinematic development.

AVOIDING 'HORROR'

The programmatic dismissal of horror shows itself in a tendency to simply ignore the genre. If possible, Belgian critics will not use the word 'horror' (or any equivalent in any of the languages) – one exception being children's stories, where words like 'griezelig' do occur – generally avoiding any reference to the horrific *tout court*.[2] Second, when confronted with films so ostensibly horrific, critics have used elegant ways to avoid framing them as such. As their inclusion in encyclopaedias and online canons demonstrates, the films of our case study are generally seen as horror films by international critics (see Schneider 2007); yet local critics rarely, if ever, discussed them as horror films and hardly ever compared them to other examples of the genre. Instead, Belgian critics replaced the word horror with various synonyms which means they do not have to engage with individual works as horror films.

It is tempting to argue that this critical rejection relates to the 'un-Belgian' nature of the genre. There is certainly an unfamiliarity with the tradition of horror in literature and the other arts, both amongst the higher echelons of culture and more lowbrow cartoons, comics or fanzines.[3] A scarcity of books dedicated to the genre has merely served to reinforce a lack of a tradition of public sphere exploration and negotiation of the concept of the horrific in Belgian culture. However, as anyone who has even briefly looked at Belgian art and culture will notice, there are plenty of options: the works of Jean Ray (whose *Malpertuis* [1943] was adapted by Harry Kümel in 1972), Hubert Lampo and, more recently, Pieter Aspe carry an abundance of horrific overtones. Yet they are classified without touching the 'horror' word. Even those works that do deal explicitly with horror are first predominantly to 'magical realism', itself a long-established critical trope in Belgian film criticism. Given that magical realism ordinarily implies 'an interest in the representation of the split between the real and the imaginary, or a dialectic between life and allusion' (Nysenholc 1985: 221), we might expect this to lead to explorations of the horrific, but Belgian critics have always avoided that leap. This rigid adherence to magical realism as a means through which to understand films that verge on the fantastical has meant ignoring the important issue of a film's cultural relevance in favour of linking the surreal/real dichotomy to wider aesthetic considerations.

That is certainly true for 'magical realism'. Magical realism initially appeared in relation to film with reference to the debut features of both André Delvaux (*De man die zijn haar kort liet knippen/The Man Who Had His Hair Cut Short*

[1965]) and Harry Kümel (*Monsieur Hawarden* [1968]), based as they were on magical realist literature. From this point onwards magical realism was to become a key reference point to which critics would consistently return in appraising both the 'Belgianness' and artistic pretensions of its domestic cinematic output. When explicit horror films appeared, they could easily be contained within the discourse of magical realism (especially since there were 'lineages' that could legitimise such a treatment). For instance, Danny De Laet, a long-time defender of the genre in Belgium, sees E. G. De Meyst, Norbert Benoit and Marcel Jauniaux's *La maudite/ The Damned* (1949) as being a predecessor of magical realist cinema, before continuing to discuss horror and fantasy. In other words, in *some* cases horror could be accepted in the margins of the critical discourse, *if* its connection with legitimate frames of reference *could* be established.

One reason why this kind of connection has hardly ever occurred lies in the construction of Belgium's cinematic history – and the way it is generally linked to other art forms rhetorically. The first serious attempts at filmmaking, and the first 'golden' moment in domestic motion picture production were linked to the creation of the Belgian documentary tradition, by Charles Dekeukeleire and Henri Storck in the early 1930s. Importantly, this association with the documentary form as truly 'Belgian' served to tie critical debates to both realism and art. Inevitably then, 'realism' and 'documentary' and ontological tensions between 'real' and 'fiction' became essential keystones in any discussion of cinema. Indeed, it is tempting to think that Belgium's relationship to the surrealist art movement, which produced artists such as René Magritte and Paul Delvaux (whose careers were blossoming just at the point in which Belgian cinema saw its first serious attempts at film production), only reinforced this notion of cinema as just another medium for realistic artistic expression. It is not much of a surprise then that one of the ways in which horror films have been criticised is that they fall in between tropes of realism, surrealism and magical realism: not 'real' enough to represent reality and too fantastical to be truly surreal.

MORALITY: VIOLENCE AND SEXUALITY AS DETRACTIONS FROM HORROR?

Belgian critics' resistance to employ a discursive framework that would look favourably upon – and even use – straightforward references to the horrific goes further than mere semantics. Such an approach ignores the intrinsic link between film and culture that is essential – even if only in its perception – for small film cultures, where everything is linked to everything, and where evaluating films also means judging them, and their attitude towards life. In other words, there is a moral component. In Belgian film criticism, this moral element has been present since its inception (see Biltereyst and Van Bauwel 2004). The strong tradition of centring appraisals of national films in relation to moral issues has meant that the levels of sexual and violent scenes in horror films have led to condemnation on moral terms. Gilbert Verschooten, writing in the Catholic Film League's *Film & Televisie*, has noted that 'horror has always been dismissed by the film press and "right-minded" public opinion because of the way it challenges morality' (1983: 24). In such a climate it is no great surprise that horror has been both marginalised and ill-received.

Curiously, given Belgium's Catholicism and its catholic taste culture, critics have generally avoided exploring the religious representations present in these films. A fact rendered even more intriguing when one considers the prominence of religious imagery in the history of Belgian cinema. *The Devil's Nightmare* and Emmanuel Kervyn's *Les mémés cannibals/Rabid Grannies* (1988) both contain prominent roles for priests and *The Ordeal* is replete with religious metaphors (though 'god' in the shape of a priest is absent from the village featured in the film). Likewise the quasi-religious vampire tonality of *Daughters of Darkness* and the problematic stance taken toward religion in *S.* (Guido Henderickx, 1998) demonstrate a distinct presence for religion in Belgian horror cinema. Religion is, then, both present as a prominent textual element and acts as wider general background and atmosphere against which events are painted. The fact that discussions of such explicit imagery and topics are missing from Belgian reviews is conspicuous. And yet, reviewers do not comment upon any of these elements because to do so would be to acknowledge the films' functions as forms of social commentary. To do so would be to question the foundations and stability of Belgian moral and religious thinking.

So for Belgian critics, horror was consistently reduced to basic functions of morality, exempt from cultural application or representation. It allowed critics to avoid seeing horror or the horrific as in any way representing cultural reality (the idea that any given film is 'not like any reality I know'). Naturally enough, commercially exploitative films, which tended to feature sex and violence prominently, were seen as ephemeral 'trash' not just because they were found aesthetically wanting, but also because they lacked any structuring moral concern (see Thys 1995: 542). This has, in effect, meant that reviewing practices consciously failed to adopt a frame of reference that could or would link horror films to national culture in a wider sense (for to do so would imply a failure of moral standards). Within Belgian film criticism such readings (or non-readings) are, then, arguably part of a tradition of interpretation which excludes social commentary from the critical agenda. Horror has therefore always been considered culturally *irrelevant*. Belgian film criticism has not substantially explored the trends affecting other national and international film, such as psychoanalytic, (post-)structuralist or even feminist theories of film criticism that seek to link film texts to contemporary culture (with a few issues of *Andere Sinema* between 1977 and 1983 as notable exceptions – but even here the praise was limited to the new wave of American horror, more a reflection of Robin Wood's discussions of the genre than an attempt to link it to local culture).

THE 1970S: *DAUGHTERS OF DARKNESS* AND *THE DEVIL'S NIGHTMARE*

If the moral condemnation made some sense up to and until the 1970s, because there was hardly any horror to write about, there is no reason why it would extend beyond that. The end of the 1960s saw a radical overhaul of the structure of Belgian film industry. State-funded film production started in the middle of the decade, which complemented a concomitant rise in commercially-financed film at the same time. A new wave of Belgian films arose, where the distinction between the artistic 'merit' film (usually auteur driven and seen as culturally relevant) and commercially oriented exploitation film was deepened even further. The decade's social liberalisation meant that changing social mores combined with a greater emphasis upon magical realism led to much more explicit representations of sex and violence.

This was also the point where several works by Belgian filmmakers moved closer to utilising the kind of thematic and stylistic devices seen in international horror cinema. The rise of sex, violence and magical realist-inspired work meant

Sexualised violence in Belgian horror cinema. Clockwise, from top left: *Daughters of Darkness* (1971), *Man Bites Dog* (1992), *The Ordeal* (2004) and *Lucker* (1986).

that part of Belgium's national film output began slowly to make contributions to a rapidly evolving horror genre. Films such as Pierre Laroche's *Il pleut dans la maison/It Rains in my House* (1968), Roland Lethem's and Jean-Louis Van Belle's short films, and even Guy Nijs's more sex- than horror-oriented *In Love with Death* (1970) marked a move toward a more explicit exploration of sexuality and violence. The beginning of the 1970s was a turning point. International co-productions bloomed, and people like Jess Franco and Jean Rollin became, albeit occasionally, involved in Belgian projects. The test case became the arrival of two films whose textual properties forced horror to be addressed by critics. *Enfant terrible* Harry Kümel's *Daughters of Darkness* and Jean Brismée's *The Devil's Nightmare* featured strong sexual and violent content (both contained lesbian plot elements, the latter containing an infamous lesbian love scene) along with a magical realist aesthetic. But they also were congruent with the prevailing European horror aesthetic from the likes of Hammer Studios, Paul Naschy, Franco and Rollin, meaning an association with horror and an exploration of the horrific was doubly hard to resist.

Yet they proved too much for most Belgian critics and both films felt the full force of domestic critical opprobrium. Their reception ably demonstrated that any connection with horror (or references to the horrific) within reviews tended to lead to a negative appraisal. So whilst *The Devil's Nightmare* gained momentum as a cult film in the US and *Daughters of Darkness* was a box office draw in the US, UK and France (topping the box office charts in all three countries), their domestic receptions were muted at best. Where they were praised it was precisely because they traversed and pushed forward genre conventions, not because they were completely congruent with them. *The Devil's Nightmare* in particular was seen to be too 'daring' in its linking of violence, sexuality and explicit lesbianism (and its suggestions of 'forced sex') and was dismissed with the derisory observation that it was nothing but 'Petit Guignol' (Thys 1999: 501). The fact the film did well – at least in its critical reception – in niche markets across Europe did nothing to prevent Belgian reviewers from dismissing it.

Daughters of Darkness suffered a somewhat ironic reception, with its label as 'Dracula in Marienbad' (in reference to the presence of *Last Year at Marienbad's* Delphine Seyrig) proving as good as it got. To understand fully the extent to which the Belgian reception differed from the rest of the world, it is useful to draw a comparison to see how *Daughters of Darkness* illustrates wider trends within Belgian film culture. From the start *Daughters of Darkness* occupied an awkward position in trying to straddle the tropes of both art and exploitation cinematic practices, with Kümel himself on record as saying that he was trying to go against the values that Belgian film culture held dear by wanting to make 'undignified trash' that would stand in contrast to the state-funded projects that were being green-lit at the time. It was initially released in the US on 28 May 1971, quickly becoming a big box office success. Its reception focused on two things. On the one hand there was an emphasis on how well *Daughters of Darkness* fitted the genre, with emphases on lesbian vampirism and predatory sexual acts, and contemporary competition, as being most often mentioned.[4] Yet there is also stress on the artistic pretensions of the film. The *New York Times* review referenced both *Et mourir de plasir/Blood and Roses* (Roger Vadim, 1960) and *L'anneé dernière à Marienbad/Last Year at Marienbad* (Alain Resnais, 1961) as comparable source material. In this sense it was not seen as typical exploitation fare.[5] In any case it generally received a critically moderate appraisal that seemed to tune into its dual address to both the aesthetic and the exploitative.

Britain was the first European territory in which the film was released, receiving a moderately positive reception, with *The Guardian* summing it up as 'a fine piece of camp' but crucially 'better than average fang yarn' (quoted in Mathijs 2005a: 462). If British critics engaged with the film as a playful entry into the horror genre, the French made deeper connections to what they saw as the film's highbrow leanings. More often than not the reviews referred to the cool distance, noting its links to *Last Year at Marienbad* and *Blood and Roses*, whilst others even attempted to make highbrow art links, citing Giorgio De Chirico, surrealism and Paul Delvaux. The film was therefore seen as part of a chain of visual art and when such references appear the subsequent reviews tended to be positive. But, importantly, this did not mean French critics shied away from calling it horror – quite the contrary, they did and yet it did not prevent them from drawing positive conclusions. Both in the UK and France *Daughters of Darkness* was a commercial success, and René Michelems writes that 'the film went on to enjoy an enormous success, in Paris as much as in Britain and the States' (quoted in Thys 1999: 483). Frederic Sojcher calls the film's box office results in Paris 'unsurpassed by any other Belgian film up until now' (1999: 69).

Daughters of Darkness was released in the Low Countries during February–April 1972 and marketed as both an auteurist exploration of artistic themes and a crude exploitation film. In line with the US publicity posters the Belgian marketing ensured that Seyrig and Danielle Ouimet featured prominently, in a careful juggling act that stressed the artistic pretensions and kinkiness of the film. The press kit emphasised both the horrific origins of the story and the literary qualities of Kümel's scriptwriting in comparison to the rest of the film, was much better publicised and much more visible among other releases. There was a fairly substantial referencing of things linked to a positive evaluation of the film (F.W. Murnau, Carl-Theodor Dreyer, Josef Von Sternberg, Roman Polanski, Greta Garbo, Louise Brooks, Marlene Dietrich and *Last Year at Marienbad*). However, whilst the Belgian reception was in line with the international one in as much as it recognised the films duality, this ambiguity was not seen as a positive quality. So although reviews generally tended to recognise some positive qualities within the film, it was said to lack vision and 'cinematographical flair'. Moreover, given the moral imperatives of the Belgian critical establishment, the explicit portrayals of sex (particularly the lesbianism) and violence stopped them from seeing *Daughters of Darkness* as a 'good' film. Even in comparison to native art films that did contain a fair amount of sex and violence, such as Fons Rademakers' *Mira, of de teleurgang van de Waterhoek/Mira* (1971) the film's lack of realism was seen to devalue any artistic bent it might otherwise have had. For Belgian critics, *Daughters of Darkness* was clearly a film by a talented and innovative filmmaker made within the context of a booming film culture, but it also lacked the realism required to make it 'art', while being too trashy to be considered a critical or commercial success. Reviews, instead, seem to have used the film as a symptom of all that was wrong with Belgian film culture. References to the international reception – which were frequent – served to demonstrate just how 'un-Belgian' the film is (that fitted into the idea that horror was an 'un-Belgian' genre). Ultimately they utilised pre-existent referencing strategies to reinforce feelings about domestic film in an oppositional sense (for a detailed analysis of *Daughters of Darkness*' reception, see Mathijs 2005a).

What is true of *Daughters of Darkness* (and *The Devil's Nightmare*) is true for Belgian films with a horrific edge up until 1992. Boris Szulzinger's *Les tueurs fous/ The Lonely Killers* (1972), Maurice Rabinowicz's *Le Nosferat/Nosferatu* (1974), Luc Veldeman's *The Antwerp Killer* (1983) and Johan Vandewoestijne's *Lucker* (1986) all elicited a steadfast refusal by critics to make references to the horrific and such references were generally replaced with synonyms wherever possible. Even in cases where textually they could not but mention horror, as with *Rabid Grannies* and Szulzinger's *Mama Dracula* (1980), critics did so only with great reluctance.[6]

THE 1990s AND BEYOND: MAN BITES DOG AND THE ORDEAL

The release of the low-budget *Man Bites Dog* in 1992, however, challenged these critical boundaries, forcing a (temporary) reassessment of existent critical frameworks. *Man Bites Dog* concerns a film crew making a documentary about local assassin and some-time serial killer, Benoit (Benoit Poelvoorde). They loyally follow his every action as he embarks upon a murder spree. As the killings increase the film crew themselves become implicated in Benoit's murders, even taking part in the rape and murder of one couple. The film ends in their death at the hands of unknown gangsters. The term horror was used by the international press frequently but only twice by the Belgian press, preferring to find another language with which to express the horrific elements of the film. This is curious as given the centrality of murder to *Man Bites Dog*'s narrative, it was difficult to even retell the plot without referencing it.

Arguably, in this case, a lack of experience of writing about horror cinema, more than a refusal, contributed to a critical hesitation in labelling *Man Bites Dog* as a horror film. Instead Belgian critics adopted the same referencing strategies as before (surrealism, magical realism and the denunciation of sex and violence – and sexual violence: another rape, this one prominent in the narrative), but in contrast to what had passed before, these elements were linked to a positive review of the film. Equally, moves were made to stress its cultural relevance, with reviews citing the self-reflexive nature of the film as forming a commentary upon contemporary Belgian media. Importantly here there was no moral condemnation of the film, although the strategy of noting the film's self-reflexivity allowed critics to see the film as something other than *just* 'horrific'. In particular it allowed them to reference and critique Belgian reality television, itself a critical *bête noir*. Shows like *Striptease* (1990–) were frequently cited, as were shows such as *Jambers* (1989–2000), *NV De Wereld/The World Inc.* (1989–93) and *Het Eenzame Harten Buro/The Lonely Hearts Bureau* (1990–92) to stress the self-reflexive nature of *Man Bites Dog*. Horror had become culturally relevant by the back door (for an elaboration of the international reception of *Man Bites Dog*, see Mathijs 2005b).

Since *Man Bites Dog*, Belgian critics have truly tried, yet continued to fail, to twist and shake the foundations of their own discourse in order to accommodate horror. Even in 1998, in the wake of one of the most pressing moral and political crises in Belgium's history – when everything from child rape to fraud was thought of as part of a 'Belgian disease', horror films – and indeed other representations of horror – were only very reluctantly allowed to be linked to the cultural malaise. A film like *S.*, which again featured a fairly explicit rape as a prominent textual metaphor, was initially championed as a return to form for a veteran director, but subsequently dropped like a hot potato when it became clear its tone and theme were downright social critiques of the cultural discourse Belgian critics had helped maintain (for an elaboration, see Mathijs 2004a; 2004b).

The latest example in the ongoing row is *The Ordeal*, a film that, like *Man Bites Dog*, combines explicit sex and violence with a highly reflexive attitude. Du Welz may have switched Easter for Christmas, but the directness with which he shows suffering is only a little less literal than Mel Gibson's *The Passion of the Christ* (also from 2004), and at least as gut-wrenching. The film references most of the modern horror canon, from *Freaks* (Tod Browning, 1932), over *Psycho* to *The Texas Chainsaw Massacre* (Tobe Hooper, 1974) (and Brigitte Lahaie, known to fans from her appearances in Jean Rollin's films, makes a cameo appearance). *The Ordeal* not only oozes biblical metaphors, it is sutured with the kind of rural abductions and rape scandals that rocked Belgian society in the mid/late 1990s. It is impossible to see the film outside that framework. Once more, the international reception was extremely positive, as were local screenings at the *L'Age D'or*, the annual festival of subversive cinema of the Belgian Film Archive (the term 'subversive' already parks the film culturally), but again Belgian critics managed to find ways to avoid highlighting the cultural relevance, instead making comparisons to other cultures' deep anxieties via references that link the Fagnes area to the Deep South of *Deliverance* (John Boorman, 1972) or the Cornwall of

Peckinpah's *Straw Dogs* (1971). *The Ordeal* demonstrates how horror can hold up a mirror to the society it reflects: decaying, stuck on absurd and violent rituals; incomprehensibly surreal, but also oh so recognisably real. But Belgian critics still will not say that.

CONCLUSION: RAPED RECEPTIONS?

When we started this research project into the reception of Belgian horror we thought the presence of sexual violence in the films we wanted to analyse was a genre's favourite cultural trope, a bit like fangs or blood, or guns in a western. At the end of the project we are genuinely confused. In every single case in which sex and violence have been combined into sexualised violence to create an atmosphere of threat and abuse in Belgian films – what most would call horror – Belgian critics have backed away from seeing those representations and metaphors as having any bearing on the culture they stem from and reflect upon. We have noted changes over time, from the 1970s to now, but we cannot help but wonder why sexualised violence – rape in other words – *as* a sensitive topic goes almost always unmentioned, even in times when the cultural atmosphere makes it highly topical. Most theories on the functions of criticism fail to explain this: it is not mere semantics, nor is it the rhetoric of an invisible college (as Bordwell has it). In Belgium, horror has fallen between the cracks of a critical framework that addresses aesthetic and moral judgements that it can rarely, if ever, satisfy. The divergence between the international and domestic receptions, as evidenced here, demonstrates the need for them to be viewed as trajectories. That is to say, receptions of films are not simply a snap-shot in time, but a constantly evolving and dynamic process, which consists of a far more integrated look at the ways in which discourses can 'clash' in particular situations and over time than has normally been the case. The reality of reception is that it is made up of multiple strands of discourses that struggle within the public sphere for dominance and are in turn influenced by discourses in other national and international public spheres.

Is it really the case that Belgium critical debates over horror are stunted because films like *Daughters of Darkness, The Devil's Nightmare, Man Bites Dog* and *The Ordeal* are directly representational of local anxieties, too sensitive to be lifted out of their immediate frame of reference? Does it explain the ironic situation of how, internationally, these films' cultural address is more easily acknowledged and celebrated *because* they are less relevant? Are they elevated to cult internationally because they are stuck in culture nationally? If so, Belgian directors should take note. After all, in an era of global receptions, horror cinema needs to combine *both* a national and international approach if it is to maximise its public presence. Until the international reception is allied to the local reception, Belgian horror cinema will truly remain a cultural 'Daughter of Darkness'.

NOTES

1 Space does not permit elaborations on several other Belgian films: *The Antwerp Killer* (Luc Veldeman, 1983), *Lucker* (Johan Vandewoestijne, 1986), *Rabid Grannies* (Emmanuel Kervyn, 1990), and *S.* (Guido Henderickx, 1998). All had receptions in Belgium and internationally that are similar to the ones we note in this chapter. In fact, several of them are caricatures of the ones we discuss, with each side radicalising its position.
2 The term 'griezelig' literally means 'gruesome', 'creepy' or 'spine-chilling', but is also a verb ('griezelen') in which case it means 'to shiver'. In Dutch the term is often used as an indicator of a juvenile 'startle effect', that does not cut as deep as 'horror' (which is the term reserved for more adult material).
3 Two rare examples are *Le Journal de Jonathan Harker* (publishing eight issues between 1967 and 1968) and *Fantoom* (publishing six issues between 1975 and 1979).
4 Common points of comparison were *The Vampire Lovers* (Roy Ward Baker, 1970), *Lust for a Vampire* (Jimmy Sangster, 1971) and *Twins of Evil* (John Hough, 1971).
5 *Variety* noted that the film's duality would require a 'special sell' if it wasn't 'going to be lost in the mire of the conventionally bloody exploitation market'.
6 *Lucker* had a storyline that focused upon *nothing but* the escape of a psychopathic prisoner from a secure mental health institution and his subsequent killing spree. The plot, which also included scenes of both rape and graphic necrophilia, was purely a device to allow for representations of violence, which in itself invited clear references to the horrific. Yet it too was carefully dissected and positioned so as not to reflect these elements. Conversely, several of these films were received relatively favourably outside of Belgium (*Lucker*, for instance, was commercially successful in both France and Switzerland) and the horrific elements were seen as a boon for *Rabid Grannies*, which was heralded as a 'gore fest for aficionados' by *Variety*.

BIBLIOGRAPHY

Altman, R. (1999) *Film/Genre*. London: British Film Institute.
Biltereyst, D. and Van Bauwel, S. (2004) 'Whitey', in E. Mathijs (ed.) *The Cinema of the Low Countries*. London: Wallflower Press, 49–58.
_____ (2007a) 'Cine Clubs en het geheugen van de film', in D. Biltereyst and C. Stalpaert (eds) *Filmsporen, Opstellen over film, Verleden en Geheugen*, Ghent: Academia Press, 30–50.
_____ (2007b) 'Filmclubs en de explosie van Potemkin: Storck en Eisenstein', in J. Swinnen and L. Deneulin (eds) *Henri Storck Memoreren*. Brussels: VUB Press, 96–111.
Bordwell, D. (1989) *Making Meaning: Inference and Rhetoric in the Interpretation of Cinema*. Cambridge, MA: Harvard University Press.
Klinger, B. (1994) *Melodrama and Meaning: History, Culture and the Films of Douglas Sirk*. Bloomington, IN: Indiana University Press.
Labio, C. (ed.) (2003) *Belgian Memories: Yale French Studies 102*. New Haven: Yale University Press.
Mathijs, E. (2004a) 'Nobody is Innocent: Cinema and Sexuality in Contemporary Belgian Culture', *Social Semiotics*, 14: 1, 85–101.
_____ (2004b) 'Alternative Belgian Cinema and Cultural Identity: *S.* and the Affaire Dutroux', in E. Mathijs and X. Mendik (eds) *Alternative Europe: European Exploitation and Underground Cinema*. London: Wallflower Press, 64–76.
_____ (2004c) 'Daughters of Darkness', in E. Mathijs (ed.) *The Cinema of the Low Countries*.

London: Wallflower Press, 96–106.
_____ (2005a) 'Bad Reputations: the Reception of Trash Cinema', *Screen*, 46: 4, 451–72.
_____ (2005b) '*Man Bites Dog* and the Critical Reception of Belgian Horror (in) Cinema', in S. J. Schneider and T. Williams (eds) *Horror International*. Detroit, MI: Wayne State University Press, 315–35.
_____ (2007a) 'Henri Storck en de Culture Identiteit van de Belgische Cinema', in J. Swinnen and L. Deneulin (eds) *Henri Storck Memoreren*. Brussels: VUB Press, 57–66.
_____ (2007b) Entries for *Malpertuis*, *Le Calvaire*, *The Lift*, in S. J. Schneider (ed.) *100 European Horror Films*. London: British Film Institute, 144–6, 173–4.
Mosley, P. (2001) *Split Screen: Belgian Cinema and Cultural Identity*. New York: SUNY Press.
Nysenholc, A. (1985) 'André Delvaux ou les visages de l'imaginaire', in A. Nysenholc (ed.) *Special Edition of the Revue de l'Universitee de Bruxelles*. Brussels: Editions de Université de Bruxelles, pp. 91–6.
Schneider, S. J. (2003) *Fear Without Frontiers: Horror Cinema Across the Globe*. Godalming: FAB Press.
Schneider, S. J. and Williams, T. (eds) (2005) *Horror International*. Detroit: Wayne State University Press.
Schneider, S. J. (ed.) (2007) *100 European Horror Films*. London: British Film Institute.
Sojcher, F. (1999) *La kermesse heroique du cinema belge (Vol. II: 1965–1988)*. Paris: L'Harmattan.
Thys, M. (ed.) (1999) *Belgian Cinema – Le cinema belge – de Belgische film*. Ghent: Ludion.
Van de Craen, P. (2002) 'What, if Anything, is a Belgian?', *Yale French Studies*, 102, 24–33.
Verschooten, G. (1983) 'De fantastische film: op de drempel van de erkenning?', *Film & Televisie*, 318, 24–5.

DEPRESSING, DEGRADING!
THE RECEPTION OF THE EUROPEAN HORROR FILM IN BRITAIN 1957–68

David Huxley

In 1954 the comic postcards of Donald McGill were prosecuted in Lincoln with McGill pleading guilty on four counts of publishing 'obscene matter' as defined under the Obscene Publications Act. In the same year seven of the pulp novels of 'Hank Janson' were prosecuted at the Old Bailey on grounds of obscenity and their publishers were fined £2,000 and sentenced to six months imprisonment.[1] A year later the Museum Press of London published American psychiatrist Frederic Wertham's anti-horror comic polemic *The Seduction of the Innocent*, which helped to bring about The Children and Young Persons (Harmful Publications) Act in 1955.[2] These and other prosecutions in the 1950s constituted a climate of 'moral panic' about the effects of various media largely based on a straightforward 'hypodermic' model of cause and effect. This type of influence, in Britain at least, is seen as being particularly dangerous if the given medium is available to the working classes. The Obscene Publications Act (1959) included a revealing definition of obscenity stating that an obscene text was something that 'will tend to deprave and corrupt *persons who are likely to read it* [emphasis added]'. Thus presumably it made a difference if a book was available in a popular paperback rather than a limited edition printed in Paris and the material only 'became' obscene when it was in a form available to the 'lower orders'.[3]

Dick Hebdige has characterised the opening phase of a 'moral panic' as creating a hysteria in the press'; this hysteria is 'typically ambivalent; it fluctuates between dread and fascination, outrage and amusement. Shock and horror headlines dominate' (1979: 93). This is then inevitably followed by the second stage, 'incorporation', where the perceived 'aberration' is made safe. In the field of subcultures this involves both moving from outrage to amusement, and making versions of the subculture marketable to the mainstream audience. Hebdige describes the process: 'its vocabulary becomes more and more familiar ... brought back into line, located on the preferred map of problematic social reality' (1979: 94). I would argue that much of this process of demonisation was applied to the horror film in Britain in the 1950s. Both the domestic output of Hammer films and imported horror films from continental Europe were castigated by a wide range of reviewers and critics during the late 1950s, before being 'made safe' and finally accorded some kind of approbation by the 1960s.

THE CENSORS

Before considering the critical reception of horror films in Britain it is important to remember that all horror films, whatever their country of origin, were subject to a strict censorship regime. John Trevelyan, President of the British Board of Film Censors, was widely regarded as a liberal and intelligent man who was prepared to discuss censorship issues with filmmakers in a rational manner. However, his autobiography, *What the Censor Saw*, reveals that Trevelyan believed he could clearly distinguish between serious 'art' films and commercial 'potboilers'.[4] Only five pages of the book are devoted to the horror film, and Trevelyan explains: 'Horror films were rarely a problem since most of them came to us from Hammer films, the most successful production company in this field, from whom we always had full co-operation' (1973: 165).

Thus Hammer films were in effect pre-censored at the script or first treatment stage. An internal BBFC memo of 14 October 1957 described Jimmy Sangster's screenplay for *Dracula* as: 'uncouth, uneducated, disgusting and vulgar' (*Dracula: The House that Hammer Built Special* 1998: 36). Later fourteen cuts were required by the BBFC at both script and first cut stages of the film. With *Dracula Prince of Darkness* in 1965 a communication from the Board asked for fourteen separate amendments to the script. Some scenes had to be removed completely, whilst other requirements were more minor, such as the final instruction: 'Care should be taken with the soundtrack when Dracula's wrist breaks. We would not want to hear nasty cracking noises' (quoted in Pirie 1980: item 27). American horror films also get short shrift in the book with Trevelyan describing Roger Corman as, 'most co-operative', but Continental European horror films were seen as much more problematic and were regularly cut or even banned outright. Antonio Margheriti's

Danza macabra/Castle of Blood (1963), for example, was cut by five minutes in 1968, Massimo Pupillo's *Cinque tombe per un medium/Terror Creatures from the Grave* (1965) was cut by seven minutes in the same year and Jean Rollin's *Frisson des vampires/Shiver of the Vampire* (1970) was cut by a full eighteen minutes in 1970. Nevertheless the process of 'incorporation' was underway as demonstrated in Trevelyan's comment that 'a film called *Black Sunday* [*La maschera del demonio*, Mario Bava, 1960] was refused a certificate in 1961 on the grounds of disgust, but was eventually passed by the Board in 1968 because by this time it looked rather ridiculous: if was then distributed under the title of *Revenge of the Vampire*' (1973: 166).

Trevelyan's attitude to European horror films reveals not only arrogance but also a complete misunderstanding of the European milieu when he adds that: 'One help to us was that nobody took these films seriously: this included the people who made them as well as the audiences' (ibid.). As we shall see later, Mario Bava, the director of *Black Sunday*, whom Trevelyan doesn't even deign to name, was viewed very differently by later British critics. To summarise, the attitude of Trevelyan and the BBFC to British, Continental European and indeed American horror films was remarkably even handed. Rather simplistically they assumed that as mere horror films these products could not possibly be 'art' and therefore they could be censored at will. The only exception to this rule was when a director whom Trevelyan regarded as a 'serious' director delved into horror (such as Roman Polanski) and even then, through negotiation, the Board would still insist on cuts.

THE CRITICS

As Peter Hutchings has pointed out, the critical response to Hammer horror films from 1957 onwards was actually quite mixed. The more vitriolic responses tend to be quoted more frequently because of their sensational tone. Hutchings (1993) and Steve Chibnall and Julian Petley (2002) have each looked at a number of early newspaper reviews of Hammer films for somewhat different ends. Hutchings, in *Hammer and Beyond*, to set British horror film production in its social context; Chibnall and Petley, in *British Horror Cinema*, to look at the implications of the furore for the censorship and status of later British horror films. My intention here is to extend the time frame, the nationality of films and media sources under consideration. In this way it should be possible to assess not only any changes in critical opinion over time, but also to discern any differences between various types of publication and their attitude to films from different European countries. If a range of early reviews in newspapers and film journals is examined, it is possible to discern five distinct strategies which are used by critics to condemn the horror film. These early reviews concentrate on the impact of Hammer films' switch into horror with their adaptations of *Frankenstein* and *Dracula*. It can also be seen that after 1963 a new series of strategies begin to be deployed by critics favourable to the horror film.

The first strategy of the anti-horror film critics and in many ways the most extreme is a dismissal of the entire genre. Thus Peter Dyer's review of Hammer's *Dracula* (Terence Fisher, 1958) in *Films and Filming* begins: 'There are boring horror films, and there are tasteless horror films'; having condemned the whole genre he continues: 'The new version of *Dracula* is a boring, tasteless horror film' (1958: 27). The second strategy is to suggest that all horror film is risible, as Hutchings describes it 'a need to push the film away through distancing laughter' (1993: 9). Nina Hibbin's (1958) review of *Dracula* seems to be taking this line when it opens with the comment: 'I went to see *Dracula* [...] a Hammer film, prepared to enjoy a nervous giggle. I was even ready to poke fun at it.' But the next sentence, 'I came away revolted and outraged' moves the review into the third form of attack: the accusation of bad taste. This is probably the most common of the tactics used by those who disapproved of these horror films. R. D. Smith's (1957) review of the Hammer's *The Curse of Frankenstein* (Terence Fisher, 1957) in the *Tribune* ends: 'The logical development of this kind of thing is a peep show of freaks, interspersed with visits to a torture chamber. It is a depressing and degrading thought for anyone who loves the cinema'. Campbell Dixon (1957) ends his review of the same film in the *Daily Telegraph*: 'when the screen gives us severed heads and hands, eyeballs dropped in a wine glass and magnified, and brains dished up on a plate like spaghetti I can only suggest a new certificate – 'SO' perhaps, for Sadists Only'. The fourth form of attack is allied to this in that it questions the intelligence of the horror film audience where, as Peter Hutchings describes it, the audience is constructed as: 'completely Other, primitive, childlike, easily exploited' (1993: 7). This is epitomised by Derek Granger's (1957) review of *The Curse of Frankenstein* in the *Financial Times*, which claims: 'Only the saddest of simpletons, one feels, could ever get a really satisfying frisson'.

The final and perhaps most subtle strategy was an 'attack by comparison'. Here it was accepted that good horror films could be made, but then the example under consideration was found to not live up to the requisite standard. Thus Dilys Powell, reviewing Hammer's *Dracula, Prince of Darkness* (Terence Fisher, 1966) in the *Sunday Times* combines ridicule with the 'attack by comparison'. She claimed: 'I admit to a guffaw, not stifled, now and then. But a guffaw isn't enough; if I am to have horror in Technicolor I want the kind of Gothic dream-horror which Roger Corman can do, e.g. *The Fall of the House of Usher*' (1966).

There is no distinct political or status pattern in these reviews – quality broadsheets and serious film magazines were almost as likely to condemn horror films as were the tabloids, and left-wing papers could be as condemnatory as those from the right. It is true, however, that the very few positive reviews occur in more popular newspapers, and Paul Dehn's (1957) review of *The Curse of Frankenstein* in the *Daily Herald* is so perceptive it actually reads as if it was written some thirty years later when Hammer (particularly early Hammer) had achieved widespread critical acclaim. Despite all the vitriol aimed at Hammer from other quarters, there is, perhaps surprisingly, little or no condemnation of any sexual overtones in horror films of this period (though of course the more obvious sexual content was being cut from many Continental European films on their release in Britain). There was, however, a lively discussion in the letter columns of *Films and Filming* which did touch on this issue. In March 1960 a Miss D. V. Ayles asked: 'Why is it necessary to team a perfectly good horror film (and some of them are) with nauseating sex dramas from across the channel?' (1960: 3).

In reply D. J. Ebberson raised the possibility that horror films were actually much more suspect: 'Everyone deplores the more lurid cheap sex melos ... but even the worst of these are generally less disgusting, sadistic, unhealthy and unnatural than the average good clean British or American horror opus' (1960: 3). In terms of editorial policy, however, there does seem to be some difference between 'highbrow' and more popular film journals, with the latter much more likely to defend the contemporary horror film. In 1959 *Sight and Sound* published an article by Derek Hill entitled 'The Face of Horror'. It opens with the assertion: 'Only a sick society could bear the hoardings, let alone the films' (1959: 6). Having attacked on the grounds of disgust, Hill then goes on to attack these films on the grounds of incompetence. He says: 'There is little to frighten in *The Curse of Frankenstein* ... "Horror", in fact, is the wrong term for the majority of films that Hammer's successes have inspired. Most are so ineptly written and directed that every chance of genuine suspense is botched in a way that suggests ignorance of cinematic possibilities' (1959: 9).

These two forms of attack are broadly contradictory. If, on the one hand, Hill finds these films, 'repellent, disgusting, repulsive, deliberately nauseating, sadistic, repugnant and revolting' (as he does), then why is there, 'little to frighten' in them (ibid.). Forced into a corner, he has to argue that only suspense can create horror. This is a traditional argument that many early writers on the horror film such as Ivan Butler (1970) and Carlos Clarens (1971) have used. Hill also quotes from Frederic Wertham's *Seduction of the Innocent* and implies that Wertham's analogy about the degradation of taste caused by horror comics can be applied to the horror film. Wertham wrote: 'Supposing ... you get used to eating sandwiches made with very strong seasonings, with onions and peppers and highly spiced mustard. You will lose your taste for simple bread and butter and for finer food' (quoted in Hill 1959: 10).

Again, this is a widely used argument that has been applied to everything from television coverage of the Vietnam War to children's cartoons. Despite its apparent appeal to 'common sense' it has not been proven, and perhaps cannot be proven that the media works in this way.[5] Elsewhere in the article Hill also attacks one-off horror issues produced by *Films and Filming* and *Picturegoer*. The 1 November 1958 issue of *Picturegoer* to which he refers contains the article, 'Chillers a Menace?'

Picturegoer Horror Special: a popular magazine makes the connection between horror and sex.

Rubbish says Christopher Lee' (Stoddart 1958: 5) and an article by 'Picuregoer's psychiatrist' which claims that, 'Horror interests normal teenagers', and an article about horror heroines which comments: 'No matter how abnormal a monster may look, he's usually quite normal in his instinct for sorting out the pretty girls from the rest' (*Picturegoer* 1958: 10–11).

The entire issue is very positive with a letter asking for, 'more super horror' and interestingly in the articles no distinction is made between recent horror films and the Universal versions of the 1930s. Here it can be seen that if there is little difference between left- and right-wing papers response to the horror film, the same is not true of 'higher class' and popular film periodicals. *Picturegoer* was a popular, arguably 'lower class' weekly with star profiles, gossip and reviews. The magazine clearly demonstrates its unbounded enthusiasm for horror, and even includes a specially commissioned short story by the 'uncouth' screenwriter Jimmy Sangster. Also the cover of the magazine and its article on heroines clearly show that *Picturegoer* (and presumably its audience) saw the mix of sex and horror in these films as being central to their appeal.

By 1958 specialist magazines devoted purely to the horror film had begun to appear in America. Perhaps because these magazines were preaching to the converted, they do not seem to have felt the need to defend the new horror films. They are characterised by excruciating puns, as in, 'Only thirty chopping days left to Halloween' (*Famous Monsters of Filmland*, November 1960) and uncritical enthusiasm for all things 'horrific'. In America Hammer's early films had not scandalised critics, despite the fact that C. A. Lejeune (1958) had felt, 'inclined to apologise to all decent Americans for sending them a work in such sickening bad taste', in her *Observer* review of *Dracula*. However the *New York Times* review of the same film was mainly tongue in cheek, commenting that, 'you can't keep a good ghoul down' (Weiler 1958: 24).

From 1963 onwards reviews in all kinds of journals gradually become much more favourable. This may be due in part to the cycle of the moral panic, whereby horror films were now undergoing the process of incorporation, as well as the wider cultural changes which had taken place in Britain between 1958 and 1963. But it is also the case that some critics who were much more sympathetic to the horror film had begun working for various review journals, such as Peter Cowie and David McGillivray (later the screenwriter of such films as *Frightmare* [1974] and indeed *I'm Not Feeling Myself Tonight* [1975]). These critics used a new range of strategies to explain the nature of the horror film. The first of these was the 'auteur defence'. Here the auteur theory was broadly applied to argue that certain directors rise above what might still be seen as a minor genre. Thus Cowie (1965), reviewing Mario Bava's *La maschera del demonio/Black Sunday* in 1965 claims that it is: 'a good deal better and more thoughtfully worked out than most horror films, and the final story ... is really imaginative. The Byronic landscapes, the bloody sunsets and the piles of ruins are absolutely convincing and ideal'.

Interestingly Cowie here concentrates on the *mise-en-scène* of Bava's work and it was the perceived lyricism of Bava's films that helped to establish his reputation as a major practitioner, perhaps second only to Terence Fisher in the field during this period. Indeed this revisionist view was not limited to continental European directors, and Robin Bean's review of Hammer's *Kiss of the Vampire* (Don Sharp,

1962) comments: 'All credit to Sharp for turning what could have been a creaking, monotonously predictable story into an exceptionally well made (with some beautifully framed shots) and entertaining film' (1964: 32). Again the concentration here is not so much on the elements of horror *per se* as the creation of an effective gothic atmosphere which can be perceived as beautiful rather than grotesque.

The second strategy was a 'budgetary defence', where some of the shortcomings of a given film could be explained by a simple lack of resources. Thus *Terrore nello spazio/Planet of the Vampires* (1965), which is often regarded as a minor Mario Bava film, is described in the *Monthly Film Bulletin* as 'the triumph of mind over matter, or of Bava over a shoe-string budget and appalling dubbed dialogue [...] he does atmospheric wonders with pastel-shaded ground fogs and cunning camerawork' (Anon. 1968: 204). Thirdly certain stars were now perceived as being able to transcend the limitations of low-budget horror, and to have some qualities particularly appropriate to the genre. In the *Monthly Film Bulletin* review of *I lunghi capelli della morte/The Long Hair of Death* (Antonio Margheriti, 1964), Rank Charm School graduate Barbara Steele was singled out: 'If Margheriti hasn't quite the same gift as Bava for this kind of thing, he acquits himself very creditably; Barbara Steele is her usual extraordinary self' (Anon. 1967:143). Although she appeared in films by directors as diverse as Roger Corman and Federico Fellini, Steele's generic stardom rested on her roles in Italian horror films and she remains a cult figure with the longevity of a Christopher Lee or Peter Cushing.

CONCLUSION

In conclusion it can be seen that some popular sources were broadly favourable toward contemporary horror films even as early as 1957. The moral panic created by some reviewers had run its course by the mid-1960s and any critical reviews after that date tend to be mocking rather than vitriolic. This could be, to an extent, the process which Dick Hebdige describes as 'incorporation' (see Hebdige 1979). Following his model of the 'taming' of subcultures by moral panic, the horror films of this period underwent the same process of outrage, followed by ridicule and finally, when made safe, they were incorporated into mainstream culture. However, films which were willing to stretch generic conventions and show more morbid or extreme horror could still cause problems. In 1968, for example, Michael Reeves' dystopian English Civil War tale of witch-hunts and torture, *Witchfinder General* caused something of a furore, at least in newspaper reviews. But the extent to which times had changed is demonstrated in the *Monthly Film Bulletin*, which explained: 'Not since *Peeping Tom* has a film aroused such an outcry about nastiness and gratuitous violence as this one. Difficult to see why' (Milne 1968: 100).

The *Films and Filming* review, by David Austen, was very favourable and complimented the film on its power, even calling for it not to be censored, adding that:

'But the censor, like Mathew Hopkins, has very little to do with justice' (1968: 36). But the way in which this film was advertised also indicates the extent to which general attitudes toward horror film had changed in Britain between 1957 and 1968. In the same issue of *Films and Filming* there is a half-page advertisement for the film. Above the title and an image of Vincent Price the readers of this august journal are persuaded to patronise the film on the grounds that it is: 'The Most Violent Film of the Year'.

NOTES

1 'Hank Janson' was a pseudonym for Stephen Frances. New Hank Janson novels continued to be published, written by a number of other writers, without censorship problems, well into the 1970s.
2 Geoffrey Wagner's *Parade of Pleasure* (1954) which argued for censorship in film, comics, pin-up magazines and paperbacks also contributed to this debate, as did a series of newspaper and magazine articles.
3 This, of course, is exactly what happened in probably the most famous obscenity trial of this period, when the Penguin paperback edition of D. H. Lawrence's *Lady Chatterley's Lover* was prosecuted in 1960. The book, written in 1928, had been available in small print run, unexpurgated editions printed in Europe, for many years.
4 Trevelyan's book only briefly discusses horror in chapter twelve, 'Odds and Ends' and chapter eleven, 'Violence'. In contrast forty-three pages are devoted to the topics of nudity, sex and obscenity.
5 Studies which appear to prove these kinds of direct links need to be approached with great caution. In the field of children's cartoons the methodology and conclusions of a famous 1963 piece of research by Albert Bandura is called into question in Ben Crawford's essay 'Saturday Morning Fever.' (1991)

BIBLIOGRAPHY

Anon. (1968) Review of 'Planet of the Vampires', *Monthly Film Bulletin*, 204.
____ (1967) Review of 'The Long Hair of Death', *Monthly Film Bulletin*, 142.
Austen, D. (1968) Review of 'Witchfinder General', *Films and Filming*, July, 36.
Ayles, D. (1960) 'Boy meets Ghoul', letter in *Films and Filming*, March, 3.
Bean, R. (1964) 'Kiss of the Vampire', *Films and Filming*, February, 31–2.
Butler, I. (1970) *Horror in the Cinema*. London: Zwemmer.
Chibnall, S. and J. Petley (eds) (2002) *British Horror Cinema*. London: Routledge.
Clarens, C. (1971) *Horror Movies: An Illustrated Survey*. London: Panther.
Cowie, P. (1965) 'Black Sabbath', *Films and Filming*, January, 32–3.
Crawford, B. (1991) 'Saturday Morning Fever', in A. Cholodenko (ed.) *The Illusion of Life: Essays on Animation*. Sydney: Power Publications, 113–30.
Dixon, C. (1957) Review of 'The Curse of Frankenstein', *The Daily Telegraph*, 4 May.
Dehn, P. (1957) Review of 'The Curse of Frankenstein', *The Daily Herald*, 3 May.
Dyer, P. (1958) 'Dracula', *Films and Filming*, July, 27.

Ebberson, D. (1960) 'Sex with Horror', letter in *Films and Filming*, April, 3.
Granger, D. (1957) Review of 'The Curse of Frankenstein', *The Financial Times*, 6 May.
Hebdige, D. (1979) *Subculture: The Meaning of Style*. London: Routledge.
Hibbin, N. (1958) 'Dracula's Macabre Decline', *The Daily Worker*, 24 May.
Hill, D. (1959) 'The Face of Horror', *Sight and Sound*, 6–11.
Hutchings, P. (1993) *Hammer and Beyond: The British Horror Film*. Manchester: Manchester University Press.
Lejeune, C. A. (1958) Review of 'Dracula', *The Observer*, 5 May.
Milne, T. (1968) Review of 'Witchfinder General', *Monthly Film Bulletin*, 100.
Picturegoer (1958) 'Horror Special', London: Odhams Press, 1 November.
Pirie, D. (1973) *A Heritage of Horror: The English Gothic Cinema 1946-1972*. London: Gordon Fraser.
Pirie, D. (1980) *Hammer: A Cinema Case Study*. London: British Film Institute.
Powell, D. (1966) Review of 'Dracula, Prince of Darkness', *The Sunday Times*, 9 January.
Smith, R. D. (1957) 'Depressing, degrading!', *The Tribune*, 10 May.
Stoddart, S. (1958) 'Chillers a Menace? Rubbish', *Picturegoer*, 1 November, 5.
Trevelyan, J. (1973) *What the Censor Saw*. London: Michael Joseph.
Weiler, A. H. (1958) Review of 'Horror of Dracula', *The New York Times*, 29 May, 24.
Wertham, F. (1954) *The Seduction of the Innocent*. London: The Museum Press.

BRITISH HORROR CINEMA

BRITISH HORROR CINEMA

Patricia Allmer, Emily Brick and David Huxley

Horror in Britain is strongly anchored in and emerges out of the literary Gothic and Romantic tradition. Writers such as Mary Shelley, John Polidori, Bram Stoker and M. R. James provided the initial narratives still haunting twentieth and twenty-first century horror film audiences. Horror was also a significant genre for early British film pioneers such as George Albert Smith, who filmed a ghost for the Society of Psychical Research in 1898, and Walter Booth, whose *The Magic Sword* (1901) and *The Haunted Curiosity Shop* (1901) featured haunting skeletons and moving mummies. Sources for early British horror narratives lie in the country's colonial history, as can be seen in films such as T. Hayes Hunter's *The Ghoul* (1933), tracing the 'return of the repressed' of British imperial rationalism which regarded the exoticised spaces of the colonies as threatening. Another source was 'real life' murder narratives like that of Jack the Ripper, which influenced Hitchcock's early British horror film *The Lodger* (1926).

Few horror films were produced in Britain in the 1930s, partially due to America's domination of the film market. The decade saw a significant migration of a number of directors and actors, including Hitchcock, Bela Lugosi and Peter Cushing, to America. However, a series of cheap stage adaptations starring Tod Slaughter, such as *Sweeney Todd: The Demon Barber of Fleet Street* (George King, 1936) showed that there was still an audience for a home-grown product, even if it could not compete with the budgets of Universal's American horror films. Slaughter continued, with less success, after the Second World War, but his work preserves the Victorian stage melodrama tradition on film.

Whilst British horror cinema's subsequent development was restricted by competition from the American film market, the biggest threat to it emerged from Britain itself through a censorship campaign comparable to a witchhunt, little rivalled in the rest of the world. British horror cinema was punished from the 1920s onwards, by an ongoing campaign led mostly by the British Board of Film Censors (BBFC), the political right and popular tabloid newspapers, indoctrinating and controlling British audiences who were treated as 'little more than advanced children' (Kermode 2002: 11).

The campaign involved the introduction of ratings and certificates legitimising the cutting and banning of films to an extent that 'home-produced British horror was forbidden from being "disgusting or revolting" from the 1950s through to the early 1970s' (Kermode 2002: 14). Most horror films fell into this category. Ironically, in this climate of censorship and media concern it was the highly respected director Michael Powell who received the most opprobrium for his study of a voyeuristic serial killer, *Peeping Tom*, in 1960 (the released film was heavily censored). Now highly regarded, the reception of the film was nevertheless instrumental in destroying Powell's career.

However, as Peter Hutchings remarks, 'the last part of the 1950s, into the 1960s and then on to the 1970s, British horror was one of the most commercially successful areas of British cinema' (1993: 1). This was due to prolific production of gothic horrors (often harking back to the literary tradition mentioned above) by companies like Amicus, Tigon and, most famously, Hammer, featuring actors such as Christopher Lee and Peter Cushing. That these companies were allowed to produce horror films in an ideological climate hostile to horror, is largely due to their resemblance to costume and historical dramas, their avoidance of overt sexual or political meanings and their conventionality of language and action. Despite their commercial success (Hammer was awarded the Queen's Award for Industry in 1968) these films were not critically reappraised until David Pirie's seminal book *A Heritage of Horror* in 1973, just as the cycle was in decline. Since that date early Hammer films in particular have been regarded as 'classics', along with films like Tigon's (heavily cut) *Witchfinder General* (Michael Reeves, 1968) and British Lion's (heavily cut) *The Wicker Man* (Robin Hardy, 1973). Significantly, Europe is repeatedly constructed in these films (made during the historical moves towards European union) as a regressive, superstitious and atavistic space.

The most relentless campaign against horror cinema was in the 1980s and 1990s, in the wake of the Conservative Party's landslide election victory in 1983, consisting of the clamping down on the new, unregulated video market which introduced previously unseen horror films to British audiences. Tabloid newspapers christened these films 'video nasties' and the 1984 Video Recordings Act gave the BBFC *carte blanche* to classify and cut all video releases. In 1993–94 a further attack against horror cinema was launched by the tabloid press and the Conservative Party, linking the murder of the toddler James Bulger by two boys to the horror film *Child's Play III* (Jack Bender, 1991).

The dominance of conservative ideologies in Britain becomes apparent through this brief outline. British horror films have responded to this situation: Clive Barker's *Hellraiser* (1986) explores British colonial history and contemporary conservative ideologies (see Allmer 2008). The chapters in this section focus on this potential of British horror film as an exploration, sometimes reactionary, sometimes subversive, of British cultural conservatism. John Sears' discussion of Wolf Rilla's *Village of the Damned* (1960) unearths a range of British post-war anxieties and conservative fantasies about patriarchal authority, paternity, immigration and reverse-colonisation – the class politics of the film are an allegory for 'an English class system in crisis'.

Recently, there have been several internationally successful contemporary low-budget British horror films such as *28 Days Later* (Danny Boyle, 2002), *Dog Soldiers* (Neil Marshall, 2002) and the cross-generic ('rom-zom-com') *Shaun of the Dead* (Edgar Wright, 2004). Linnie Blake's chapter explores some of these films in relation to the New Labour government elected in 1997, drawing parallels between these films' re-visioning of 'earlier zombie, werewolf, vampire and monster movies' and 'New Labour's own re-formulation of Old Labour and Neo-Conservative positions'.

BIBLIOGRAPHY

Allmer, P. (2008) '"Breaking the Surface of the Real": The Discourses of Commodity Capitalism in Clive Barker's *Hellraiser* Narratives', in M. Holmgren Troy and E. Wennö (eds) *Space, Haunting, Discourse*. Cambridge: Cambridge Scholars Publishing, 14–24.

Hutchings, P. (1993) *Hammer and Beyond: The British Horror Film*. Manchester and New York: Manchester University Press.

Kermode, M. (2002) 'The British Censors and Horror Cinema', in S. Chibnall and J. Petley (eds) *British Horror Cinema*. London and New York: Routledge, 10–22.

Pirie, D. (1973) *A Heritage of Horror: The English Gothic Cinema 1946–1972*. London: Gordon Fraser.

THE BOUNDARIES OF HORROR IN WOLF RILLA'S *VILLAGE OF THE DAMNED*

John Sears

Wolf Rilla's *Village of the Damned* has invited allegorical readings ever since its initial release by MGM in 1960. Directed by an émigré German director (who died in October 2005) whose subsequent films included sex comedies like *Secrets of a Door to Door Salesman* (1973) and *Bedtime with Rosie* (1974), *Village of the Damned* was filmed in the village of Letchmore Heath near Watford, and made nearby at Borehamwood Studios. The film interrogates the hazy generic boundary between science fiction and horror, consisting of a relatively conventional science fiction/horror narrative, the kind summarised by Susan Sontag as combining 'unremitting banality and inconceivable terror' (1987: 224). After an unexplained outbreak of fainting in a sleepy English village, apparently alien children are born of all the women of child-bearing age, and quickly proceed to establish a colony (the word is used twice in the script), rapidly developing, via what one internet reviewer calls 'escalating mayhem' (http://twtd.bluemountains.net.au/Rick/votd.htm), into potentially superior and destructive beings who must somehow themselves be destroyed in an extended version of the Oedipal struggle. Much political wrangling takes place; the crisis deepens, with a sequence of deaths in the village, and eventually the hero, Professor Gordon Zellaby, putative 'father' of David, the apparent leader of 'the Children', is forced to commit suicide in order to eliminate the threat.

The film, made for budgetary reasons in black and white, draws on atmosphere and devices established in the 1950s by Nigel Kneale's *Quatermass* series (*The Quatermass Experiment*, BBC, 1953; *Quatermass II*, BBC, 1955; *Quatermass and the Pit*, BBC, 1959) and prefigures later British science fiction/horror crossovers like *A for Andromeda* (1961) and, eventually, *Doctor Who* (1963–89; re-launched 2005–present). A sequel, *Children of the Damned*, followed in 1964, and the original was remade, unsuccessfully, by John Carpenter in 1995. As with other roughly contemporary science fiction/horror films (Don Siegel's *Invasion of the Body Snatchers* [1957] being the most obvious) the narrative and the text open up spaces for potentially endless interpretation, indicating the polysemic richness of the generic space afforded by science fiction/horror and suggesting fruitful ways in which theoretical and contextual analyses can respond to the horror film.

The film's anxieties are overt and simple to summarise, responding as they do to contemporary social and cultural changes and concerns. It allegorises post-war English anxieties about patriarchal authority, family and paternity – the central protagonist is aware that his son is his mother's more than his: 'I have no evidence that he is mine', he states. This anxiety is also clearly a potential condemnation of female promiscuity; the planned filming in America was abandoned after protests by the censorious Catholic Defamation League; the film presents several images of frustrated, violent masculinity, men excluded from the manifest procreative process and therefore, implicitly, from the family structure and from conventional ideologies defining masculinity in relation to paternity. It explores English anxieties about immigration, invasion and reverse-colonisation; the alien Children are conspicuously pale-skinned and white-haired, in an inverted representation of the racial appearances causing most cultural anxiety in England in the 1950s. This semiotic inversion also gestures back to fascist iconographies of the Aryan *übermensch* and invokes memories of the then still recent invasion threats of the early war years. The film furthermore addresses concerns about children who are clearly distinct from their parents, a difference marked in their appearance and behaviour, signifying the new 1950s phenomenon of the generation gap described and theorised by Richard Hoggart (1957) and others. At thematic levels, it presents us with a staple science fiction fear, the communal mind, clearly alluding to Cold War ideological anxieties and concerns about individualism and capitalist identities (see Seed 1996). And it allows, like so many post-war British films (for example, Basil Dearden's *The League of Gentlemen* [1960]), a symbolic re-enactment of the War, a nostalgic, temporary return to the good old days of troops on the streets, although now with Geiger counters and radiation suits – the same old war, with all its myths of community and shared duress, updated for the nuclear age, the old war as Cold War. Above all, the film addresses anxieties about the changing English class system, which will be the primary focus of this chapter; the class politics of the film allegorise an English class system in crisis, this crisis both standing for and subsuming other levels of significance in this remarkably polysemic text. Each potential reading contributes to the others, confirming *Village of the Damned* as a film that demands complex cultural-critical responses. Each reading, in turn, centres on the film's readings of its own contexts, figured in the recurrent visual and plot motif of the crossing of different kinds of generational, political, historical or social boundary.

The genre of horror can be understood as being defined by boundaries and their crossing. The boundary, Martin Heidegger argues, 'is that from which something begins its essential unfolding' (1993: 356); what unfolds from the boundary, in the context of its symbolic functions in horror films, is difference and delimitation. Boundaries delimit and discriminate, or mark the difference between, the acceptable and the unacceptable, the representable and the unrepresentable, the permitted and the punishable, the explicit and the implicit, the known and the unknown, the natural and the supernatural. Underneath such structures lie primal boundaries between self and other, clean and contaminated, inside and outside, living and dead, past and present – boundaries that constitute the material of such theoretical frameworks as Kristevan abjection. The boundary marks the limit of each term, but belongs to neither, existing outside of and yet structuring these binary divisions. The boundary establishes difference as both defining of, and threatening to, identity; difference unfolds from boundaries. Horror typically oscillates back and forth across the material and symbolic boundaries it establishes, moving us between the familiar and the unfamiliar and from identity to difference in a destabilising manner that works to unsettle and to inculcate fear by alerting us to differences that simultaneously establish and threaten identities. The more integral the boundary to the identity constructed by a conventionally 'stable' ideological position, the more powerful the destabilisation by horror's generic movement. Boundaries themselves are, simultaneously, undermined and reinforced by the genre's relentless repositioning of them in relation to tradition (and specifically the tradition of the genre itself), audience expectation (a product of marketing as well as of narrative structure), and perceptions of ideological acceptability (what Stephen King calls 'the gross-out level' of horror [see 1988: 17–9], the visual and visceral challenge it presents, in its representations, to the hitherto acceptable). The boundaries of horror, and the things which begin incessantly to unfold from them, are mobile, polysemic, fluid in response to shifting ideological territories; consequently the genre itself is mobile, its limits changing historically and culturally.

The boundary of the horror film is always allegorical, in that it speaks of, and therefore brings into symbolic presence, the interminable and threatening presence/absence of the Other. The word 'allegory' derives from *allos*, other and *agoreuein*, to speak openly (see Warner 1985: xix). The boundary always marks the limits of the possibilities of familiar conception, and the potential for conception to be otherwise, in relation to the social and cultural world depicted in the film (and that to which the film responds). Boundaries work by inclusion and exclusion to construct the ideological thresholds against which the horror genre continually presses, and beyond which it insistently spills. In *Village of the Damned* boundaries function in powerful and explicit ways in relation both to the contexts that the film addresses, and to the possibilities for reading that the film presents. The film adapts John Wyndham's remarkable novel *The Midwich Cuckoos* (first published in 1957), itself a tightly plotted, suspenseful narrative that operates centrally within an œuvre of key British science fiction novels that constructs what Roger Luckhurst has called 'an echo-box of post-war anxiety' (2005: 132). The film adopts the novel's range of expression and its overall, typically English, struggle to contain emotion and to sustain rational engagement and enquiry, suggesting an ideological urgency being continually repressed, boundaries continually being pressed against. The novel is explicit about this pressing urgency and its various explicit allegorical functions – the Children present, for example, 'a racial danger of a most urgent kind' (Wyndham 1960: 191) – while affording ambiguous space for other potential interpretations – for example, its events 'had a somewhat queer beginning' (Wyndham 1960: 132), Major Bernard reminds us, signifying the potential damage to heterosexual conceptions of masculinity lurking within the film's boundaries.

The film itself is replete with literal and figurative boundaries. These range from the inexplicable 'barrier' surrounding Midwich and cutting it off, to the 'brick wall' imagined by the 'hero' Zellaby to defend his mind against the cuckoo Children; from the image of that brick wall that is reflected back by the internal walls of Kyle Manor to the external brick wall at the edge of the estate into which Paul's car smashes when he is punished by the Children and from the barrier set up by the Civil Defence Guard to 'protect' people arriving at Midwich to the political and bureaucratic barriers alluded to in the debating of the Children's future. These boundaries offer a series of responses to the historical contexts from which the film emerges, allegorising perceived social divisions, the experienced differences within post-war English society. They constitute barriers that either are apparently uncrossable and yet demand crossing, or are impenetrable, or alarmingly absent; the image of the brick wall around which the *dénouement* evolves is both a defence and a containment, a barrier to crash into and a boundary to be crossed, a demarcation of territorial identity and a blockage or arresting of development. These boundaries establish the liminal or 'in-between', signified in the name *Midwich*, as that which resists clear differentiation and therefore mobilises the film's anxieties. These in turn provide templates for a series of generic markers integral to the film's allegorising of English class anxieties.

The film constructs its version of England as a liminal, imaginary space circumscribed and divided by these barriers. Englishness itself is the ideological territory being mapped and interpreted; the ideological construction of post-war

Paul's car crashes into the wall surrounding Kyle Manor

Englishness comes under intense scrutiny and is found continually to be problematic. The English class system and its reification of English identities, while seemingly under threat in the film, are also clearly repeated by the social organisation of the Children, who are 'naturally' led and spoken for by David Zellaby, son of the lord of the manor. In turn, the social world of Midwich and of England is wholly available to Gordon Zellaby – he has access to private information, such as who has consulted with the vicar about their pregnancy, and he demonstrates easy familiarity with the working men and women in the village as well as with the Home Secretary and senior military and scientific figures. Zellaby is a professor of an indeterminate discipline, and functions as a reassuringly English version of the 'scientist' archetype, combined with elements of the detective (Basil Rathbone's Sherlock Holmes lurks somewhere in the background). Other key characters perform similar simple functions within the social terrain (vicar, soldier, gossipy telephonist, village bobby) that demarcate a society structured around seemingly ancient, reliably familiar roles and hierarchies.

Within this rigidly limited social framework the film announces an interconnected rhetoric of the horrific, a *résumé* of key horror motifs and resonances that will adumbrate and delimit the political unconscious of much late twentieth-century horror, and which indicates the full force of the repressions necessary to sustain this ideological vision of post-war England. This rhetoric includes murderously ungrateful children and infanticide (recurrent in subsequent horror films like *The Omen* [Richard Donner, 1976] and *Children of the Corn* [Fritz Kiersch, 1984]), apparently uncontrollable feminine sexuality and the consequences of new technologies of birth control (numerous films from *Rosemary's Baby* [Roman

Polanski, 1968] and *The Exorcist* [William Friedkin, 1974] to *Species* [Roger Donaldson, 1995]: the contraceptive pill was legalised in America in 1960, the year of *Village of the Damned*'s release), miscegenation (an overt concern of films like the *Alien* tetralogy [various directors 1979–97] and Bernard Rose's *Candyman* [1992]), reverse colonisation (integral to the narratives of films like *Poltergeist* [Steven Spielberg, 1982] and *Hostel* [Eli Roth, 2005]), telepathy and mind-control (*Carrie* [Brian De Palma, 1976], *The Shining* [Stanley Kubrick, 1980], *Scanners* [David Cronenberg, 1981], even a puzzle box (the central motif of Clive Barker's *Hellraiser* series [1987–2005]) and a character who says 'I'm afraid – so afraid' (a version of the tag-line of Cronenberg's *The Fly* [1986]).

The film establishes its critique through the ways in which these motifs and figures thematically and symbolically disrupt its conventional scenario. The opening sequence establishes rural bliss and class stability as primary signifiers of rigid and yet invisible boundaries: a pan shot delimits the initial territory of the ideological vision of England that the film will depict as challenged and defended, leading us to the manor house via scenes of shepherds and tractors, icons of modern pastoral. Midwich, its name redolent of centrality (and the village is foregrounded in the titles of both book and film), is thus established as a pastoral, oddly anachronistic territory, in which anachronism – time 'out of joint' – assumes powerful significance. The opening sequence leads into the title credits via the church tower and its clock face, the hour being tolled, marking, perhaps, the end or limit of this idyllic prehistory and the emergence of rural England (an Edenic fantasy) into the new, momentary temporality of the strange event. This is the radical deterritorialisation of the 'time-out' (as it's called in the novel), a different kind of anachronism which is eventually replaced or reterritorialised by the repressive, ordered time of modernity. This new time is signified by the invasion of military activities and technologies, and therefore paradoxically already old, the return of a historical moment in the belated re-enactment of a war that finished fifteen years earlier. This reterritorialisation competes with and counters other efforts to reterritorialise the village – specifically those of the Children to defend their own deterritorialised version of Midwich, a space that diminishes, as the film progresses, into a single room bounded by the mental wall that Zellaby imagines.

The film's tranquil opening is, then, confused and disrupted, as, in a re-enactment of the myth of the Fall, the village moves from the symbolic pre-temporal Eden of 'before', to the unknowable, imaginary or unconscious atemporality of the 'time-out', while the real, material temporality of modernity is momentarily excluded, only to assert its presence in the post-Lapsarian world that unfolds at the end of the 'time-out'. The 'events' of the 'time-out' – the impregnation, while unconscious, of all women of child-bearing age – thus suspend Midwich in an unknowable space of horror, an absence or lack, before plunging it abruptly into a version of modernity to which it must immediately respond – which is perhaps why the village can signify such a range of modern anxieties so quickly. The 'time-out' is thus the boundary-event in which the disruption of conventional temporality, and of symbolic versions of temporality and historical sequence encoded in ideologies and mythemes of paternity and maternity, primogeniture and inheritance, constructs the template for the narrative which follows, in which those mythemes are relentlessly re-imposed in response to the film's conservative ideological demands. From this event unfolds the fallen (contemporary) world of generational, sexual and social division that allegorises the early stages of conservative fantasies of the consequences of permissiveness – single and virgin mothers, children fathered impossibly by absent or unnaturally elderly men. These metonyms of unnatural parenthood are quickly reified, in the film, as the iconic unnatural Children.

The film's opening boundaries are clearly ideological and invite audience complicity. The relentless message of this opening sequence concerns the invisible, intangible persistence and apparent naturalness of English social class divisions and their explicit imbrication within another invisible, intangible network of power, the military-industrial complex. The first dialogue consists of Zellaby's telephone call requesting 'Major Bernard at his Whitehall number'. Telephones are, throughout the film, ambiguous signs of both communication and its failure. The opening sequences are characterised by telephone, rather than direct, dialogue exchanges; the telephone signifies the modernity and dynamism of the external world, communication as the vehicle of the new. The failure of the Midwich telephone exchange/Post Office to respond to incoming calls provides the first indication of the 'cutting off' of the village, establishing a new boundary around the village. The telephonist, Miss Ogle, later confuses the soldiers analysing the street outside with people 'from the telephone company'. The Post Office is one of the centres around which village life is metonymically constructed, along with the General Store and the Church. Indeed, when Major Bernard fails to contact his brother-in-law in the village, he tries 'the vicar, the general stores and the post office', in that order; not, as might have been expected, the police or the army.

The opening telephone call is thwarted by the second invisible boundary in the film, as the caller, Zellaby, seems, before being connected, to faint. The boundary between wakeful activity and unwilling sleep, and thus between normal and abnormal, is broken, and each person in Midwich is a victim of this breach, a disconnection of communication and consciousness; consequently, a new series of ideological and material boundary transgressions are set in motion, extending from willingness, agency, self-determination and self-control (which emerge as key elements of the ideology the film seeks to defend) to ownership of women, paternity and patriarchal authority. Boundaries here work to contain and exclude; they are present and absent, and differentiate between the possibilities of presence and absence in terms of agency and knowability within the film, raising questions about the status and possibility of knowledge – what is 'present' or 'presented' within the boundary of Midwich during the 'time-out'? What is excluded, and therefore absent? What absent fears and anxieties are made present by the unwanted pregnancies? What is presented, gifted, to the women of Midwich by such presentation? The film's responses to such questions are largely strategic and repressive, movements of exclusion and containment that respond to one set of boundaries by setting up another – characteristically, those required in order for the military-industrial complex to reterritorialise the pastoral idyll of English social relations with which the film opens. Such a reterritorialisation is of course also a deterritorialisation, a transformation of the social from a space of apparent security into, precisely, something other.

Midwich itself is established by these opening events as different, differentiated from the outside world of soldiers and policemen, implying an indeterminate and unknowable – even unconscious – lawlessness within the village. Within the 'cutting-off' of Midwich difference is momentarily erased by the imposition of an imaginary state (all people and animals sleep), only to be reified in the new and rapid mobilisation of repressive state apparatuses outside of the boundary. The boundary established around Midwich, which inaugurates the film's exploration of horror motifs, is itself intangible and invisible: as Major Bernard announces, 'It was static, odourless and invisible, and didn't register on any of our Geiger counters.' Such a boundary (a metaphor for ideology itself, perhaps) is a staple of science fiction – one thinks of the 'force field' common in *Star Trek* or, more interestingly, the invisible wall erected around the hospital treating the alien in Alan Bridges' minor classic *Invasion* (1966), itself a film very much in the tradition of *Village of the Damned*. The barrier insists upon its allegorical status; it marks a transformation, the imposition of a new spatiality and temporality and a new social structure and organisation upon the ancient world of order previously embodied by Midwich.

If the telephone signifies the potential of communication to establish order and to indicate disorder, communication itself is more problematic. The 'incidents' of violence that begin to accumulate in Midwich occur, we are told, 'in each case after some contact with the Others'. Zellaby's direct questioning of the Children ('Are you aware of life on other worlds?') meets with silence and evasion. His final statement to his wife concerns the possibility of communication: 'I think I've found a way of getting through to them', he says. Anthea, of course, realises too late the real message in this statement. Communication and its failure are, of course, figures of the boundary, of the ways media and words work to convey or fail to convey information across the boundaries between men, women and Children in the film. Inarticulacy belongs, largely, to the men in the village; the Children, by contrast, are expressly clear in their articulation. One significant subtext of *Village of the Damned* concerns the vulnerability of the human media of communication – and of human language itself – when compared with the telepathic mind-reading abilities of the Children.

This is signified clearly in a central scene where the Child David Zellaby first demonstrates that his remarkable development far outstrips that of an equivalent

David spells his name using wooden bricks

human child. He is shown, at the age of a year old, spelling out his name on a series of wooden bricks. Quite apart from offering a graphic image of the difference and power of the Children encoded as knowledge, this is an action rich in significance for the rest of the film. Firstly it indicates David's arrival at subjectivity, his premature 'mirror-stage' accession into the symbolic world of human language and, implicitly, his readiness to colonise and reterritorialise that world and all it contains. Secondly it reinforces, through metonymic insistence, the centrality of the brick wall as a motif that extends its significance to the function of a medium of communication. David spells his name with wooden bricks; the Children kill Paul by forcing him, by the power of their minds, to crash his car into a brick wall; Zellaby thinks of a brick wall to defend his thoughts against the mind-reading abilities of the Children. The brick wall is thus, in the film's fluid rhetoric, both a medium of communication and a barrier to communication that nevertheless communicates. It figures the function of the boundary in *Village of the Damned* as profoundly ambiguous, as both necessary and deplorable.

Furthermore the brick wall is a signifier of the class difference that both separates the Children from the villagers, and connects them symbolically, via their reading of the image in his mind, to the man who will be their nemesis, Zellaby. Zellaby's surname figures nowhere in any English nomenclature (a Google search reveals, in fact, that outside of this film and the novel it is based upon, the name seems not to exist); it therefore resides, like the Children, outside the film's nominal mapping of English identities. Zellaby signifies the temporarily acceptable presence of otherness (intellectual, aristocratic, marked by an alien name, residing, in post-war democratic England, in a manor house) within and yet outside the established social order, an otherness which, of course, he shares with the Children (also intellectually superior, aristocratic in their enunciation, marked by differences of appearance and residing at 'the Grange'). Because of his otherness, but also because of his identification with the Children as their sympathiser, protector and defender in key scenes in the film, he can be sacrificed along with the threatening otherness of the Children. He is identified with them as a thing to be destroyed. This drastic social expenditure, through the establishment of an economy of the equivalence of differences, of all sources of difference within the film's limited geography portends the return of some kind of social order. The film's closing image, of a burning stately home, can, again, be read in a variety of ways – as a standard Gothic image of the burning house of patriarchy familiar from Charlotte Brontë's *Jane Eyre* (1850) to Daphne du Maurier's *Rebecca* (1938); as an image of the need for the old to destroy the new; or as an allegory of a class structure that can only envision its own persistence through the erasure of difference.

Fredric Jameson notes of Stanley Kubrick's *The Shining* (another horror film concerned with anxieties about class identities acted out in a confined social space) that its 'lesson' is 'peculiarly disturbing for Left and Right alike. [...] The glossy simulacrum of this or that past is here unmasked as possession, as the ideological project to return to the hard certainties of a more visible and rigid class structure' (1992: 95). *Village of the Damned* similarly articulates a violently simplistic and reactionary response to a variety of modern cultural crises in terms of a destructive fantasy of Englishness possessed and dispossessed by otherness, a fantasy which culminates in the connection of Zellaby's personification of liberal thinking with both external, threatening social forces and pseudo-aristocratic, indigenous values. Its 'ideological project' perceives all forms of otherness as threats requiring elimination, so as to return the society of Midwich and England to the 'visible and rigid class structure' of its opening sequence. Its 'ideological project', like that of films like *The Shining*, is fundamentally nostalgic, consisting of seeking a regressive, destructive solution to seemingly irresolvable contemporary problems which include the different manifestations of social change presented in the film. Zellaby's destruction, along with the Children he has tried throughout to educate, protect and understand, is the final, violent gambit in a game of setting up and breaking down brick walls, played in defence of a social order that saw itself as already, as the film's title indicates, damned.

BIBLIOGRAPHY

Heidegger, M. (1993) *Basic Writings*, edited by D. Farrell Krell. London: Routledge.
Hoggart, R. (1957) *The Uses of Literacy*. Harmondsworth: Penguin Books.
Jameson, F. (1992) 'Historicism in *The Shining*', in F. Jameson, *Signatures of the Visible*. London:

Routledge, 82–98.
King, S. (1988) *Danse Macabre: The Anatomy of Horror*. London: Futura.
Luckhurst, R. (2005) *Science Fiction*. Cambridge: Polity Press.
Review of 'Village of the Damned', On-line. Available HTTP: http://twtd.bluemountains.net.au/Rick/votd.htm (15 May 2006).
Seed, D. (1996) *American Fiction and the Cold War*. Manchester: Manchester University Press.
Sontag, S. (1987) 'The Imagination of Disaster', in S. Sontag, *The Imagination of Disaster and Other Essays*. London: André Deutsch, 209–25.
Warner, M. (1985) *Monuments and Maidens: The Allegory of the Female Form*. London: Picador.
Wyndham, J. (1960 [1957]) *The Midwich Cuckoos*. Harmondsworth: Penguin.

NEW LABOUR, NEW HORRORS:
GENETIC MUTATION, GENERIC HYBRIDITY AND GENDER CRISIS IN BRITISH HORROR OF THE NEW MILLENNIUM

Linnie Blake

In the United Kingdom, the 1980s were characterised by the avaricious individualism of the Thatcherite agenda, which dismantled the industrial economy on which the nation's class-based and regionally-distinctive culture had historically rested, promoted narcissistic consumerism as the acme of human aspiration through wholesale valorisation of the cultural products of American capitalism and turned to military action in the Falklands and the Gulf as a means of ensuring electoral victory and cementing the much-vaunted 'special relationship' with the United States. As Jeffrey Richards has put it, the *zeitgeist* of the Thatcher years was that of 'aggressive and uncompromising individualism' that glorified combat whilst rejecting 'consensus and concern as wet and wimpish' (1997: 23). Needless to say, it was a worldview entirely inimical to cooperative social endeavour, the nation being encouraged to view itself, again in Richards' words, as 'a mass of struggling individuals each out for what they could get' (1997: 24). With the fall of the Berlin Wall in 1989 and the collapse of the Soviet empire two years later, the victory of Conservative ideology seemed assured and a sense of right-wing triumphalism saturated British social life: from the Porsche-driving Yuppies of the de-regulated City of London Stock Exchange to an increasingly rootless working class aspiring to participation in Britain's new property-owning, share-owning democracy even as the nationalised industry and the welfare state were dismantled around their ears.

Film culture was not slow to respond to such a perilous state of affairs – numerous films, many made with the financial support of Channel 4's Film Four label, despairing at the depths of social injustice, intolerance and hatred to which the nation had unashamedly descended; they included, of course, films like Lindsay Anderson's *Britannia Hospital* (1982), Stephen Frears' *My Beautiful Laundrette* (1985) and *Sammy and Rosie Get Laid* (1987) and Derek Jarman's *The Last of England* (1987). But even as the liberal left railed against the horrors of the present age in ways broadly in keeping with Britain's history of cinematic realism, new developments in video technology were introducing a mass audience to a range of innovative cultural products that would come to alter the ways in which filmic narratives were conceived of, structured and shot. Breaking down traditional distinctions between music, television and film, music videos thus conflated their own glamorous fictionality and the greedy, self-seeking intolerance of the real world into a single simulacral realm of fun and sunshine, glamour and glittering economic rewards. Thus setting out, in Peter Wollen's words, to 'plunder the image bank and the word-hoard for the material of parody, pastiche and in extreme cases, plagiarism' (1986: 169), the 1980s music video encapsulated that ideologically saturated flattening of history visible across contemporary visual and political culture. Enthusiastically consuming such products whilst displaying a decidedly equivocal response to the politics of contemporary British cinematic realism, the public appeared to concur with Thatcher's outlandish assertion that it was no longer possible to speak of 'society' at all, only of 'individuals and their families' (see Thatcher 1987). As real life and its representations collapsed into a single simulacral realm, it became possible to claim that despite the deaths of some 40,000 soldiers and 113,000 civilians (see Andrews 1992: A7), as Baudrillard would put it, the Gulf War did not take place.

By the 1990s then, it was apparent that the legacy of the Thatcher years had been to make the rich richer and the poor poorer by destroying the nation's industrial base and promoting a culture of self-seeking social irresponsibility that valued hyper-masculine characteristics such as aggressively individualistic ambition over all others. It was equally apparent that any political party that sought to overturn eighteen years of Conservative rule must engage not only with mass popular culture's polyphonic and multi-genred celebration of the signifier, but with the crisis in masculine identity that was all too visible within that culture; a crisis engendered not only by the mere existence of the dominatrix-encoded Thatcher (whose wholesale dismantling of British industry had not only dissipated traditional models of masculine identity formation but had dispersed patriarchal authority across a number of social and commercial institutions) but by the cultural consolidation of earlier equal rights legislation such as the Equal Pay Act of 1970 and the Sex

Discrimination Act of 1975, legislation which further called the efficacy of the patriarchy into question.

On the first of May 1997, a party purporting to address the crises of the previous two decades swept to power; Tony Blair's New Labour won a record number of seats, a record majority and a record swing in votes, ending a run of four successive electoral defeats for Labour. Or so it seemed; for from the very outset New Labour was a hybrid entity; its 'third way' professing to synthesise economic growth with a concern for social justice whilst repudiating any 'Old' Labour-style attempts to actually redistribute wealth. Similarly hybridised was New Labour's conception of gender identity, Blair being keen to embody in his public persona those 'dominant constructions of masculinity' that under Thatcher had 'dictated that assertiveness, toughness, decisiveness and, when necessary, the capacity for violence' was said to lie 'at the core of what it is to be a man' (Hatty 2000: 173). He was nonetheless keen to temper such qualities by presenting himself as a nurturing family man, working in tandem with his professionally successful wife to raise their children in keeping with Labour's own history of social justice for all.[1] Responding to the challenges that feminism and gay liberation had made to both the hyper-masculine ethos of the warrior ideal of Britain's imperial past *and* the ways that 'patriarchal structures of authority, domination and control were currently diffused throughout social, economic, political and ideological activities' (Kaufman 1995: 15), Blair set out to promote a political culture that was simultaneously tough *and* caring, pro-active *and* stable, decisive *and* nurturing. Whilst heading a government that boasted record numbers of female MPs, Blair thus sought to retain a 'traditional left concern for equity and social cohesion' whilst insisting on the proactive virility of the neo-liberal emphasis he placed 'on economic efficiency and dynamism' (White 1998: 17). In a world in which the British man's traditional role as familial provider has been dissipated both by the destruction of the nation's industrial base and by increasing numbers of working wives and mothers, themselves demanding equal rights in civil society and the workplace, New Labour set out to appeal to a post-patriarchal demographic.

If we look, then, to the horror films of this period we can see an engaging exploration of the seismic social changes that faced the British people as the nation's industrial culture was destroyed by Thatcher's love of the service industry and its socialist traditions were similarly eroded by Blair's penchant for right-wing Christian-inflected social democracy. It is no coincidence, in other words, that numerous horror films of Blair's first term of office would set out to explore the total and horrific mutation of British people into what Noël Carroll would term 'fusion monsters' (see 1990). Generated, in part, as Marina Warner put it, by a fear of 'millennial turmoil, the disintegration of so many political blocks and the appearance of new national borders, ferocious civil wars, global catastrophes from famine to AIDS, threats of ecological disasters – of another Chernobyl, or larger holes in the ozone' (1994: 17–18) such monsters would embody a socially-sublimated post-Thatcherite awareness that under certain circumstances Britons have the capacity to behave in utterly monstrous ways. Hence, Neil Marshall's *Dog Soldiers* (2001) would depict how otherwise 'good people' could transform into bloodthirsty werewolves whilst *Shaun of the Dead* (Edgar Wright, 2004) would see the dead returning as flesh-eating zombies. Virulent infection would change ordinary human beings into rage-driven maniacs in *28 Days Later* (Danny Boyle, 2002) whilst *The Descent* (Neil Marshall, 2005) and *Creep* (Christopher Smith, 2005) would illustrate how closely related we all are to blind, cannibalistic and evolutionarily regressive subterraneans.

Arising to fight such fusion monsters, of course, was the post-Thatcherite 'fusion hero,' one whose qualities were drawn from the British cinematic tradition and range, in Andrew Spicer's formulation, from the debonair gentleman to the action hero, from the common man to the Byronic romantic, from the fool to the stoic to the criminal. Thus testing the ways in which gender identity is shaped by the historically specific needs and imperatives of the national culture, the composite heroes of films such as *Cradle of Fear* (Alex Chandon, 2000), *Long Time Dead* (Marcus Adams, 2001), *The Bunker* (Rob Green, 2001), *Reign of Fire* (Rob Bowman, 2002) and *Deathwatch* (Michael J. Bassett, 2002) do battle with malevolent spirits, demons, dragons and themselves in their exploration of gendered national identity. And repeatedly, they emerge as the 'product of a [distinctively New Labour] culture that is decentred and heterogeneous, no longer recognising clear national, ethical or sexual boundaries, where forms of masculinity are becoming increasingly hybrid and audiences delight in the knowingness and self-reflexivity of popular culture' (Spicer 2003: 204).

Appropriately, then, Edgar Wright's *Shaun of the Dead* is self-consciously steeped in the iconography of both contemporary British life and American horror cinema. From its opening in The Winchester, a pub named for the iconic American rifle, we are slowly steeped in the cultural stasis of the contemporary UK, this being a smoke-filled traditionally-styled venue complete with fruit machines, pool table, nicotine-stained walls, red velvet curtains, a heavy wooden bar, juke-box, brown-painted cast iron radiator, decorative plates on the walls and numerous pints of lager. 'Things will change,' opines our hero Shaun to his discontented girlfriend Liz, but he says it to the strains of 'The Specials' *Ghost Town* as 'time' is called on his unconvincing optimism. Unsurprisingly, Liz's main complaint is that Shaun and his best friend Ed refuse to grow up and embrace the responsibilities of manhood. In their late twenties they are still living in a student-style shared house, itself trapped in time – with its saggy 1970s-brown sofa, its coffee table groaning with unidentifiable detritus and its overgrown garden. Theirs is a mode of masculinity endlessly trapped in its own fast-receding adolescence; a life of computer games and cornershop lager, dead-end jobs and small-scale dope deals, fart gags and cowardly avoidance of the biological family that men such as Shaun are too afraid to leave.

Shaun and Ed playing computer games (*Shaun of the Dead*, 2004)

This is a way of life admirably encapsulated in the two scenes in which Shaun makes his morning visit to the cornershop – once before and once after the events that will come to be known as 'Z Day'. In the first, Shaun leaves his house, passes a boy playing football, a beggar with a dog, a man washing a car, the row of mopeds on display at a bike shop and a National Lottery advertisement outside the corner-shop where the Asian proprietor greets him with 'Hello my friend, no beer today?'.[2] The second occurs after a heavy night's drinking when Shaun, who has failed to notice the escalating military presence, the sirens in the street and the running terrified people, braves the morning to buy a Cornetto and a Coke to assuage his terrible hangover. The street this time is oddly empty, though the beggar from earlier is now a zombie who shuffles on a clearly broken ankle down the road, holding a lead but walking no dog. Burglar and car alarms are going off, bollards are knocked over, the windscreen of the now-clean car is smashed, a terrified man runs down the street past the knocked-over National Lottery sign and a pile of tumbled mopeds. In the shop, Hindi pop still plays but the floor is sticky, there is a bloody handprint on the refrigerator and no newspapers have been delivered. Shaun notices none of this. As assorted zombies shuffle about Shaun returns safely home. Entirely blind to all that surrounds him he is one of the atomised and isolated living, cut off from each other by their iPod-wearing lack of interest in anything beyond their own immediate gratification. In this, of course, he is remarkably like the dead.

Such pseudo-subjectivity is admirably served by mass culture, here gratifyingly evoked by the film's references to and inclusion of real-world television programmes. Shaun's refusal to engage with current events thus leads him to ignore tabloid headlines that warn of a 'New Super Flu', 'Mutilated Remains' and the 'GM Crops Blamed' for recent unfortunate events. Even at work in an electrical goods store, as army trucks roll down the street outside, Shaun ignores the news on the banked television screens, preferring a (student-like) diet of *Teletubbies* (1997–2001). Following his lucky avoidance of zombies at the cornershop, Shaun still insists on channel-hopping to avoid anything as serious as news. This results in a wonderful montage of TV genres, ranging from football to a wildlife documentary to a music show; the juxtaposition of which admirably evokes the climate of anodyne disposability that distracts us all from the horrors of actuality. Like Thoreau's nineteenth-century Americans, the vast majority of contemporary Britons lead lives of quiet desperation; men in particular being trapped within a stultifying present that prevents them from developing beyond their teenage years. One might as well be a zombie. And certainly the quality of television programming offered to the British public is seen as appropriate for such an audience. The national culture is a pastiche of simulacral representations, a triumph of style over content where anaesthetising platitudes and clichés stand in for genuine thought, engagement or interaction. It is truly horrific and yet grimly funny. Described in its own publicity as 'a romantic comedy with zombies', this generic hybrid is happy to juxtapose in its opening sequence a bleached-out supermarket checkout (drawn from Bryan Forbes' *The Stepford Wives* [1974]) and shopping-centre car park (from George Romero's *Dawn of the Dead* [1978]) with hooded youths whose rhythmic shuffling is reminiscent of *West Side Story* (Robert Wise, 1961). And throughout, playful references to films within and without the horror genre abound. The swinging bathroom cabinet door, revealing the zombified flatmate Pete is a delightful tribute to *An American Werewolf in London* (John Landis, 1981). The shot through the hole in the zombie-girl's stomach echoes a very similar piece of cinematography in the remade *Texas Chainsaw Massacre* (Marcus Nispel, 2003). Shaun's headband, donned when under siege in The Winchester evokes, of course, that of the Russian roulette-playing Christopher Walken in *The Deer Hunter* (Micheal Cimino, 1978). David is pulled out of the window to his doom just like Barbara in Romero's *Night of the Living Dead* (1968) and is eviscerated like Captain Rose in his *Day of the Dead* (1985) – the opening of which is repeatedly referenced in Shaun's foot-shuffling early morning walk, the end of which is neatly inverted at this film's *dénouement* as the elevator in the pub cellar lifts Shaun and Liz to safety. But references to British comedy culture are equally frequent, most notably when our band of survivors encounters Shaun's friend Yvonne, whose own accompanying group exactly mirrors them in terms of age, physical type and dress. Furthermore, each is a significant figure in British radio and television comedy culture.[3] There is no such thing as authentic and autonomous human subjectivity in Britain of the present, it seems; only media-constructs aware of their own stereotypical status.

Shaun of the Dead thus seems to explore how mass cultural late capitalist society infantilises its males, bombarding them with simulacral images of their own desires so insistently that they exist in tranquillised isolation from each other;

unable to think, act or live for themselves. In the light of this, 'Z Day' becomes the best thing that ever happened to Shaun. Admittedly he loses his mother and stepfather, but this is necessary if he is ever to move on to attain an autonomous adult subjectivity free of the past. From a man unable to book a restaurant table or buy a gift for his mother's birthday, Shaun evolves into a capable decision-maker. That these decisions result in the death of his friends and family is of course testament to the destructive potential of such incisive and purposeful masculinity. And it is for this reason that Shaun's potential for hyper-masculinity must be tempered by Liz, who moves into his flat and takes over his domestic arrangements in classic gender-defined ways. By the end of the film Shaun's house has been transformed by new lighting, cushions and throws. His friend Ed, now a zombie, has been exiled to the garden shed where his video-gaming, meat-eating, fart-unleashing life continues much as before. Only by repressing his adolescent yearning for homosocial camaraderie and redirecting his desire towards heterosexual romance, domesticity and putative paternity can Shaun come fully to life and face his destiny and his responsibilities as a man.

But as Danny Boyle's *28 Days Later* is also keen to explore, such a journey is not without risk: specifically from the overweening machismo that underpins decisive and authoritative masculinity but is normally tempered in society by those qualities of co-operative endeavour and altruistic nurturance that, as we have seen in *Shaun of the Dead*, is traditionally associated with the conventionally feminine spheres of child-rearing, education, healthcare and welfare provision. Thus exploring the ways in which patriarchy is embodied in and perpetuated by hegemonic institutions such as the military, *28 Days Later* is a fascinating exercise in generic hybridity, being a highly effective amalgam of science fiction's 'end of the world' preoccupations, body horror's interrogation of the nature and culture of humanity and the quest narrative's recounting of the hero's voyage to adult masculinity in the face of overwhelming odds. As such, it echoes and references British films such as *The Day the Earth Caught Fire* (Val Guest, 1961) and *The Day of the Triffids* (Steve Sekely, 1962) whilst providing a very British take on eschatological fantasies like *The Omega Man* (Boris Sagal, 1971). But unlike cult offerings such as *Cradle of Fear*, this film is far more than a collection of references to other cinematic works, being an engaged and engaging exploration of the ways in which the modern world is shaped both by the material manifestations of the state (such as the government, the police or the army) and the state's ideological apparatuses (such as television, radio or film). The horrors of twenty-first-century life are on display from the opening sequence's visually arresting documentary-realist montage of acts of human violence. These range from small-scale private-enterprise lynchings to the state-sponsored homicide that is an execution. Ironically the footage is being watched by our closest primate relative, a chimpanzee trapped in a laboratory. Although he is the ostensible experimental subject, it is really humanity that is under scrutiny. For only humanity naturally experiences the rage depicted on screen and only human beings would be sufficiently scientifically adept and socially irresponsible to synthesise a viral agent capable of destroying its own species.[4]

Some four weeks after the release of the virus, then, a naked young man awakes in an intensive care unit. Staggering from the hospital into the silence of a deserted London dawn he moves like *Reign of Fire*'s Quinn through a city made strange by its total lack of inhabitants.[5] In time, having accepted the death of his parents, our hero Jim is forced to move on – in time forging a surrogate family with the pharmacist Celina, the taxi driver and alpha male Frank and Frank's teenage daughter Hannah. It is Frank who persuades the group to travel north in response to a military broadcast urging survivors to make their way to the forty-seventh blockade on the M602 outside Manchester, a city now burned to the ground. But Jim's role as Frank's surrogate son is soon to end as Frank is infected and shot dead by soldiers and Jim is forced to become a man by doing battle with the evocatively named Major Henry West who asserts 'women mean a future' whilst sanctioning Celina and Hanna's rape by his troops. From being a boyish bicycle courier living with his parents in an affluent London suburb, Jim must now become a new kind of hero for a post-apocalyptic age. As such, he will reject the soldiers' hyper-masculine equation of manly force and sexual violence, redirecting his energies to preservation of the family unit. As such his actions echo those of the classical figure Laocoön, whose statue stands in the hall of the soldiers' billet, being a priest of the healing-god Apollo who lost his life defending his two children from giant serpents sent to destroy them. Clearly, the aggressively phallic 'serpents' in this tale are the forces of military might unchecked by any authority higher than their commanding officer, a professional soldier who proudly asserts that normality is 'people killing people.' That Jim destroys West's platoon by adopting the guerrilla tactics of an insurgent functions as something of a tribute to the powers of the freelance freedom fighter who acts in the service of those he loves and thus through that love triumphs over the might of the military machine.[6] As the Apollonian references make clear then, his actions are not destructive but redemptive; leading to the infected over-running the artificial sanctuary the soldiers have constructed for themselves and illustrating in their murderous rage the logical consequence of their hyper-masculinism. Only with its eradication can the future be contemplated; Jim, Celina and Hannah being spotted by a military plane from Finland, the least aggressive of nations. Celina's conjecture that the virus had wiped out the entire world was clearly wrong, as was that of the ill-fated Sergeant Farrell who believed that the planet was purging itself of humanity's harmful presence. The last of the infected are now dying in the streets and our heroes are set to return to the 'civilised' world that engendered the disaster. Their survival has clearly been bought at a price, though. Not only have Jim, Celina and Hannah been forced to kill everyone who stood in their way of their survival but they have attained a profound personal knowledge of the horrors of unchecked machismo and the necessity of social co-operation and personal self-sacrifice if one is to survive as a civilised human being and in Jim's case a man.

The overweening preoccupation with the military world of men without women visible in British horror under New Labour (in films such as *The Bunker*, *Deathwatch* and *Dog Soldiers* in particular) clearly indicated a certain discomfort with Britain's imperial past and a reluctance on behalf of contemporary men to identify unquestioningly with the hyper-masculine ethos that underpins nationalistic war. It also bespeaks an awareness that over the course of the last thirty years or so the social world of men's experience has so altered that that traditional models of masculinity are in need of substantial reconceptualisation. For not only has there been a radical increase in the number of British households headed by women and a corresponding decrease in the number of traditional families headed by a sole male breadwinner in recent years, but as the comprehensive failure of the Child Support Agency has illustrated, men appear increasingly reluctant to accept even financial responsibility for the children they have fathered. With the mechanisation of domestic labour taking the drudgery out of homemaking, and with consumer capitalism enabling men to become their own status objects, the desirability of maintaining a non-productive trophy wife could also be said to have decreased. Accordingly, it is now uncommon for men to advocate a return to the responsibilities of patriarchal authority preferring, as Susan Faludi (1992) has indicated, to complain about the oppression they are now suffering at the hands of women and to wish for a kind of 'hegemonic-masculinity-lite' – with all the privileges of hierarchical superiority over women and children but few of the responsibilities such paternalism entails. From a patriarchal and post-patriarchal perspective, of course, the increasingly visible power of women is both horrific and frightening; the fear of the totemic mother being a consistent feature of recent British horror. Certainly, in the films considered here, the mother is either absent, (as in *Creep*, *Dog Soldiers* and *Cradle of Fear*) or already dead (as in *28 Days Later* and *Long Time Dead*). She may die within the course of the film (as in *Reign of Fire* and *Shaun of the Dead*) or be excluded by definition from the militaristic world of men (as in *Deathwatch* and *The Bunker*). Such narrative punishment of the maternal figure clearly bespeaks an ongoing set of problematic attitudes towards women that remain in contemporary British society, for all Blair's attempts to promote a political culture that synthesises traditional gender positions. In an age in which traditional masculine lifestyles, modes of work and patterns of leisure have been transformed by socio-economic and cultural changes that have challenged traditional gender hegemonies to the clear advantage of women, Blair's attempts to head a government that appeared simultaneously tough and caring, pro-active and stable, decisive and nurturing now appear doomed to fail; especially given the strength of masculine discontent with post-patriarchal realities and the elusiveness of genuine equality for women. It is in horror cinema of this period, then, that we attain an almost visceral engagement with the terror of the trans-historically monstrous feminine that bubbles away beneath the endlessly proliferating signifiers of our entrenchedly simulacral culture.

NOTES

1 It was, of course, the Labour Party that had been responsible for the introduction of the Welfare State, including the foundation of the National Health Service (1945–51), the introductive of Comprehensive education (1964–70), the State Earnings Related Pension and universal Child Benefit (1974–79) and the decriminalisation of abortion and homosexuality (1967).
2 *Shaun of the Dead*, like *28 Days Later*, was funded in part with grants from the National Lottery and, in return, carries several advertisements for it.
3 Yvonne herself is played by Jessica Stephenson, co-star and co-writer with *Shaun of the Dead*'s Simon Pegg of the surreal sitcom *Spaced* (1999–2001). Her best friends are played by Tamsin Greig (who appeared in the comedy *Black Books* [1999–2001] with Dylan Moran who plays David, Lucy Davis of *The Office* [2001–03]) and Reece Shearsmith of *The League of Gentlemen* (1999– 2002). Her mother is played by Julia Diakin, also of *Spaced*, whilst Matt Lucas of *Little Britain* (2003–05) brings up the rear.
4 The parallels between this film and Terry Gilliam's time-travelling dystopian horror *12 Monkeys* (1995), where twelve billion people are wiped out by a similarly man-made virus are clear from the outset, not least in the introspective and bewildered central performance from Bruce Willis, whose disoriented hero James Cole is clearly a conceptual forefather of Cillian Murphy's Jim in the present film.
5 He crosses Westminster Bridge, trampling Big Ben souvenirs underfoot. Passing an overturned Routemaster bus on The Mall he moves along Horseguard's Parade to pause by the bronze statues of fallen British soldiers at the Cenotaph. He stops to collect bundles of cash littering the stairs next to the ICA, central London's premiere arts venue, before heading to Trafalgar Square, past the National Gallery and up Charing Cross Road to Centrepoint.
6 Interestingly, a very similar impulse can be seen to be at work in *The Patriot* (Roland Emmerich, 2000) that pits Mel Gibson's Revolutionary War freedom fighter against the massed force of the British Empire for like Gibson's Benjamin Martin Jim also has to learn to control and direct his rage in service of his new-found family.

BIBLIOGRAPHY

Andrews, E. L. (1992) 'Census Bureau to dismiss analyst who estimated Iraqi casualties,' *The New York Times*, March 7, A7.
Baudrillard, J. (1995) *The Gulf War Did Not Take Place*. Trans. P. Patton. Bloomington, IN: Indiana University Press.
Campbell, J. (1949) *The Hero with a Thousand Faces*. Princeton, NJ: Princeton University Press.
Carroll, N. (1990) *The Philosophy of Horror or Paradoxes of the Heart*. New York: Routledge.
Faludi, S. (1992) *Backlash: The Undeclared War Against American Women*. New York: Anchor.
Hatty, S. E. (2000) *Masculinities, Violence and Culture*. Thousand Oaks, CA: Sage.
Jones, D. E. (2000) *An Instinct for Dragons*. New York and London: Routledge.
Kaufman, M. (1995) 'The Construction of Masculinity and the Triad of Men's Violence', in M. S. Kimmel and M. A. Messner (eds) *Men's Lives*. Boston: Allyn and Bacon: 13–25.

Ludlum, S. (2001) 'The Making of New Labour', in S. Ludlam and M. J. Smith (eds) *New Labour in Government*. Basingstoke and New York: Palgrave.

Richards, J. (1997) *Films and British National Identity From Dickens to Dad's Army*. Manchester: Manchester University Press.

Rigby, J. (2002) *English Gothic: A Century of Horror Cinema*. London: Reynolds and Hearne.

Schwalbe, M. (1995) 'Mythopoetic Men's Work,' in M. S. Kimmel and M. A. Messner (eds) *Men's Lives*. Boston: Allyn and Bacon: 507-519.

Spicer, A. (2003) *Typical Men: The Representation of Masculinity in Popular British Cinema*. London: I.B. Tauris.

Thatcher, M. (1987) *Woman's Hour Interview 31 October 1987*. Online. Available HTTP: http://www.margaretthatcher.org/speeches (15 September 2007).

Walcsak, Y. (1988) *He and She: Men in the Eighties*. London and New York: Routledge.

Warner, M. (1994) *Managing Monsters: Six Myths of Our Time*. New York: Vintage.

White, S. (1998) 'Interpreting the Third Way: Not One Road, But Many', *Renewal*, 6: 2, 15–25.

Wollen, P. (1986) 'Ways of Thinking about Music Video (and Postmodernism)', *Critical Quarterly*, 28: 1–2, 167–70.

FRENCH HORROR CINEMA

FRENCH HORROR CINEMA

Patricia Allmer, Emily Brick and David Huxley

French cinema is often perceived as having a strong tradition of the fantastic, rather than of horror film *per se*. Although there are scenes which could be categorised as 'horrific' in some of Georges Méliès' early silent films such as *Barbe-bleue/Bluebeard* (1901) and *Les quatre cents farces du diable/The 400 Tricks of the Devil* (1906) or Jean Cocteau's *La belle et la bête/Beauty and the Beast* (1946), the humour of Méliès and the lyricism of Cocteau have tended to mitigate against them being included in the horror canon. Rather than a continual, interrelated horror tradition French cinema has produced a series of outstanding individual horror films, normally by directors who did not specialise in the field. Thus, as well as Cocteau's *Beauty and the Beast* and *Orphée* (1950) (although both of these could be seen as part of other generic tropes) there is Henri-Georges Clouzot's *Les diaboliques/The Fiends* (1955). Again, the latter film and also Clouzot's *Le corbeau/The Raven* (1943) can be seen as generically peripheral to horror and the former film in particular is often described as being part of an 'Hitchcockian' thriller tradition. Nevertheless a whole chapter of Ivan Butler's book *Horror in the Cinema* (1970) is devoted to Clouzot's films. The same book only mentions in passing a film which clearly does draw unequivocally on horror conventions, *Les yeux sans visage/Eyes Without a Face* (1959), directed by Georges Franju. In this influential film a plastic surgeon tries to graft the faces of girls he has murdered onto the disfigured face of his daughter. The comparative explicitness of the removal of the faces involved led to a media backlash, particularly in Britain and France itself. Less controversial was Roger Vadim's *Et mourir de plaisir/Blood and Roses* (1960), a loose adaptation of Sheridan Le Fanu's vampire novella *Carmilla* (1872). Its 'artful approach' (Schneider 2007: 25) meant that it attracted little of the opprobrium that Franju's more graphic film had received, although British critic Derek Hill did comment that 'to find as sick and silly a film one only has to think back to the last production of the once great Georges Franju, *Eyes Without a Face*. Our horror films may be no healthier, but at least no real talents waste themselves on them' (1961: 54).

The one area where French horror cinema has flourished is in low-budget exploitation films, particularly in the work of Jean Rollin. Partially inspired by the success of Hammer films and the Spanish director Jess Franco, Rollin produced a series of four vampire films, culminating in *Vierges et vampires/Virgins and the Vampires* (1971), and went on to make ten more horror films in the 1970s. The emphasis on the visual over dreamlike, often confused narratives and Rollin's mix of sex and horror confounded critics but earned him both early financial success and continuing cult status. But these very qualities also seem to have consigned him to the periphery of serious critical consideration. In the encyclopaedic overview of French cinema, Remi Fournier Lanzoni's *French Cinema: From Its Beginnings to the Present* (2002) for example, Rollin is not even mentioned in passing – not even to dismiss the quality of his œuvre.

Yet the French aversion to popular horror film may run deeper, as Alexandre Aja believes that, 'The problem with the French is that they don't trust their own language (when it comes to horror). American horror movies do well, but in their own language, the French aren't interested' (quoted in Jones 2005: 226). However Aja's own *Haute tension/Switchblade Romance* (2003) and Lionel Delplanque's *Promenons-nous dans les bois/Deep in the Woods* (2002) and Virginie Despentes and Coralie Trinh Thi's *Baise-moi* (2002) appear to be part of a mini boom in French horror production since 2000 that contradicts this view.

The chapters in this section discuss two of these films. Emily Brick analyses *Baise-moi* and *Irréversible/Irreversible* (Gaspar Noé, 2002) in relation to the figure of the 'killer woman' and the cycle of 'rape-revenge' films, in particular Meir Zarchi's American film *I Spit on Your Grave* (1978). Brick argues that there is a particularly strong tradition of the figure of the *femme fatale* in French cinema. Matthias Hurst examines Alexandre Aja's *Switchblade Romance* and the ways it differs from contemporary American horror films. The film uses an apparently recognisable 'slasher' format but subverts expectations in both narrative and structural terms. Taken together these chapters suggest that rather than talking about individual French horror films it is now possible to speak of a French horror cinema.

BIBLIOGRAPHY

Butler, I. (1970) *Horror in the Cinema*. London: Zwemmer.
Hill, D. (1961) 'Turn of the Tide?', *About Town*, April, 51–4.
Jones, A. (2005) *The Rough Guide to Horror Movies*. London: Penguin.
Lanzoni, R. F. (2002) *French Cinema: From its Beginnings to the Present*. New York: Continuum.
Schneider, S. J. (ed.) (2007) *100 European Horror Films*. London: British Film Institute.

BAISE-MOI AND THE FRENCH RAPE-REVENGE FILMS

Emily Brick

The rape-revenge film often sits on the boundaries of horror/exploitation cinema. In American cinema in the 1970s Wes Craven's films such as *Last House on the Left* (1972) and *The Hills Have Eyes* (1977) are essentially horror films which contain rape. Carol Clover notes that 'by the mid 1980s, rape moved virtually offscreen' and that rape is generally absent from the slasher film (1992: 154). Representations of rape moved outside of horror to big budget productions such as *The Accused* (Jonathan Kaplan, 1988) (courtroom drama), *Sleeping With the Enemy* (Joseph Ruben, 1991) (melodrama) and *Thelma and Louise* (Ridley Scott, 1992) (road movie). Approaches to looking at the rape-revenge film typically fall into two broad categories: psychoanalytic models of visual pleasure, and exploring it as a socio-political text which engages in feminist discourse. Although analysis of the genre has focused primarily on American films, a recent cycle of films known as 'French Shock Cinema' or 'New French Extreme' has produced examples such as *Baise-moi* (Virginie Despentes and Coralie Trinh Thi, 2000) and *Irréversible/Irreversible* (Gaspar Noé, 2002). This chapter will look at *Baise-moi* in relation to the rape-revenge narrative and female spectatorship as well as its relationship to images of violent women within French cinema, and to contemporary France.

The rape-revenge film appears across many national cinemas, and goes through parallel historical shifts in many of them. Jacinda Read charts the development of the rape-revenge film in American cinema into stages: in rape-revenge films from the silent era until the 1970s, women were largely defined in relation to men, and their rape was avenged on their behalf by a male protector; in the films of the post-1970 period, women took violent revenge for themselves – 'in the post-1970 period, the rape-revenge film can be seen as telling increasingly feminine, and even, feminist, stories' (2000: 242). She argues that the rape-revenge films of American cinema represent an engagement with feminist politics by Hollywood. Jyotika Virdi maps a similar development of the rape-revenge narrative across Hindi cinema: 'The 1980s rape-revenge film, fuelled by women's rage, dramatizes a public discourse which repudiates victimisation and patriarchy and is distinct from the pre-1980s '"inscription" and "erasure" of sexual violence' (1999: 36). Japanese horror also commonly features abused women turned agents of violence in films such as such *Ôdishon/Audition* (Takashi Miike, 1999) and *Freeze Me* (Takashi Ishii, 2000). All of these films share similarities of narrative structure, ideology and symbolic economy. Although there are examples of prominent rape-revenge narratives in European cinema such as *Jungfrukällan/The Virgin Spring* (Ingmar Bergman, 1960), *Straw Dogs* (Sam Peckinpah, 1971) and *Dirty Weekend* (Michael Winner, 1993) they have not been explicitly linked to a historical moment and feminist movement in the same way as American cinema. It is worth noting here that feminist activism and legislation relating to rape came at different times within Europe so it is hard to identify a linear link to socio-political events in the same way as a specific national cinema.

Most of the critical discourse on rape-revenge films acknowledges *I Spit on Your Grave* (Meir Zarchi, 1978) as the narrative paradigm. Textual analysis of the genre as a whole has focused on this film, which has been read as both misogynist and feminist. All of the structural, ideological and symbolic elements of the rape-revenge film that exist in more subtle forms in mainstream versions are exposed and laid bare in *I Spit on Your Grave*. The plot is simple and brief: Jennifer leaves the city for the country to write a book. She is stalked by four men who rape her and leave her for dead. She then hunts them down one by one and kills them. The film is shot primarily from her point of view throughout. The first two deaths are staged as elaborate seductions; the first man is hanged, the second is castrated and left to bleed to death. The last two are stalked and hacked to death with, respectively, an axe and boat propeller. The film ends there. It devotes equal time to the rape sequences and to Jennifer's revenge, and is built around a three act structure consisting of 'RAPE / TRANSFORMATION / REVENGE' which produces a dynamic in which men are punished for sexual crimes in a sexual way.

Critical readings of the film tend towards interpreting the heroine as a masculine figure. Carol Clover links the victim/hero of the rape-revenge on a continuum with the 'final girl' of the slasher film. Like the slasher film, the rape-revenge film sets up a one-sex model of gender, setting a feminised male against a masculinised female. For Clover, the heroine is 'a male surrogate in all things Oedipal, a homo-erotic stand-in, the audience incorporate: to the extent that she means 'girl' at all, it is only for the purposes of signifying phallic lack [...]. The discourse is wholly masculine, and females figure in it only insofar as they "read" some form of male experience' (1992: 119). While this is a beautifully constructed model of male visual pleasure, it is ultimately reductive because there is no space for women to be active and sadistic subjects on screen without re-constructing them as masculine. Femininity represents only passivity. Peter Lehman's article 'Don't Blame This on a Girl', also discusses the heroine as a screen surrogate for the male audience, representing 'a male subjectivity which is both heterosexually masochistic and homosexually sadistic' (1993: 105). The expression of male masochism in the rape-revenge text also represents repressed homosexuality – since Jennifer is figuratively male, her eroticised attack on the rapists is a homosexual/homophobic act (see Lehman 1993: 114–16). Within this reading, not only is Jennifer symbolically male, she is also symbolically homosexual. For Phillip Green, *I Spit on Your Grave* is 'a simple inversion of the Death Wish saga' and 'the genre's invocation of the phallic woman in the guise of killer seems to suggest not so much a different, frightening way of being a woman, as a different, more universalised way of being a man' (1998: 194). All of these readings also repress the heroine's placing as erotic object (a position which male critics are particularly keen to distance themselves from) to support their reading of her as masculine.

Barbara Creed, however, reads the heroine of *I Spit on Your Grave* as a trope of the Monstrous-Feminine. Castrating women appear in different guises across genres and in the rape-revenge film she seduces and literally castrates. The rape-revenge film operates as a conduit for male castration anxiety via its representation of woman in the twin roles of castrated and castrator (1993: 122). Jacinda Read (2000) argues that the psychoanalytic focus of both Creed and Clover are too ahistorical and overlook the significance of the social-political influences on the films. This chapter will approach *Baise-moi* from both perspectives – as a text which exists as a 'universal tale' type as part of a continuum of other rape-revenge films, and one which is grounded in the time and place which produced it.

Creed's work offers a way of re-reading the rape-revenge heroine as symbolically feminine, but still in a phallic economy and produced from within a framework of male fantasy. The emphatic emphasis on male visual pleasure and the masculinisation of the heroine within critical accounts of the rape-revenge film has meant that female agency, in particular the notion of sadistic female agency, has been all but erased from the text. None of these readings really address the rape-revenge story or the female avenger in relation to what visual pleasure they may offer to women (if any). So against this background *Baise-moi* is particularly interesting because it was written, produced and directed by women, and therefore I am firstly looking at how this rape-revenge drama operates in relation to feminine rather than masculine fantasy.

Baise-moi was based on the 1999 novel by Virginie Despentes who also directed the film together with Coralie Trinh Thi. It is a hybrid of genres; in her *Sight and Sound* review Linda Williams calls it 'neither a horror nor a porn film' (2001). The connection with pornography is enhanced by the film's production values – the two female stars (Karen Lancaume and Raffäela Anderson), one of the rapists (Ian Scott) and Coralie Trin Thi herself had all worked in pornography before making this film. Its reputation is built on the extreme sexual and violent content, and it was not given a release certificate in numerous countries, including, for a while, France.[1] The DVD case promotes its own controversy, and all reviews discuss it in relation to censorship. Graphic sex and violence form key aesthetics.

Like *Thelma and Louise*, *Baise-moi* begins as a dual focus narrative, converging to a singular point of view. Manu is raped and shoots her brother. Nadine is working as a prostitute and goes on the run after killing her flatmate in a fight. They meet by chance at the station and go on a road trip, picking up men for sex and killing indiscriminately. Eventually, Manu is shot, Nadine burns her body and is arrested as she is about to shoot herself. The two women's stories begin separately and although they separate at brief points, once they meet they are together in every scene.

The producers insist that the rape scene must be brutal and hard to watch because rape is horrible. Clover (1992) argues in relation to *I Spit on Your Grave* that the rape must be experienced by the viewer because without it, the revenge makes no sense. The most notable departure of this film from its narrative origins, however, is that the revenge is indirect: the rapists themselves are never hunted down and punished. Manu's brother says he will take revenge, so she shoots him. Instead Manu and Nadine embark on a series of random killings interspersed with casual sex. In the traditional rape-revenge film, sex is violent and violence is sexualised. A key feature of this film is that for the women there is a clear separation of sexual fantasy and violent fantasy. There is only one incident where they seduce a man and then kill him, and Manu attacks him because he will not have sex with her without a condom; the sex and subsequent violence are not co-dependent.

Across genres, violent female protagonists often take pleasure in identifying with the image of the violent woman. There are numerous examples of films in which violent women are positioned as spectators before they kill people – either in relation to their own image in a dressing-up sequence, or by watching another film. Brian De Palma's *Femme Fatale* (2002) opens with its heroine watching *Double Indemnity* (Billy Wilder, 1944). The heroine of *The Last Seduction* (John Dahl, 1994) also identifies herself with the same film by using the pseudonym 'Mrs Neff'. In *The Assassin* (John Badham, 1993), the remake of Luc Besson's *Nikita* (1990), the heroine plans her kill while watching *Repulsion* (Roman Polanski, 1965). Nadine and Manu comment that they need better lines, as if they were in a film. There is a pleasure in performing the image of the violent woman, which is

Nadine poses in the mirror

separated from the violence itself. The image above shows Nadine posing with her gun, looking at herself in the mirror. A similar image is used on the poster of the film, which has visual similarities to *Nikita*.

The narrative of transformation here also has a physical dimension. The film very clearly eroticises the image of the violent woman but there is an important narcissistic element to this scene which depicts the pleasurable acting out of an identification with her own violent image. The autoerotic nature of this performance in the mirror reinforces the placing of the women as narrative subjects.

This process of identification also happens in *Baise-moi* in relation to sex as well as violence. Nadine is positioned as an active consumer of porn. In one of the early scenes, she is watching a film and masturbating and later she tells Manu that she has seen her in a porn film. In the scene where they seduce two men together the camera emphasises the women watching each other: for Nadine this is a 'live version' of what she has already seen on screen. When one of the men suggests that the women put on a show with each other, Manu throws him out. This scene constructs the women as both voyeurs and exhibitionists in a scenario in which masculine desire is subjugated.

Manu and Nadine kill on eleven occasions. In keeping with the politics of rape-revenge, some of these deaths are explicitly linked to male abuse of women, but mainly, they are random acts of violence. The nature of rape involves a penis which means that it is hard to divorce rape-revenge films from a phallic economy, but *Baise-moi* does achieve this in an unusual way in relation to both the sex scenes and the rape. This film makes a visual spectacle out of the penis in the sex scenes. It is not just 'unhidden', it is overtly on display. Male bodies function in relation to female visual pleasure. Fetishising the penis and reducing it to a sexual object make it devoid of phallic power. Similarly, after her rape, in which the penis and penetration are shown, Manu describes the experience as 'just a bit of cock'. It could be worse, they could be dead.

Baise-moi differs from the symbolic economy of the rape-revenge in that it barely uses castration, either literal or symbolic as a response to male sexual violence. The equation of 'rape = castration' is one which usually saturates the genre marking notorious scenes in films such as *I Spit on Your Grave, Last House on the Left, The Hills Have Eyes, Ladies Club* (Janet Greek, 1986) and *Hostel II* (Eli Roth, 2007); all answer rape, or intended rape, with castration. There is only one instance where *Baise-moi* makes this reference. In an early scene, Nadine is having sex with a punter as they watch the Gasper Noé film *Seul contre tous/I Stand Alone* (1998). Two shots from this film are shown and juxtaposed with each other: a man hitting a woman, followed by a salami being sliced. These two images put together form the narrative essence of *I Spit on Your Grave*. Their inclusion here is almost parodic and underscores the differing responses to rape in male and female authored texts.[2] If images and fantasies of castration dominate male-authored rape-revenge films, then overall it is conspicuously absent as an obvious metaphor within this film. Unlike *I Spit on Your Grave*, which presents female violence in the framework of male fantasy, *Baise-moi* in many different ways eradicates masculine in favour of feminine agency.

However, this is a film about class politics as much as gender. Carol Clover reads *I Spit on Your Grave* and the 1970s rape-revenge films such as *The Hills Have Eyes* and *Deliverance* (John Boorman, 1972) in relation to an urban/rural axis. She states that 'going from the city to the country in horror film is like going from village to forest in traditional fairytales' (1992: 124), to a world of sexually dysfunctional and uncivilised families which produce rapists. In *Baise-moi*, however, this is reversed, the rape takes place in the city in a bleak industrial landscape, and the women escape the city and go on the road.

In many rape-revenge cycles, women are raped to punish them for moving beyond their 'natural' gender or class position. There is a double revenge axis which relates to class politics. Jennifer Hills is raped because she is rich and her rapists are poor. The class politics in *Baise-moi* are very different and it is this political dialogue which grounds it in contemporary France. Unlike the other films, Manu and her friend are raped not because they have climbed above their place in the social order, but because they are already at the bottom of it. She says, 'we're just girls. It is the natural order of things', challenging the 'natural order' via the killing spree which is, for Manu, as much about class rage as male abuse. In the opening scenes she is dealing drugs and doing porn because 'there is no work in France'. The first woman they kill together is smartly dressed and obviously rich. Many reviews discuss the inclusion of this woman's death as important because it is indiscriminate and lifts the film beyond the simple equation of women killing men because men abuse women, but this overlooks the overt class dialogue prompted by its inclusion. Unlike *I Spit on Your Grave*, this woman is shot because she is rich and Manu is raped because she is poor. Nicole Brenez recognises a specifically European aesthetic within the film, citing Frederic Nietzsche's 1887 note on European nihilism being 'a symptom that the underprivileged have no comfort left; that they destroy in order to be destroyed; that without morality they no longer have any reason to "resign themselves"' (quoted in Brenez 2003). *Baise-moi* has a bleakness that the rape-revenge films of other national cinemas lack; the revenge is empty and destroys them, it is hardly a triumphant ending.

The high profile of this film and *Irreversible* (discussed below) and the focus on the rapes within them link the cycle to contemporary France. Gang rape on urban Paris estates became known as *'tournante'* or 'pass around', and the set up of *Baise-moi* echoes the landscape and dynamics of *tournante*. In 1991, it represented ten to twenty percent of serious cases in French juvenile courts.[3] Rose George explains that when the depiction of 'torched cars, violence against the police, deep-seated fury' in *La Haine* (1995) provoked concerned outrage but little change, 'the *banlieue* imploded instead. The stronger minority – frustrated, furious young men – turned on the weaker women' (2006a: 4). Any girl who had sex with her boyfriend was seen as fair game for other men. Catherine Breillat argued that 'there is no strong feminist movement today. Instead, there's a very strong misogyny. When the fact of the gang rapes came out, no-one protested because of fatalism. They said "it's cultural." No it's not!' (quoted in George 2006b). This fatalistic acceptance of rape is articulated by Manu; it is what happens to women at the bottom of the social order. This is in sharp contrast to films which engaged with the same issue in the 1970s – women may have suffered but they always emerged victorious and justice was done.

Contemporary French cinema does not share the same horror history as America and until recently with the success of *Haute tension/Switchblade Romance* (Alexandre Aja, 1993), the absence of the slasher film also meant an absence of the 'final girl' as a common narrative figure. *The Bride Wore Black* (François Truffaut, 1968), in which a wronged woman takes violent revenge against the men who killed her husband, offers a narrative antecedent of sorts although rape does not feature as a motivator. Although the mix of sex and violence in *Baise-moi* does not translate as sexualised violence, the most obvious reference point for the eroticisation of violent women is the *femme fatale*. Noël Burch and Geneviève Sellier argue that the figure of the *sale garce* or 'evil bitch', 'who uses her powers of seduction to exploit, enslave and/or destroy me' (2000: 47), appears in 25 percent of films made in France between 1945 and 1955. They link this prevalence to both male fears about women and the impact of the occupation on male national pride: 'The symbolic violence against women expressed in the *grace* figure was no longer necessary once patriarchal authority, badly shaken by defeat and occupation had (temporarily) recovered its serenity' (2000: 48). One group of women who came in for particularly harsh treatment was those accused of having sexual relations with the enemy; they were punished by having their heads shaved, 'a reminder to women that their bodies did not belong to them and could be repossessed symbolically on behalf of the nation' (ibid.). The appearance of this figure in post-war French cinema, and the concurrent *film noir* era in America, firmly grounds the image of the sexually dangerous woman to masculine anxieties, expressed via women. A common difference between the French *femme fatale* and her Hollywood counterpart is her relation to other women. Burch and Sellier argue that whereas American films often pit the *femme fatale* against a saintly woman, when she appears in French cinema it is commonly within narratives in which all women are evil.

Irreversible also features a controversial rape scene and revenge-based narrative. The revenge here, however, is taken by the victim's boyfriend on her behalf, as in the pre-1970s, pre-feminist mode of the genre. As in *Baise-moi*, the rapist himself is not punished, although as director Gaspar Noé points out in the DVD commentary many people think that he is and a false memory occurred because that is what the audience expect. The film's narrative is shown backwards (although shot in chronological order) which immediately and obviously alters the narrative structure in that the revenge precedes the rape. Like *Baise-moi* and *I Spit on Your Grave*, the film was controversial primarily because of its nine-minute rape scene. All three films share similarities in the way that they depict rape – long takes, lack of editing and a static camera to produce a documentary feel. All are also notably long scenes, and the length of the rape scene is mentioned frequently in reviews. The inclusion of graphic, extended rape scenes on the grounds that, for the revenge to be understood and the violence justified, the rape has to be seen, is an argument consistently repeated by filmmakers, film censorship boards and reviews. *Irreversible* differs considerably in the way the rape scene was constructed. *Baise-moi* and *I Spit on Your Grave* are low-budget productions and while *Irreversible* utilises a realist aesthetic (no make-up, natural lighting, no shot list and some non-professional actors) the rape scene has surprisingly complex and expensive production values – the most notable being the post-production addition of a CGI penis. This simulated and conscious visibility of a penis is curious – the absence is perceived as a lack and added in afterwards. This is in sharp contrast – literally and symbolically – to the constructed absence enacted via castration in the traditional formula.

Although the rape-revenge film is not strictly horror, the appearance of two high-profile films does link in with a wider trend within contemporary horror in relation to the representation of rape. As stated earlier, actual rape is in the main absent from horror. However in contemporary horror, particularly ultra-violent films such as *Hostel* (Eli Roth, 2003) which have come to be known as 'torture porn', rape has resurfaced as an implicit rather than a symbolic threat. *From Dusk Till Dawn* (Robert Rodriguez, 1996) features an almost comedic rape, and in *Wolf Creek* (Greg McLean, 2005) and *The Devil's Rejects* (Rob Zombie, 2005), violence against women includes sexual violence.

All of these films, in common with the cycle in the 1970s, are rural horrors, but unlike the originals these girls don't escape and there is no vengeance taken either by themselves or on their behalf. They just get threatened with rape, and then killed with no revenge. These films are more bleak and brutal in their representation of rape than their 1970s ancestors. The final scene of *I Spit on Your Grave* leaves Jennifer triumphant and unpunished, but *Baise-moi* kills off its heroines and the rape victim in *Irreversible* gets no revenge. The films' pessimism and shift in narrative structure ground them firmly in the tensions of the time and place they represent.

NOTES

1   *Baise-moi* was released in the UK in 2000 under recently relaxed censorship laws with ten seconds (including a penetration shot) cut from the rape scene.
2   It is worth noting that *Thelma and Louise*, written by Callie Khouri, and *Dirty Weekend*, based on the novel by Helen Zahavi, both also avoid using castration as revenge for rape.
3   See J. Henley, 'Gang Rape on Rise Among French Youth', *The Guardian*, 3 May 2001.

BIBLIOGRAPHY

Brenez, N. (2003) '*Baise-moi* - Girls Better than Maenads, Darker than Furies', *Screening the Past*, 15. On-line. Available HTTP: http://www.latrobe.edu.au/screeningthepast/classics/cl0703/nbcl15.html (13 February 2008).

Burch, N. and G. Sellier (2000) 'Evil Women in the Post-War French Cinema' in U. Sieglohr (ed.) *Heroines Without Heroes: Reconstructing Female and National Identities in European Cinema 1945–51*. London: Cassel, 47–61.

Clover, C. (1992) *Men, Women and Chainsaws: Gender in the Modern Slasher Film*. Princeton, NJ: Princeton University Press.

Creed, B. (1993) *The Monstrous Feminine: Film, Feminism, Psychoanalysis*. New York and London: Routledge.

Despentes, V. (1991) *Baise-moi*. Paris: J'ai Lu.

George, R. (2006a) 'Revolt Against the Rapists,' *The Guardian*, 17 July, On-line. Available HTTP: http://www.guardian.co.uk/world/2003/apr/05/france.gender (19 July 2006).

_____ (2006b) 'Ghetto Warrior' (Interview with Fadela Amara), *The Guardian*, 17 July, On-line. Available HTTP: http://www.guardian.co.uk/world/2006/jul/17/france.politicsphilosophyandsociey (19 July, 2006).

Green, P. (1998) *Cracks in the Pedestal: Gender and Ideology in Hollywood*. Amherst, MA: University of Massachusetts Press.

Henley, J. (2001) 'Gang Rape on rise among French Youth', *The Guardian*, 3 May, On-line. Available HTTP: http://www.guardian.co.uk/world/2001/may/03/jonhenley (19 July 2006).

Lehman, P. (1993) 'Don't Blame This on a Girl: Female Rape Revenge Films', in S. Cohen and I. R. Hark (eds) *Screening the Male: Exploring Masculinities in Hollywood Cinema*. New York and London: Routledge, 103–17.

Nietzsche F. (1968) *The Will to Power*. Trans. W. Kaufmann and R.J. Hollingdale. New York: Vintage.

Read, J. (2000) *The New Avengers: Film, Femininity and the Rape-Revenge Cycle*, Manchester: Manchester University Press.
Vincendeau, G. (2002) Review of *Baise-moi*, *Sight and Sound*, May, On-line. Available HTTP: http://www.bfi.org.uk/sightandsound/review/1715/www.baise-moi.co.uk (23 February 2006).
Virdi, J. (1999) 'Reverence, Rape – and then Revenge: Popular Hindi Cinema's Woman's Film', *Screen*, 40, 1, 17–37.
Williams, L. R. (2001) 'Sick Sisters', *Sight and Sound*, July, On-line. Available HTTP: http://www.bfi.org.uk/sightandsound/feature/406 (25 July 2006).

SUBJECTIVITY UNLEASHED:
HAUTE TENSION

Matthias Hurst

The phenomenon of subjectivity and the crisis of identity are topical cornerstones of modern art. With the loss of religious faith, traditional values and philosophical reassurance in the modern age one can also sense a growing threat of destabilisation of both the conditions of individual human lives and social order in general. Individuality, identity and the self have become insecure and unreliable. The realisation that objectivity is more often than not a mere social or cultural construction and that subjective perception and subjective convictions shape and dominate our sense of reality has made the world a more ambiguous place and our lives, our personal agendas and our self-perception a more unsettling endeavour. There seems to be no certainty; instead we have to accept a deep and irreconcilable gap between our ideas of identity and the obscure, unfathomable reality of our selves. We have to accept the notion that we are split personalities by nature and that living in society means a constant struggle to maintain some form of unity.

The rise of psychoanalytical theories did not solve the problem, but instead put the whole issue on a more crucial level and deepened the problematic aspects of subjectivity and perception. Now we know – thanks to Sigmund Freud and his successors – that there are forces and hidden urges that rule our consciousness and determine our perception, our thinking and our actions without being conscious or easily detectable and without being shared by any objective or general understanding. The duality of man might be common knowledge, but it has not become easier to endure this existential experience.

Art, of course, reflects the feeling of uneasiness related to this duality. Modern literature presents characters in abundance who suffer from the lack of objective truth and the inadequacy and unreliability of human subjectivity. Cinema too has produced visions of subjectivity that stress the power of individual imagination and perception, cinematic discourses that transcend any notion of a filmic restriction to plain physical reality. They reflect the dilemma of our critical epistemological situation in which compulsive ideas of objectivity and the forces of subjectivity clash and undermine our perception of stable identity. Especially in the European cinema of horror and the fantastic there is a long tradition of the topic of subjectivity and its disturbing implications. In 1920 Robert Wiene's classic German film *Das Kabinett des Dr Caligari/The Cabinet of Dr Caligari* unleashed the power of subjective imagination in a tale of murder and madness. The distorted images of a nightmarish world, all painted in a unique expressionistic style, reflect the inner feelings and turmoil of the protagonist Francis, who thinks he is about to uncover the crimes of mad Dr Caligari, but in fact is the inmate of a mental hospital himself. The audience partakes directly in the madman's perception and realises only at the end of the film that it was forced to share his point of view. But the frame story in which Francis is shown telling his story to another inmate of the hospital makes the twist of the tale retrospectively clear for us. It is a story he alone is telling and he alone is responsible for, and we discover the inherent logic of this story by realising that he utilises all the people he knows from his life in the hospital as characters in his imagination. Thus his phantasmagorical story reflects his real life and his emotional relations to the people surrounding him. There is a system even to madness.

Other examples of this tradition of psychological horror films are Polanski's *Repulsion* (1965) and *Le locataire/The Tenant* (1976), in which the boundless subjectivity and the emotional insecurity of the characters lead to traumatic experiences. Again the filmic discourses confront us directly with the perception and the impressions of the protagonists, making us immediate witnesses to their terrified and terrifying world view. Mental disorder is expressed in images of terror, caused by forcing subjective feelings and anxieties upon the surrounding reality. Internal horror defines the perception of the external world. The events we see may still be weird, but the very structure of filmic narration makes perfect sense. A logic of depiction becomes visible, a coherence that shapes the imaginary world in a way we can understand, linked to the consciousness of the protagonists and described precisely with psychiatric terms like paranoia or schizophrenia.

With the French film *Haute tension/Switchblade Romance* (2003) by Alexandre Aja and screenwriter Gregory Levasseur the theme of subjectivity, mental disorder and split personality reaches a new dimension. On one hand it reflects the tradition of European horror films regarding the depiction of subjectivity and adds a new level of violence and brutality; on the other it comments on the modern American horror cinema and its implied psychoanalytical notions.

The story – about two young women, Marie (Cécile de France) and Alex (Maïwenn le Besco), the lonely house of Alex's family in the French countryside, a mad serial killer (Philippe Nahon), the slaughtering of the family, the abduction of Alex, and Marie's desperate attempts to rescue her friend – starts as an average horror film and bears a striking resemblance to Dean Koontz's novel *Intensity* (1996). It's easy to see how Aja was influenced by American horror films, namely slasher films like *Halloween* (John Carpenter, 1978) and *Friday the 13th* (Sean Cunningham, 1980) or backwoods horror films like *The Texas Chainsaw Massacre* (Tobe Hooper, 1974) and *The Hills Have Eyes* (Wes Craven, 1977).[1] Structural elements and motifs in this tradition of modern horror films, that has seen a gruesome renaissance since the mid-1990s, are obviously part of the effectiveness of *Switchblade Romance*: the mysterious appearance and ruthless behaviour of the killer, the depiction of disturbing violence and the strict focus on the very simple main plot. There are no subplots that could distract from the confrontation between Marie and the killer. This concentration and the skillful use of cinematic means of storytelling – the *mise-en-scène*, the editing and the suggestive sound – create a high degree of tension which pulls the spectator totally into the action.

The solution of the film, the realisation that Marie and the mad serial killer are but one person, offers a spectacular story twist and makes *Switchblade Romance* a new distinguished entry in the cinematic canon of psychological horror. Creating a controversial debate among critics and fans and stirring up passionate Internet activities, this revealing twist has proven to be the crucial element of either the film's unique effectiveness or utter failure.[2] However, this revelation in itself might not be too surprising.

It's very common to analyse the confrontation between victim and perpetrator, between human beings and monsters in horror films as a confrontation between the conscious and the unconscious. It has become a traditional reading to understand the antagonist as an externalisation of repressed feelings or urges, as a part of the protagonist's own psyche or as a sublimated part of his cultural context. The other – no matter how strange and how disturbing his appearance may be – seems to represent the darker half of human nature.

Robert Louis Stevenson's novel *The Strange Case of Dr Jekyll and Mr Hyde* (1886) conveys the duality of human beings and their affiliation to both good and evil by the physical transformation of the protagonist: he is Jekyll, the well educated and respected member of society, and he becomes Hyde, the outcast who satisfies his lust without remorse – the evil twin who lives out all the emotions and desires that Jekyll is constantly repressing. Stevenson's seminal novel about the split personality of Jekyll/Hyde did not invent the idea of the unconscious double, but it can be seen as a summary and a disclosure of all the stories that reflect the duality of man. It is, as it were, a manual for interpreting classical and modern horror stories in psychological terms, defining a new degree of horror in the most evident way: 'To be haunted by another, by a spectre, is uncanny enough, but to be haunted by yourself strikes at the foundations of identity' (Dryden 2003: 41).

Psychoanalytic thinking has provided a key to understand both the familiar-looking double and the loathsome monsters and maniacs of horror fiction who stalk innocent people with sharp knives and chainsaws. In his essay 'The Uncanny', first published in 1919, Sigmund Freud points out that it is the repressed that comes back to haunt the individual; the 'uncanny is in reality nothing new or alien, but something which is familiar and old-established in the mind and which has become alienated from it only through the process of repression ... something which ought to have remained hidden but has come to light' (1990: 363–4). The double is just the most illustrative case in the perennial return of the repressed; the monster, the vampire, the werewolf, the serial killer – they all embody the dark forces and desires, sexual and aggressive urges that were put aside by civilised man.

The psychoanalytic reading is obvious in regard to some classical European and American horror films, for instance *Peeping Tom* (Michael Powell, 1960), *Psycho* (Alfred Hitchcock, 1960), *Hands of the Ripper* (Peter Sasdy, 1971), *Sisters* (Brian de Palma, 1973); it is less obvious, but still possible, in regard to the slasher films and the tales of backwoods horror that inspired Aja's *Switchblade Romance*. These films keep the distinction between protagonist and antagonist; they hide the narrative device of externalisation or projection. By this they stress the difference and the strangeness of the other, the deviation from the norm (see Wood 2003: 63–84, 168–79).

Keeping the distinction between man and monster means to establish clear boundaries between *us* and *them*, between the innocent and the evil, and to shut out feelings of responsibility for what's going on and what's going wrong: it's always the other, the fiend in various disguises who is threatening society, it's not our own vicious and destructive nature. This dualistic belief generates a whole philosophy of life, a simplistic worldview of arrogance and boastfulness and habitually misguided accusations that becomes perceptible not only in petty everyday situations, but also in major social conflicts and sometimes even in global politics.

The tendency to maintaining the dualistic structure and corroborating the related connotations is particularly demonstrated by the strange way in which the new American horror films either stubbornly repeat the simple plot of bloody conflict between the usual bunch of teenagers and the terrifying group of weird backwoods dwellers or East European torturers – like in the 2003 remake of *The Texas Chainsaw Massacre* (Marcus Nispel), *Wrong Turn* (Rob Schmidt, 2003), *House of 1000 Corpses* (Rob Zombie, 2003) and *Hostel* (Eli Roth, 2005) – or construct complicated and absurd whodunit scenarios and solutions to single out the least expected to be the crazy killer on campus – like in *Scream* (Wes Craven, 1996), *I Know What You Did Last Summer* (Jim Gillespie, 1997) and *Urban Legend* (Jamie Blanks, 1998) and all the sequels, of course.

Switchblade Romance, on the other hand, makes the standard psychoanalytical interpretation, the Jekyll and Hyde solution, absolutely clear in its final part. Marie *is* the brutal killer, overwhelmed by her own desire, her repressed love for Alex and her fear of losing her. She and everyone else become victims of her raging violence; she does not know what she is doing, because she does not realise the difference between objective reality and her feverish imagination. Everything we see before the revelation is just an expression of her very subjective perception, an illusion, a dream she is caught in, a nightmare of unleashed subjectivity. The film could consequently be characterised as a visualised process of (failed) repression: the heroine is confronted with her own aggressive impulses, and she accepts the challenge; she engages in a duel against the dark, forbidden forces within herself. She seems to win, killing her enemy and thus trying to repress the unwanted urges. Unfortunately, this enemy keeps coming back. As the depiction of a nerve-wracking battle against evil that comes from within and as a testimony to human monstrosity Aja's film is like a blueprint of horror fiction in its basic, essential and most revealing form.

From the beginning the film establishes a strong identification between the audience and Marie by using numerous close-ups and point of view shots. Consequently the spectator is surprised and confused at first, realising that Marie has a split personality and that the second self of this slender, delicate girl is portrayed by a disgusting, brutish, stocky man. He is a Hyde character who does not only differ in appearance and behaviour but also in sex.

Describing the idea of the 'final girl' in modern horror films, i.e. the heroine who survives only because she neglects and denies her femininity and acts like a man instead, Carol Clover points out that in this genre 'gender is less a wall than a permeable membrane' (1993: 46). Gender has become an even more unstable and significant factor in contemporary horror cinema; the specific qualities or social functions of men and women and their roles as victims or perpetrators seem to shift, but the constellation of dominant male power and the oppression of female interests and values, fuelled by the voyeuristic nature of cinema itself, i.e. the male gaze of the camera (see Mulvey 1986), is still an issue. Independent of the characters' physical appearance, gender categories influence their behaviour and their meaning, based on deeply rooted social conventions and traditions. By making these common ideas and normative traits of gender and sexual identity available for both male and female characters and by offering the spectators of the filmic discourse both sadistic identification with the (male) perpetrators and masochistic identification with the (female) victims, the gender-related aspects of behaviour, of dominance and submission become even more significant and more debatable.

Externalised duality: Marie, the 'final girl', attacks her male alter ego

And indeed, Marie, the heroine of *Switchblade Romance*, excels as the 'final girl' who adopts male qualities, learns to fight and literally strikes back smashing the face of her enemy with a barbed wire club. But at the same time she transgresses the model of the 'final girl' in a subversive and almost mocking way, because this 'final girl' not only acts like a boy and thus reveals herself as a masculine female, she even generates a masculine alter ego displaying in abundance all the 'bad phallic' (i.e. aggressive) habits we know from serial killers in slasher films. She herself is creating the enemy she has to face and to overcome; she is responsible for the horror and the challenge of gender aspects in the first place. In the end Aja's film is yet another version of the figurative equation of women and monsters as a (sexual) threat to patriarchal society, another version of the monstrous feminine (see Creed 2003), that has become a perennial topic of the horror genre (see Williams 1984; Freeland 2000: 55–86), but the disclosure of the misogynistic male killer as an image of female subjectivity and ferocity seems to make the genre's playful and intriguing confusion with gender representations more complex and disturbing.

On a more basic level the duality of Marie demonstrates one of the central elements that Noël Carroll applies to define the creatures of horror fiction and thus one of the crucial elements of horror in general, namely impurity and interstitiality:

> 'Many cases of impurity are generated by what ... I called interstitiality and categorical contradictoriness. Impurity involves a conflict between two or more standing cultural categories. [...] On the simplest physical level, this often entails the construction of creatures that transgress categorical distinctions such as inside/outside, living/dead, insect/human, flesh/machine, and so on' (1990: 43).

The distinction male/female is not on this list, but there is no doubt that – according to the rigid logic of horror fiction – it belongs to this catalogue of imperfection.

Marie's transgression of gender categories makes her an impure, interstitial creature; because the filmic discourse presents her as both female and male, she is a monster.

Her externalised masculine self is representing her repressed sexuality. Similarly to some American slasher films, in which the killers prefer to hunt down promiscuous teenagers, this vengeful force is stirred up by sexual arousal: having seen Alex naked under the shower, Marie is listening to a song with the lyrics 'just another girl...'[3] and masturbating, and at the same time we see – in a parallel montage of several alternating shots – the truck of the killer approaching on the road and finally arriving in front of the house. Marie's sexual climax correlates with the coming of the brutal murderer. The message seems to be a conservative one: beware of this kind of desire! Keep these unwanted and socially unaccepted emotions under control.

The depiction of repressed lesbian sexuality that suddenly turns into frenzy has caused disapproving reactions by the audience. But does Aja really hate lesbians? He rather wanted to achieve the maximum effect of tension and surprise by showing two young women in trouble, threatened by a man in a stereotypical horror film situation, and then reveal the female protagonist to be the killer herself. His intention is more likely to tell a gripping story of outrageous subjectivity than to denounce lesbian love. Still, it cannot be denied that *Switchblade Romance* confronts the spectator with an extreme case of female sexuality running amok and thus features an impressively shocking example of the monstrous-feminine; 'sexual longing, some films suggest, can turn women into terrifying juggernauts' (Hogan 1997: 38). This time, however, the violence of the schizophrenic woman does not only nourish male anxiety, but also female anxiety of a sexual threat. The frightening male representation of her lesbian desire and the related phallic aggression turn Marie into an impure and interstitial perpetrator with confused gender aspects. Consequently her fury affects men and women alike; the terror works in both directions. In this excessive display of gender dynamics the identification process of the spectator shifts, as it were, from a position of sadistic voyeurism – as described by Mulvey (1986) – to a complementary position of masochistic victimisation – as suggested by Clover (1993) – and back again.

In this context it should not be forgotten that Marie does not only cause pain, but suffers herself from her disposition and her existence in a society which makes representations of women easily available for male desire and abuse. Before the killer leaves the house of Alex's parents, he takes a photograph of her from the mantelpiece and adds it to his photo collection in the truck. It seems obvious that all the young women on the pictures are victims of his previous crimes; by keeping their images he still has power over them: Alex is *just another girl* in this dreadful gallery. Not only the song about 'just another girl' that Marie was listening to earlier comes to one's mind in this scene, but also the fact that Alex's father mentioned upon the arrival of the girls that the family had put a photograph of Marie on the mantelpiece. Even before the family met Marie, she was already present and known at their house. Her image is available; unknowingly she is the object of the father's gaze, i.e. of the male gaze. The stealing of Alex's photograph from the mantelpiece and its addition to the killer's collection of gruesome souvenirs echoes Marie's own experience of being the object of the ubiquitous male gaze and is in a more general sense a reflection of the degrading availability of women or female representations in a patriarchal society of heterosexual voyeuristic structures.

Marie's bloody rebellion against these structures fails. Her attack is stopped when Alex, the representative of the common heterosexual order and suddenly a 'final girl' in her own right, pierces her body with an iron bar – a phallic penetration that does not kill Marie, but forces her back into the heterosexual realm of patriarchal society. Being severely scarred both physical and mentally, her fate is to become the isolated inmate of an asylum. Yes, she is a terrifying killer, a dangerous threat to society, but she also provokes pity as a failure, an outsider to the system.

As mentioned above, the revelation of the killer's true identity does not come entirely as a surprise, at least not for the attentive spectator: at the very beginning of the film Marie dreams about being chased through the woods, the same way Alex will be chased by her at the end of the film. 'Who was the guy stalking you?' asks Alex, when they are talking about the dream. Marie answers: 'It wasn't a guy. It was me. That's the weirdest part. It was me running after me!'[4] Actually, here she is already revealing the twist ending. And there are visual symbols for her split personality and her repressed duality throughout the film, such as, for instance, the cage with the twin parrots in the house of Alex's parents; the doll with the crack in the face; the split reflections of Marie in the mirror, when she is trying to escape the killer in the house; the double stripes on the car she is using to follow the killer's truck; or the two dice in the rear mirror in the car showing the number two in different shots. In the scene that introduces the truck driver, he uses a severed head to perform oral sex and throws it out of his vehicle, a shocking image that sets the tone for things to come; but this head looks like Alex's head and thus reveals the scene as a sexual fantasy of Marie.

It is not the fact that Marie is the killer that is the most disturbing aspect of the film, but the way this revelation is put into the context of the film, the way this truth affects the whole narrative structure and the previous events of the story. Suddenly so many things that occurred before seem to be totally impossible. Where did the truck come from? Was there a truck at all? How could Marie drive two cars at the same time? Were there two cars at all?

And while these questions remain unanswered and the absurdity of the whole story starts to solidify, we witness the hysterical climax of the film: Marie as the mad truck driver, covered with blood, chasing Alex with a screeching circular saw through the woods *à la* Leatherface, screaming and grunting. A filmic presentation of shot and reverse-shot is showing the running victim and the murderous maniac in a familiar situation of horror and mayhem, recreating the emblematic image of the slasher genre. This exaggerated scene, now tainted by our knowledge of the artificial construction of the plot, is near to parody. It's the clichéd situation of many modern American horror films, but presented here as the conclusion of a movie that uncovers the mechanisms and psychological implications of horror fiction to the point of sheer absurdity. At this moment the audience is made aware of the constrained artificiality of these horror scenarios, and the explosion of gross violence combined with the implosion of narrative logic literally deconstructs the genre. It's a metafilmic moment stripping the horror genre down to its bones and to the basic principles of its plain psychoanalytical construction, unabashed and ludicrous. Thus fans of the genre either hate this moment or embrace it with glee.

Tania Modleski (2001) points out that the contemporary horror film has become part of postmodern culture by its denial of easy consumable and pleasant presentation and its renunciation of traditional forms and elements of narration, like character and plot development or a satisfying closure of the story. In a similar vein Philip Brophy coins the term *horrality* to describe the elements and effects of 'horror, textuality, morality, hilarity' (2001: 277) which constitute the modern horror film and demonstrate its 'violent awareness of itself as a saturated genre' (2001: 278–9). Both approaches could explain the effectiveness of *Switchblade Romance* and its metafictional account of modern horror; however, there seems to be a specific quality, an exceptionally high degree of awareness that makes Aja's film unique.

Unlike other horror films in which the structural and psychoanalytical implications are not revealed so blatantly, or unlike David Fincher's *Fight Club* (1999) in which the duality of the protagonist does not question the previous scenes in terms of narrative plausibility, the twist in *Switchblade Romance* subverts the logic and the plot structure in a way that cannot be ignored. Films like *Repulsion, Sisters* and *The Descent* (Neil Marshall, 2005) indulge in female subjectivity too, but they maintain a clear and more homogenous structure and do not mess up the innerfictional logic of events. In Aja's film we have to accept the crucial meaning of Marie's subjectivity for the experience and visualisation of the horror; the structure of *Switchblade Romance* is so dependent on her imagination, so embedded in the turbid logic of dreams that there is no other way to understand it other than bearing in mind its origin in total subjectivity.[5] As spectators we have become part of Marie's private distorted universe, a nightmarish story that exists only *because of Marie* and her emotional state. Through the course of the film we are losing our distance to Marie and her perception and we are adopting her point of view, identifying with her – regardless of gender issues – and only at the end do we win back our own point of view by realising her duality. Once we have understood the nature of her subjective world of violence and madness we are glad to stay apart, and we don't want to lose this distance of perception again.

'I won't let anyone come between us anymore ... I won't let anyone come between us anymore...' Marie is repeating this sentence obsessively at the beginning and at the end of the film; it is meant to show her affection for her friend Alex, but in this context it sounds like a threat to the spectator of this or any other horror film. It is the threat that lies at the heart of so many modern horror tales, namely to lose the distance, to become involved in the subjective vision of a troubled and haunted being – for nothing else seems to be the nature of modern horror. At the same time this process of identification between film spectator and film character is one of the most effective principles of narrative cinema in general and thus one of the most important means of cinematic entertainment.

Jean-Louis Baudry, looking back on a long tradition of comparison between narrative arts and subjective perception, claims that there is a strong and meaningful connection between cinema – the 'simulation apparatus' (1986: 312) – and dreams, and that feature films are but regressive dreams of wish fulfilment. Both film and dream present forms of subjective reality in which regressive forces rule. A dream reveals the secret wishes of an individual dreamer, the cinema displays the longings of a collective, compelling the individual to share a vision that may appeal to him, but is definitely not his own. 'Cinema, like dream, would seem to correspond to a temporary form of regression, but whereas dream, according to Freud, is merely a "normal hallucinatory psychosis", cinema offers an artificial psychosis without offering the dreamer the possibility of exercising any kind of immediate control' (1986: 315).

This is exactly what *Switchblade Romance* is showing to be the experience of its heroine and what it is presenting self-reflexively to the spectator as a principle of modern horror fiction. Its true horror may not be the violence and the bloodshed but the implicit statement that there is no common interpersonal truth, no objectivity everyone would share and could rely on – and that we could be fooled by our own subjectivity or – even worse – that we could be fooled and absorbed by another person's subjective perception and beliefs.

Summarising the effectiveness of modern horror, Ivan Butler points out that 'when the mind is the actual stuff of horror, when madness and collapse are presented from inside, rather than viewed from without, then the solid ground itself shifts and crumbles, and we do indeed find ourselves looking into the bottomless pit' (1979: 83). Film seems to be the perfect medium to look into the bottomless pit of sinister subjectivity and delusion. But within the pit, within the cinematic discourse of subjectivity it is also the medium of film that offers a fragment of another, more objective reality, an escape route out of the pit, as it were: the surveillance camera at the gas station has recorded Marie committing the murder of the station attendant. As long as we share Marie's point of view, the video monitor is showing the truck driver as deadly foe. But when the police officer is checking the recording, we realise for the first time that Marie is the perpetrator. Now the grainy, blurred images of the video camera reveal the truth – as Marie, in yet another instant of self-reflexivity, turns her head and looks fiercely into the camera, directly towards us. The voyeuristic pleasure of the male gaze, characterising the genre in general, is confronted and undermined by the female gaze. Marie's piercing eyes repel the spectator, breaking the bond with her perspective and forcing him/her to dramatically re-evaluate the filmic discourse so far.

This is a paradoxical and ambiguous moment in our relation to the narrative structure, and nonetheless a moment of redemption: the revelation of the female gaze releases the spectator from Marie's female point of view and grants access to an objective perspective which redefines the whole narrative. Film, we are reminded here, is not only capable of generating and conveying very convincing images of egocentric perception and extreme subjectivity, it has also the power to show photographic images of physical reality and to re-establish our sense of the real.

Male and female gaze, subjectivity and objectivity – it seems as if the cinematic discourse itself is spoiled by interstitiality, a confusion of different modes of perception, and thus embodies an impure monstrosity that does not fail to subvert expectations related to the processes of spectator identification. Alexandre Aja's *Switchblade Romance* is a true horror film because it presents characters, situations and even a solution which are all familiar elements of the perennial formulae of the genre, but it is also a unique film about the essence and the construction of modern horror that does not hesitate to become an interstitial monster of effectiveness and absurd travesty in its revealing depiction of cruelty and subjectivity unleashed.

NOTES

1 Aja directed the remake of *The Hills Have Eyes* in 2006.
2 See, for example, the user comments at the *Internet Movie Database* IMDb. On-line. Available HTTP: http://www.imdb.com/title/tt0338095/usercomments (12 July 2007).
3 It's the song 'Runaway Girl' by U-Roy.
4 Quote from the English dubbed version of the film.
5 With its circular construction – the film starts with Marie sitting wounded in the hospital – and the uncertainty about the levels of reality and perception marked by the intrusion of the foreshadowing dream, *Switchblade Romance* is a close competitor to the stunning narrative structures in David Lynch's *Eraserhead* (1977) and *Lost Highway* (1996).

BIBLIOGRAPHY

Baudry, J.-L. (1986) 'The Apparatus: Metapsychological Approaches to the Impression of Reality in the Cinema', in P. Rosen (ed.) *Narrative, Apparatus, Ideology: A Film Theory Reader*. New York: Columbia University Press, 299–318.

Brophy, P. (2001) 'Horrality – The Textuality of Contemporary Horror Films', in K. Gelder (ed.) *The Horror Reader*. London/New York: Routledge, 276–84.

Butler, I. (1979) *Horror in the Cinema*, 3rd edn. South Brunswick/New York: A. S. Barnes.

Carroll, N. (1990) *The Philosophy of Horror or Paradoxes of the Heart*. London/New York: Routledge.

Clover, C. J. (1993) *Men, Women, and Chainsaws: Gender in the Modern Horror Film*. Princeton, NJ: Princeton University Press.

Creed, B. (2003) *The Monstrous-Feminine: Film, Feminism, Psychoanalysis*. London/New York: Routledge.

Dryden, L. (2003) *The Modern Gothic and Literary Doubles: Stevenson, Wilde and Wells*. Basingstoke/New York: Palgrave Macmillan.

Freeland, C. A. (2000) *The Naked and the Undead: Evil and the Appeal of Horror*. Boulder, CO: Westview Press.

Freud, S. (1990) 'The "Uncanny"', in *Art and Literature: Jensen's Gradiva, Leonardo da Vinci and Other Works*. The Penguin Freud Library Vol. 14. London: Penguin, 335–76.

Hogan, D. J. (1997) *Dark Romance: Sexuality in the Horror Film*. Jefferson, NC: McFarland.

Koontz, D. R. (1996) *Intensity*. London: Headline Book.

Modleski, T. (2001) 'The Terror of Pleasure: The Contemporary Horror Film and Postmodern Theory', in K. Gelder (ed.) *The Horror Reader*. London/New York: Routledge, 285–93.

Mulvey, L. (1986) 'Visual Pleasure and Narrative Cinema', in P. Rosen (ed.) *Narrative, Apparatus, Ideology: A Film Theory Reader*. New York: Columbia University Press, 198–209.

Stevenson, R. L. (2002) *The Strange Case of Dr Jekyll and Mr Hyde and Other Tales of Terror*. London: Penguin.

Williams, L. (1984) 'When the Woman Looks', in M. A. Doane, P. Mellencamp and L. Williams (eds) *Re-Vision: Essays in Feminist Film Criticism*. Frederick, MD: University Publications of America, 83–99.

Wood, R. (2003) *Hollywood from Vietnam to Reagan ... and Beyond*. New York: Columbia University Press.

SPANISH HORROR CINEMA

SPANISH HORROR CINEMA

Patricia Allmer, Emily Brick and David Huxley

Graphic depictions of violence and horror are strong themes in Spanish national cinema. As Marsha Kinder suggests, this is related to a wider national context referring to a history which has been marked

> by fratricidal civil war with bloody repercussions, by a long period of Francoism that glamorized death, by a deep immersion in the conventions of the Counter-Reformation that fetishized the bleeding wounds of Christ and other martyrs, and by a 'Black Legend' of cruelty and violence dating back to the Inquisition and the Conquest which Spaniards have tried to overcome for the past five hundred years. (1993: 1)

This list can be extended to include an artistic tradition which incorporates images of violence ranging from Goya's *Black Paintings* (1820–23) and Picasso's revolutionary *Guernica* (1937), to films by the Spanish surrealist filmmakers Luis Buñuel and Salvador Dalí, for example their collaboration (the French-produced) *Un chien Andalou/An Andalusian Dog* from 1929.

Whilst there are few early Spanish horror films (Edgar Neville's horror-tinged melodrama *La torre de los siete jorobados/The Tower of the Seven Hunchbacks* from 1944 is an example), the beginning of the Spanish horror boom can be located in 1968 with Enrique López Eguiluz and Paul Naschy's *La marca del hombre lobo/ Mark of the Werewolf*, triggering a period of film production from the late 1960s to the early 1970s during which horror films by directors such as Eloy de la Iglesias and Vicente Aranda attained particular significance as tools to subvert and critique the Franco regime. Under this regime (1936–75) the significance of blood was ideologically connected to valorisations of religion, family, nation and other key-stones of fascist ideology.

Whereas some Spanish horror filmmakers, such as de la Iglesia and Aranda, set their films in Spain, often settings outside of Spain were chosen due to the censorship enforced by Franco. A number of Naschy's films were set in France and Eastern Europe, and Amando de Ossario's *Las garras de Lorelei/Grasp of the Lorelei* (1973) was set in Germany. Furthermore, the Spanish horror film of this period refers to and exists in relation to both Europe and America, constructing a hybridity which undermines any simple analysis of a 'national horror cinema'. In order to appeal to an international market, the films of this period were modelled on successful American, British and Italian horror films in the style of Universal 1930s horror and Hitchcock's *Psycho* (1960), Italian gothic and *giallo* films by directors such as Mario Bava and Antonio Margheriti, and British Hammer films.

Thus the director Jesus (Jess) Franco, having seen Hammer's *Brides of Dracula* in Nice in 1961, was inspired to make *Gritos en la noche/The Awful Dr. Orloff* in 1962, and the plot of this film clearly drew on Georges Franju's *Les yeux sans visage/Eyes Without a Face* (1959). Jess Franco went on to become one of the most prolific horror directors in post-war Europe. He made *Il conde Dracula/Count Dracula* (1969), starring Christopher Lee, and many other films which increasingly moved towards exploitation and on occasion hardcore sex in the 1970s and 1980s, tying in with wider developments in the work of Spanish distributors following an overall loosening of censorship laws in Europe in the 1970s and the restoration of democracy in Spain after Franco's death.

More recently, Spanish horror cinema has experienced another renaissance with films such as Alejandro Amenábar's *Los otros/The Others* from 2001 and Juan Antonio Bayona's *El orfanato/The Orphanage* from 2007, a co-production with Mexico. These ghost films address the horror of discovering the failure or absence of ideologically-coded family structures, often pointing to a solution in which, after the loss of the conventional family, a new, hybrid family structure can evolve. The mourning of lost family structures and lost identities is similarly significant in Guillermo del Toro's films, such as *El espinazo del diablo/The Devil's Backbone* (2001) and *El laberinto del fauno/Pan's Labyrinth* (2006). These films' generically hybrid elements, ranging from horror to fantasy and fairytale, offer explorations of the historical horrors of the civil war, whilst revealing national identity as an unreliably mythic construction.

The three chapters in this section examine Spanish horror cinema in the 1970s and more contemporary Spanish horror, demonstrating some of the diversity and developments within the genre. Whilst it has often been argued that Spanish horror cinema in the 1970s is a subversive tool, Andy Willis's chapter examines its reactionary elements by offering close analysis of Paul Naschy's *Exorcismo* (1974). Phil Smith's chapter unearths parallels between the walking of the living dead in Amando de Ossorio's *Blind Dead* quartet (1971–75) and the radical functions of walking developed in European avant-garde aesthetic traditions and practices of remapping terrain, tracing in these films the 'free' walk of the European 'dead'.

Post-Franco, Spanish horror cinema offers ways to express the horrors of the regime as well as an arena for the exploration of new and emergent national and aesthetic identities. Touching on these themes, Barry Jordan's chapter explores the films of Alejandro Amenábar and their innovative use of generic hybridity to rejuvenate the genre.

BIBLIOGRAPHY

Kinder, M. (1993) *Blood Cinema: The Reconstruction of National Identity*, Berkeley, CA: University of California Press.

PAUL NASCHY, *EXORCISMO* AND THE REACTIONARY HORRORS OF SPANISH POPULAR CINEMA IN THE EARLY 1970s

Andy Willis

Whilst many of those who have written about the horror film have sought to find the radical within the genre or to read it through challenging theoretical perspectives, it is certainly the case that many horror works in fact offer rather reactionary views of the world. In this chapter, through a study of a single film, *Exorcismo* from 1974, I want to explore such reactionary tendencies within the Spanish horror cinema of the early 1970s, arguing that in order to understand the particular conservative values represented within many of these works one needs to place the films into the very specific historical and cultural contexts of their production. Here, the films were produced in a country that was moving towards the end of a right-wing dictatorship that had controlled the country for almost thirty-five years.

Spanish horror cinema of the late 1960s and early 1970s is slowly being given the critical attention it deserves. A number of writers, such as Carlos Aguilar (2000), Antonio Lázaro Reboll (2002; 2005) and Tatjana Pavlović (2003) have begun to consider the place of Spanish horror within both national and international film culture from a range of critical and theoretical approaches. As horror has become the focus of more and more sustained critical work (see Jancovich

2002: 1), so previously marginalised or even forgotten examples of the genre have found themselves under the academic microscope. Spanish horror, and in particular figures associated with cult cinema, such as director Jess Franco, have been reclaimed from the critical wilderness and their work reconsidered in a number of ways that are drawn from the body of critical work produced within film studies. Perhaps most commonly, they have been raised to the not-unproblematic pedestal of the cinematic auteur, their œuvres seen as radical and subversive examples of work within the genre, often due to their explicitly violent images and sexual content. In Franco's case they have even been celebrated due to their narrative incoherence (for example, see Le Cain 2003).

My own work in this area has focused on how, during the late 1960s and early 1970s, a number of established art film directors used the horror genre to create works that offered a clear critique of the values that maintained and were supported by the Franco regime (Willis 2003; 2005). These directors, such as Vicente Aranda, Claudio Guerin Hill and Juan Antonio Bardem, had all enjoyed significant or substantial careers in what might be labelled 'serious' cinema both before and, in the case of Aranda and Bardem, after their horror ventures making a number of seemingly more personal and less commercially driven films. Their endeavours within the horror genre used, sometimes quite explicitly, the codes and conventions of the genre to what were in hindsight clearly subversive ends challenging variously the socially accepted norms of sex and sexuality, religion, class and the family that were dominant in Spain at the time.

Other writers, such as Joan Hawkins, have argued that the mere existence of these horror films in Spain during this period should be seen as challenging the attempts of the regime to enforce their ideological position on the nation. She argues, referring perhaps unsurprisingly to Jess Franco, that, 'the existence of these films is extraordinary, given the social and political climate of the time. Even the tame, domestic versions of Franco's films hint at illicit sexuality, lesbianism, and other activities officially designated as perversions by General Franco's government' (2000: 93).

Hawkins, has, as do others on occasion, a tendency to lump Spanish horror productions from this period into one big, almost homogenous, group, claiming the radical edge she sees in Jess Franco's work for all the work produced within the genre during the period. In doing so she makes little distinction between the now-cult films of Paul Naschy and Jess Franco and those more politically driven horror films of directors such as Eloy de la Iglesia and Vicente Aranda. However, any level of textual analysis reveals that these films are in fact very different and should be approached with this in mind when one considers the radical potential of any of them. I would argue that this 'lumping together' creates particular problems due to the sheer number of horror films made in Spain, or involving Spanish production companies, at the time. This volume of output suggests that some difference of perspective is bound to exist when one looks across the genre. Therefore, due to the very particular situation in Spain during this period, some level of close textual examination must be undertaken in order to understand both the films and their very specific relationship to the political and social contexts within which they were produced and consumed.

INSERTING THE REACTIONARY TO COMPLETE THE PICTURE

With this in mind it is important to attempt to provide a fuller and more complete picture of the Spanish horror cinema of the late 1960s and early 1970s. The tendency to re-read or uncover the potentially progressive or oppositional within such films should not obscure the fact that many of the works produced within popular genres within Spain, such as the horror film, often represented rather reactionary ideas about society and specifically the shifts and changes that were occurring within the country at this time. The worldview of the Franco regime, or perspectives that seem to reflect it, certainly did appear within the popular cinema of the period and any attempt to open up the study of Spanish popular cinema of this time should be careful not to mistakenly see the act of celebrating the popular, usually in opposition to a somewhat staid art cinema, as inherently radical in itself. One should also be wary of transferring that misconceived view onto works that are, when one analyses them in any detail, far from radical in terms of their content or what they might be seen to represent. As Núria Triana-Toribio has argued in relation to the Spanish popular cinema of the period, 'in order to present Catholic and middle-class conservative values as preferable, they have to present the alternatives, even if this process is one of misrepresentation and denegation' (2003: 100). Horror cinema more than any other genre was in a position to show those alternatives as a source of fear and terror, and by extension something with the potential to destroy society as much of the contemporary Spanish audience knew it.

With this in mind, *Exorcismo*, appearing as it does towards the end of the Franco regime in 1974, offers an interesting case study. The film is, on the surface, typical of European exploitation horror of the period, designed as it clearly is to cash in on the worldwide success of *The Exorcist* (William Friedkin, 1973), and with, at least in its international export versions, lashings of female nudity. However, whilst one of the central characters is possessed from the opening sequence, the actual plot device of an exorcism does not appear until the last fifteen minutes of the film and even then feels rather tacked on, revealing its exploitation origins. For the most part, *Exorcismo* is a murder mystery with primitive rituals and pagan worship mixed with Satanism as members of a wealthy household are murdered by a killer who breaks each of his victims' necks and turns their heads around. An old-fashioned police commissioner appears to investigate the incidents and he enrols a priest and professor (played by Spanish horror star Paul Naschy) who is brought in to provide the police with expertise on Satanism and non-Christian beliefs. All this takes place in a Great Britain (Naschy passes a sign for Bristol as he drives) that, even though there was location shooting in London, for the most part looks suspiciously like Spain. Naschy claims that he initially completed the screenplay for *Exorcismo* earlier than 1974: 'I wrote the script three years before the release of *The Exorcist*, as a visit to the archives of the Sociedad de Autores (Writers' Guild) will prove' (2000: 128–9). Whilst Naschy may claim this fact to fend off criticism that the film is merely a rip-off of Friedkin's work, it also explains why the actual possession and exorcism of Layla is slightly peripheral to the main thrust of the plot. The earlier writing of the script also helps to explain the particular representations of both the clergy and young people contained within the film.

Setting a film within Great Britain, or another location that was somewhere far away from Spain, was a strategy often employed by Naschy to avoid the potential censorship of his scripts and cuts to the final film by the Spanish government censor of the period. In his biography he reflects on this noting the changes he had to make to his first major script *The Mark of the Wolfman* due to this fact: 'But then the first problem arose: the werewolf couldn't be Spanish (as I had written he was from Asturias), and we had to cut down on the religious and erotic content as well as the graphic violence. I complied with the dictates of the censors and the Polish nobleman Waldemar Daninsky was born' (2000: 92). He also argues that he set a later film, *Inquisición* (1976), in France because his research revealed that 'the Inquisition in France, Germany and Switzerland was far bloodier and much crueller than the Spanish Inquisition, for all Torquemada's reputation' (2000: 131). Even if that were true, placing the action outside Spain seems to have been a way of avoiding the censorship of the content. The assumption seems to have been that in other places such as Great Britain or France they could get up to such terrible and titillating things but showing Spaniards becoming werewolves or anything else horror-related for that matter would be just too much. It is also important to note that whilst social unrest had begun to become a little more commonplace in the early 1970s this had resulted in a re-tightening of censorship after a perceived liberalisation in the 1960s. As John Hopewell notes, in January 1972 the Minister for Information and Tourism, Alfredo Sánchez Bella, 'issues instructions for the Censorship Board to "accentuate" its rigour in classifying films' (1986: 80). It was against this background that *Exorcismo* went into production, and writer Naschy and director Joan Bosch chose to set the film in Britain.

However, whilst set in Great Britain (as already noted, we see a sign early on indicating that the characters are fifteen miles from Bristol, the police station exteriors and the uniforms they sport are clearly English and the film was partly shot on location in the UK) the film intersects with a series of issues that perhaps resonated more obviously within contemporary Spanish society. The setting of the film outside Spain therefore does not mean that it does not speak to concerns present within Spain at that time, and therefore the importance of the Spanish context to an understanding of *Exorcismo* should not be underestimated. Whilst there has been a move away from seeing films within national contexts towards placing them into an intersection of global capital and culture, films made in Spain in the early 1970s *were* produced in a very particular context unlike that of most other countries in Europe, even if the finished works were then consumed in a variety of shifting contexts that may have changed their meanings for local audiences in the countries screening them. That context in Spain was, of course, the latter stages of a right-wing dictatorship, one that had been in place since the late 1930s and as such had wielded a great deal of influence on all aspects of Spanish life. That influence would certainly have included the cultural production of popular filmmakers, such as Bosch and Naschy, who had 'grown up' professionally within a film industry that operated under the rules of the regime.

THE PRIEST AND NATIONAL CATHOLICISM

One of the major ways in which the government managed to exert that huge influence was through religion, and the Catholic Church was a major contributor to Spanish life under the Franco regime. Following the end of the Civil War in 1939 the Church moved into a close relationship with the State and the seeds of that were sown during the war itself. As Stanley Payne has noted,

> By 1936 the tone and attitudes of Spanish Catholicism were much more conservative and even reactionary, producing a spirit of religious restoration highly susceptible to the political movement of the military rebels. General Franco, leader of the new military regime, took advantage of this to re-establish a partial symbiosis of Church and State. The resulting 'national Catholicism' of the Franco regime produced, at least for a decade or so, the most remarkable traditionalist restoration in religion and culture witnessed in any twentieth-century European country. (1984: 171)

Following this period the Church rapidly became an integral part of Spanish life. In 1938 a new secondary curriculum was introduced whose clear aim was to 'restore the primacy of Catholic teachings' (ibid.).

In 1946 Franco himself explained to parliament that 'the perfect state is for us a Catholic state' (quoted in Payne 1984: 185). The consolidation of Catholicism in Spain was perhaps most fully reached when, in August 1953, a new Concordat was signed between the Spanish state and the Vatican. By the mid-1950s Catholicism was totally engrained in everyday life and culture, the position of the Church enormously strong and highly influential. According to Payne, 34 of the 109 daily newspapers available were Catholic organs and there were around eight hundred periodical publications controlled by the clergy or lay organisations. Between 1954 and 1956 over a thousand new priests were ordained each year. The level of trust the regime had in the Church is reflected in 1962 when official Catholic publications were freed from censorship by agreement.

However, as the 1960s progressed, some sectors of the Church began to shift politically as simple devotion to the Francoist cause waned and critical voices began to be heard. Key in this process was Vatican II in the mid-1960s with its more liberal view of the Church's place in the world and the social responsibility of Catholics. This shift worried right-wing Catholics in Spain and at the same time encouraged liberal young members of the clergy to move away from the regime's view of national Catholicism. Some even went so far as to embrace the developing liberation theology and so-called Catholic Marxism that developed during this period. It is against this social and historical background of a clergy seemingly willing to embrace new ideas and see a newer more liberal role for them within society that we can begin to interpret and understand Paul Naschy's character in *Exorcismo*, Reverend Adrian. He is clearly a worldly man who has attained a wide knowledge of the world outside Spain and alongside that an understanding of a variety of non-Christian belief systems. His study is adorned with images and books that clearly reflect this experience and learning, as does his position as a university Professor. As noted, this aspect of Naschy's character can be partly explained by the setting of the film in England and making him an Anglican. Indeed, Naschy has explained in an interview for the DVD release of the film that he 'wasn't a Catholic priest' as that making him one would 'have created problems'. However, the image of the freer-thinking priest would certainly have struck a cord with audiences aware of the shifts in the Church in Spain throughout the 1960s and into the 1970s even if the character on the surface was from another denomination. The Spanish context thus becomes a vital prism through which we may understand the film and the character of Reverend Adrian.

Adrian's relationship with the film's central family also needs to be placed within its specific historical context. Early in the film a number of characters comment on the fact that they have not seen much of him recently and there is a clear suggestion that there has been a division of thinking regarding something significant although this remains unsaid. According to Payne and others, the 1960s saw the rise in influence of lay organisations such as Opus Dei within the Spanish government. If elements of the clergy were moving towards liberalisation then such lay groups were becoming more entrenched in their traditionalist, conservative position. It is certainly possible to read the division between the middle-class family and the priest in *Exorcismo* as representative of these divisions within the Catholic Church in Spain at the time. The narrative of the film enables a coming together again of these two groups through the assertion that evil does exist and the need for everyone to join together in their faith during troubling times. Due to Layla's possession it is the liberal priest who is forced to challenge his own views and finally accept the existence of evil. In doing so he clearly shifts to a more conservative political position as the film progresses and the more rational perspectives he displays earlier in the story are shown as somewhat misguided when compared to a simple, unproblematic, faith in God. Indeed, they are clearly implicated in leading one of his students morally astray. Of course, it is this acceptance of simple faith which in the end saves the day and restores calm to the world as evil is vanquished and Layla returns to herself as the credits roll.

The ways in which *Exorcismo* engages with what would have been contemporary debates regarding the Catholic Church, and the relationship between the clergy and laity clearly indicates that the popular cinema of the day did indeed engage with political and social issues that were relevant to contemporary Spanish audiences. Such films did not simply provide a kind of naïve escapism for popular audiences while the serious social engagement took place within the films of the New Spanish Cinema but touched too on political issues. Ultimately, however, the position that is offered by films such as *Exorcismo* is a rather reactionary and conservative view of a rapidly changing world.

YOUTH AND YOUTH CULTURE

If the representation of the clergy seems designed to warn members of the audience that they needed to be careful how far they went with these 'new' liberal ideas, then the images of youth in the film are perhaps even more clearly reactionary. As Mark Allinson has pointed out, this was a period of some notable political unrest amongst young people: 'the 1960s were characterised by limited university protests, swiftly followed by the removal of radical professors [...]. But there was no 1968 in Spain, at least not until 1972 when student protest led to the closure of the University of Valladolid' (2000: 266). For that reason the problem of a radicalised youth would be very current when *Exorcismo* went into production and reached cinemas. From the outset of the film young people are presented as hedonistic and lacking in discipline. The opening sequence shows a group of youngsters on the beach dabbling in things they should not; from mildly rebellious activities such as pot smoking and sex, to more 'dangerous' things such as clearly un-Christian rituals. The way in which the film collapses all these activities into one during this sequence is significant if we are to further understand the reactionary politics of *Exorcismo*. Here, the fact that Layla's possession begins after attending this beach party suggests *all* such pastimes should be avoided, especially by impressionable young people, as they quite literally won't know what effect they might have and how they might change them.

The misguided nature of these pursuits is further articulated by Reverend Adrian when he states: 'you know what young girls are like today, they have a concept of liberty that isn't always nice'. This kind of negative perspective on young people is also offered by the police commissioner who becomes an important character as the murders start and his investigation begins. For example, towards the middle of the film he has a long, rather serious conversation with Adrian about young people, devil worship and political protests. It is important that the policeman is not represented in a negative way and that his position of authority not criticised. To this end he is generally shown as an honest man going about his work in the best way he knows how and, whilst his views might be seen as particularly reactionary, the film does not seem to suggest that the audience reject them in any way. This is especially the case when he explains to Adrian that it is magic that is making the kids go crazy. He does this by telling him the strange story of three individuals who ran through a school for young girls 'streaking', going on to explain that one of them was the father of one of the girls attending the school, and that he was in fact complaining that she was not getting the education she deserved. In this instance he manages to collapse devil worship, sexual liberation and protest into one. He continues his story, arguing that in his view devil worship is simply a pretext for drug-taking, sexual orgies and criminal actions. Whilst today that simplistic equation seems laughable, the opening sequence of the film, that takes place on the beach, has made such a view plausible within the world presented by *Exorcismo*. It is also worth noting that in the film's second sequence of ritual there is a clear evocation of Africa, with shots of a black man playing the drums that provide the primitive beat for the ceremony. For good measure then, the film throws Black Africa into its heady mix of things that will ruin young people's lives if they come into contact with them. Within these scenes in *Exorcismo* it is young people who are shown as being at the mercy of all sorts of possible corruptions.

Whilst Naschy's Adrian initially displays some liberal views, he soon aligns himself with the police commissioner's more clearly reactionary perspective on events. After all, Layla *is* actually possessed and she is really saved through Adrian's faith and belief in the power of God to defeat evil. His newly conservative position is perhaps best reflected when he states: 'where you can't go with science maybe you can with faith'. In the world of *Exorcismo* those who do as the Church tells them have the best chance of remaining safe. Ultimately, the film suggests that religion, combined with law and order, will save young people from the corruption and exploitation that await them in the future. That is if everyone does nothing to allay it. One can read the onslaught of ritualistic devil worship and the breakdown of morals as that potential future if faith and the role of law and order are forsaken. It is in this interpretation of the film that *Exorcismo* can be read as a clear warning to Spanish society, and in particular the young, about the choices they might make as Franco's death approached and the future of Spain became increasingly uncertain.

BIBLIOGRAPHY

Aguilar, C. (2000) *Cine fantástico y de terror Español 1900–1983*. San Sebastián: Semana de cine fantástico y de terror de San Sebastián.

Allinson, M. (2000) 'The Construction of Youth in Spain in the 1980s and 1990s', in B. Jordan and R. Morgan-Tamosunas (eds) *Contemporary Spanish Cultural Studies*. London: Arnold, 265–73.

Hawkins, J. (2000) *Cutting Edge: Art-horror and the Horrific Avant-garde*. Minneapolis, MN: Minnesota University Press.

Hopewell, J. (1986) *Out of the Past: Spanish Cinema after Franco*. London: British Film Institute.

Jancovich, M. (2002) *Horror: The Film Reader*. London: Routledge.

Lázaro Reboll, A. (2002) 'Exploitation in the Cinema of Klimovsky and Franco', in S. Godsland and A. White (eds) *Cultura Popular: Studies in Spanish and Latin American Popular Culture*. Bern: Peter Lang, 83–95.

____ (2005) '*La noche de walpurgis/The Shadow of the Werewolf*', in A. Mira (ed.) *The Cinema of Spain and Portugal*. London: Wallflower Press, 129–36.

Lázaro Reboll, A. and A. Willis (eds) (2004) *Spanish Popular Cinema*. Manchester: Manchester University Press.

Le Cain, M. (2003) 'The Frontiers of Genre and Trance: Five Films by Jess Franco', *Senses of Cinema*. On-Line. Available HTTP: http://www.sensesofcinema.com/contents/03/27/jess_franco.html (15 July 2008).

Naschy, P. (2000) *Memoirs of a Wolfman*. Baltimore: Midnight Marquee Press.

Pavlović, T. (2003) *Despotic Bodies and Transgressive Bodies: Spanish Culture From Francisco Franco to Jesús Franco*. Albany: SUNY Press.

Payne, S. G. (1984) *Spanish Catholicism: An Historical Overview*. Madison, WI: University of Wisconsin Press.

Triana-Toribio, Nuria (2003) *Spanish National Cinema*. London: Routledge.

Willis, A. (2003) 'Spanish Horror and the Flight from Art Cinema, 1967-1975', in M. Jancovich et. al. (eds) *Defining Cult Movies: the cultural politics of popular taste*. Manchester: Manchester University Press.

Willis, A. (2005) 'Spanish Horror as Subversive Text: Eloy de la Iglesia's La semana de asesino', in S. Schneider and T. Williams (eds) *Horror International*. Detroit: Wayne State University Press.

HISTORY, TERRAIN AND TREAD:
THE WALK OF DEMONS, ZOMBIE FLESH EATERS AND THE BLIND DEAD

Phil Smith

When addressing the shamble of the movie zombie from the perspective of walking as an art practice, certain ambivalent relations between European and US aesthetic walking practices and their respective national-cinematic portrayals of the walking dead begin to take shape. With few exceptions, notably Edgar Allan Poe's *The Man of the Crowd* (1840), North America lacked a tradition of subversive, urban, ambulatory art before the de-colonialised, irradiated Cold War zombie of the 1950s was radicalised by George Romero in the late 1960s. In contrast a radical aesthetic walking tradition *had* developed in Europe as part of the avant-garde response to total war in early twentieth-century Europe rendering the innocence of the everyday and the virtues of the aesthetic questionable. The responses of European filmmakers to the opportunity of Romero's new zombie walk were variable, often opportunist and self-contradictory as I will describe below. When considered in relation to developments within a longstanding European aesthetic walking practice and theorisation, these qualities are starkly revealed, though the nature of that relation is not always the expected one.

The story is well known: in 1968, Romero threw off history as manifest in the burden of back-story. Scream and you will miss the yarn about a satellite in *The*

Night of the Living Dead (1968), it means little or nothing to the film. The authorities in the film who propose this explanation are portrayed as unreliable. More importantly, this 'cause' has no power to explain, nor is it shown. The zombies walk because they walk – not because they're 'reds', or affected by radiation, or been victims of voodoo. The zombies are representative of the patterns of the movie rather than an external cause. If they have any 'cause' it is in the sense of a mission, a drive, a condition, a hunger. The stripping away of causality allows for a more poignant zombie. The dead walk because they are a version of us as well as our fictional 'other'.

In Europe's most significant early response to Romero, this process is reversed. Rather than being stripped away, history is dug up in Amando de Ossorio's *Blind Dead* quartet, Spanish productions filmed in Portugal. The dead here split the ambiguity – the 'us/them' – of Romero's zombie. These 'Blind Dead' are an elite male group of dead Templar Knights. Nowadays, courtesy of Dan Brown, the Templars are increasingly re-imagined as an oppositional elite guarding inconvenient secrets of female divinity, but de Ossorio draws not on countercultural esoterica, but on unreliable confessions of magic and deviance extracted from fourteenth-century Templars under torture.

Rather than a dispersed alternative population of living dead, crossing the American landscape in straight lines, led by strange hungers, or meandering like urban explorers or '*dérivistes*' in empty buildings and corridors, in de Ossorio's films the dead are a vengeful elite, emerging like a punishment squad from ancient ruins to cluster on their victims. They ride. They process and queue to feast on their victims. They are tied to a bogus past. Their inarticulate, skeletal hands suggest a husk-like corporeality, a dogma travestied and emptied. Their predatory adventures at the expense of young adults, usually female, have been portrayed as analogous, in Nigel J. Burrell's account, to 'the repressive fascism of the Franco regime ... versus the youth of the day' (1995: 10). But there is little real struggle. This is the punishment of the already defeated. The Templars' victims already suffer self-loathing, the curtailing of sexual contact, self-doubt, rape and loneliness. The Blind Dead do not punish enjoyment as they might in a slasher movie, instead they resolve their victims' frustrations by death, turning their victims to the camera as their bodies are mutilated: 'putrefying zombies and the bloodless corpses of their victims are what remains after people have been drained of desire' (Hardy 1993: 239). In de Ossorio the zombie is a force against appetite.

In one of the few really effective sequences of the *Blind Dead* quartet (aside from the slow-motion rides of the horseback zombies), de Ossorio invests a modern space, a mannequin workshop in *La noche del terror ciego/Tombs of the Blind Dead* (1971), with his sclerotic and morbid vision. This is already a jolt, as the *Blind Dead* series is largely shot in old villages and rotting ships – a jolt knowingly deployed. But there is no youthful life in this modernity. Released from a cinematic space in which death always rises from below, de Ossorio evokes a dread space of overwhelming possibility across a plane. Even before the zombie's arrival, death is already present in the workshop's fashionable commodities and dismembered dummies; dead labour, fashion that 'couples the living body to the inorganic world. To the living it defends the rights of the corpse' (Benjamin 2002: 7), garments out of date before their production. In the ironic interplay of fashion-centred human, modern zombie and mannequin, the connection, indeed equivalence, of consumer and commodity is forged.

Such an accumulative hollowness pervades the *Blind Dead* project, but is rarely expressed so explicitly. The quartet does have a gloss of originality, indeed the Templar zombies are a clear and qualitative break from tired re-treads of the Universal monsters in Spanish movies such as *El vampiro de la autopista/ The Horrible Sexy Vampire* (Jim Delavena & José Luis Madrid, 1970) or *La noche de walpurgis/The Werewolf's Shadow* (Leon Klimovsky, 1970), but there is nothing like the break of *Night of the Living Dead* from its voodoo and Cold War predecessors.

The Romero zombie is a modern character, consumed with appetite (unfulfilled in life), so dead and so metaphorical as to be commodity itself (reproducing itself in consumption, infecting by its own mastication), a walking critique of everyday life, 'nothing left ... but accomplishment – no scenery, no pleasure, few encounters', as Rebecca Solnit has written of destination-fixated long-distance walker Ffyona Campbell (2000: 132). Those who are victims in de Ossorio's movies are zombies in Romero's. Crossing the fields of *Night of the Living Dead*, and here in de Ossorio's mannequin workshop, this zombie is an embodiment of Guy Debord's characterisation of the morbid commodity (see *The Society of the Spectacle* 1992). De Ossorio's dead art is *détourned* by bleak, modern terrain.

The 1968 zombie blurs the reactionary countryside with the anonymity of the city, slides between organisations, resists a world of spimes. It represents no superstructure of ideas, but one idea: the stamina of appetite. It is a resolutely materialist monster. A zombie's history may be at an end, its fundamental conflicts resolved, but its utopian situation (free to wander the world as playground) is not eternal. Its final decay is delayed. It shambles in a Bhabhaian Third Space of suspended dialectic, between the idea of what death should be and cellular collapse.

Critic Jamie Russell has sought to make the Templar zombies something more universal - 'the literal embodiment of death's relentless and completely implacable approach ... the inevitability of the end' (2005: 90). Such attempts to take the territory of the universal is what the individualised, but 'un-selfed', 1968 zombie resists, wandering rather than occupying, 'dressing' in gore not symbols; its ragged uniforms, robes and overalls an indictment of a world of functionality, longing not belonging. Against this, the recalcitrance of the Templar 'dead' is too specific to be universal.

There is, however, such a morbid universality in the work of some European walking artists, overleaping history rather than making art in relation to it. Richard

Long – seeking 'places where nothing seems to have broken the connection to the ancient past' (Solnit 2000: 272) – and Hamish Fulton, seeking a bleakness removed from community. Target-fixation has reappeared in aesthetic walking, spectacularly in He Yun Chang's 2,000-mile-long *Touring Round Britain With a Rock* (2006–07), during which the artist, unlike his curators, hardly engaged with the environment, focusing on his task.

The art of such walkers is an ascetic, abstracted removal from the human quotidian, where the human figure is, at best, left to be imagined. Only the task is figured. Any residue is denied primacy – the walk (sometimes characterised as route or mileage) is the thing. On the other hand, Situationist-inspired walkers like Anna Best, Drew Mulholland or Jim Colquhoun reference communality and 'holey' histories. For *Occasional Sites: A London Guidebook of Missed Opportunities and Things That Aren't Always There* (2003) Anna Best recruited friends, volunteers and passers-by to help her explore and record the trashed and ignored city. In Mulholland's and Colquhoun's 'drifts' around Glasgow and Edinburgh, history is an elusive and provocative one, characterised by anomaly and deviancy.

Romantic traditions of rural walking, European and North American – of George Borrow and John Keats and Henry David Thoreau – cited a spurious history of Greek 'pedestration', an overleaping connection to a classical past, but in 1916 the Dada cabaret broke from such precedent-seeking, from back-story, rejecting all previous culture as implicated in total war. What Søren Kierkegaard had done, wandering the city socially and self-contained, subjecting it to a rural botanising, turning the inside outwards by making the streets his 'reception room', the Dadaists, arranging tours of derelict sites, and the surrealists and International Lettristes did again, collectively, curating the city's anomalies and decays, floating and reassembling its fragments, detaching the city's imaginary identity from its historical past, detaching themselves even from alphabets – and began rearranging these things for the future.

By distancing his zombies from explanation (although in *Day of the Dead* [1985] he would briefly speculate on a moral origin to the crisis) Romero gives us no 'where' and no 'when' to blame but here and now. He refuses to set at a distance our involvement in the walk of the dead. He forces living and dead to walk towards the future. Or at least try. Any resort to the bunker is clearly mistaken. On the bleakest map, Romero points his characters towards utopia. Like a *détourned* archaeology, the post-*Night of the Living Dead* zombie movie digs its way up towards time, not through an ancient landscape, but out of a radical, avant-garde dereliction, out of the panic-room of contemporary fears.

De Ossorio's zombies, on the other hand, *are* History and they have their scapegoats – the weak, the inadequate, the vain, the unfulfilled, whose crime is to desire without authority. They are punished for their failures to conform either to insensibility or sadism. This is a history of power, residing in ruins. This historical 'presence' is discrete; whatever the present may have gained from it, that present (the cinema-spectators' as much as the characters') is absolved of any responsibility for its good fortune by the past's archaic sadism, compressed into a living corpse that can be restrained or destroyed without culpability. On the other side of the coin, the corpses' attacks on the living are licensed for enjoyment as a pseudo-transgression, of the past against the modern.

By 1968 European aesthetic-walking had long since stripped itself of such a discrete history. Even before the Dadaists, the unflinching dislocations of the magical writers of Prague – Paul Leppin, Alfred Kubin and Gustav Meyerink – had begun this floating-free. Such preliminary work was reinforced by the reverie of the mostly imaginary *flâneur*, 'a loiterer, a fritterer away of time' (Solnit 2000: 198), alienated from domestic life, hanging around Parisian arcades (precursors of the malls to which Romero would lead his dead window shoppers). There was always something predatory about *flânerie*: 'wandering souls who go looking for a body ... enter[ing] as [they] like ... into each man's personality. For [them] alone everything is vacant' (Baudelaire 1947: 20). The disrupted pedestrian is an appetite-driven wanderer, a window-shopper who resists the commodity itself.

It is significant that when Francesco Careri, of Rome-based *'dérivistes'* Stalker, invokes history in *Walkscapes* (2002), his account of walking as art, it is not as a history of origins or identity, but of trajectories, a narrative of the architecture of nomadism. Translated into Careri's historiography, the wandering zombie would not appear as an anomaly, but as an every-body, a walking menhir, a trajectory in trajectory that continues to move and yet is dead – a reminder of primal human meanderings, even as it rots and crumbles – a reminder that, as Doreen Massey has argued, space should be defined not by border or boundary, but trajectory (see 2005: 9).

When Italian director Lucio Fulci responded to the success in European movie theatres of Romero's *Dawn of the Dead* (1978) with his unofficial sequel, *Zombi 2/Zombie Flesh Eaters* (1979), and then a series of loosely-related zombie movies, playing the role of de Ossorio for a new decade, it was similarly problematical treatments of space and history to those of de Ossorio's that compromised Fulci's intermittently distinctive project. In *Zombie Flesh Eaters*, the initial promise of the opening sequences is soon collapsed into history – *cinema* history. The film is neatly summarised by Kim Newman: 'less an imitation Romero than a bloodier return to the zombie "B" pictures of the 1940s' (1988: 190) – the voodoo movie is resurrected. Yet before it collides with its back-story, the early sequences in New York harbour do evoke the dispersed and remorseless wander of the appetite driven trajectory. Fulci's 'flesh eaters' come in all shapes and sizes – members of a *demos*. One comically flops over the side of a boat, presumably to resume its shamble on the harbour bottom towards the New York skyline. As the portentous soundtrack builds, this skyline is infected with zombie menace, ironically and sublimely 'alive', part predator/part victim. There is no doubt what flesh this film would like to eat – American flesh – a parasite upon its origins.

It is the banality of this straight line – driven by appetite across the harbour floor – that disrupts the boundaries and visuality of property and distribution in the cinema-landscape. This unselfing and democratising of the zombie, cutting a straight trajectory through fields and cities, is reflected in the popularity of the straight line in a walking-related avant-garde art seeking to reconnect itself with everyday life. In Nam June Paik's *Zen For Head* of 1962, a response to La Monte Young's Fluxus instruction 'Draw a straight line and follow it' (Young & Jackson 1970), the artist dipped his head in a bucket of red goo and drew a straight line on paper, his head as paint brush. Not dissimilar in appearance to a scene from a zombie movie. Richard Long's 1967 iconic but unremarkable *A Line Made by Walking* – a straight line trodden into a field – is now a myth of origin for a walking that pronounces itself exceptional. Simon Pope walked east to west across London, from sunrise to sunset, staying within a single row on the grid of his London A–Z map.

The transgression of boundaries, routes and markers hypersensitises the walker to what Debord called 'the sudden change of ambience in a street' (1981: 5). This straight line is complemented by the meander. The zombie's meander is stimulated by remnants of memory and familiarity. It grazes along symbolic rather than physical contours, staring intently at banal and simplistic signs as if seeking multiple layers of meaning. This is similar to the destination-less wander of the Situationist *'dériviste'*, taking 'the path of least resistance which is automatically followed in aimless strolls (and which has no relation to the contour of the ground) [...]' (Debord 1981: 5).

Romero zombies and Situationist *'dérivistes'* have no final destination to reach, they follow the atmospheres, dislocated from the everyday functioning of the city and its decision-making, their shambling walks reveal usually invisible boundaries, unexpected gaps in the fabric. Just as the zombie has a way of suddenly becoming very close, the *'dériviste'* may attend to the fine detail of the city, but also move at speed in order to sense the changes of atmosphere from one urban space to the next.

The female Romero zombie is as much a consuming dead commodity as the male, and equally freed from the social conventions of that consumption. She walks with a freedom through sites that her counterpart in the cinema audience might avoid. Hence the betrayal of this opportunity when – as with the Templar dead – the zombie is defined male. Then the zombie becomes a supernatural policeman, a punisher of the unproductive and non-reproductive.

A decisive factor here is terrain. In a workshop, on the floors of a mall, in the fields of Pennsylvania, in the corridors of the hospital in Fulci's *E tu vivrai nel terrore – L'aldilà/The Beyond* (1981), the terrain is a plane on which the zombie can *dérive*. But in the hulk of de Ossorio's Templar ship, in the watery cellar of Fulci's Louisiana Hotel, in graves and ruins, the living corpse becomes burdened with back-story and discretion. This discretion is policed by a 'portal' – a cylinder of chemicals, a ruined mausoleum, a gateway to hell. In Lamberto Bava's made-for-TV *Una notte alla cimitero/Graveyard Disturbance* (1987), with living dead as washed up as Universal monsters fallen among The Three Stooges, these portals are significantly multiplied: a police scene-of-crime tape, a weird inn, a trapdoor to the dead. Such portals serve to disenfranchise the past, to remove it from the responsibilities of the present. On the other hand, Romero's movies invite their audiences to take responsibility for causeless horror, implicitly originated for their viewing. Their looking is made democratic, responsible, civil. It has consequences which cannot be handed back to the plot.

Just as the fragmentation of linear narrative and accidental strangeness in Fulci's *The Beyond* and *Quella villa accanto al cimitero/The House by the Cemetery* (1981) make them more like exercises in lyrical pattern-making than storytelling, so the morbidity of the vertical in the geography of Romero's movies (studio, loft and cellar are deadly prisons for the living, not portals of hell) renders the horizontal plane a virtuous abstraction. As Situationist architect Constant planned a city of continual *dérive*, and architect Jan Gehl emphasised the primary importance for citizens of the space between buildings rather than the buildings themselves, so Romero's films, and fragmentary sequences in the European movies they triggered, are about the making of dread playgrounds, a utopian plane, present in the European ambulatory-imagination since de Chirico. This plane is parodied at the end of *The Beyond* when a crude, Tanguy-like landscape painting becomes geographical. This materialisation is, significantly, a subterranean one. The dead of the de Ossorio/Fulci zombie movie have risen from the grave only to lurch back to it. Romero's zombies live in order to plane.

Spectatorship is similarly distinguished: in de Ossorio and Fulci the pleasure is accumulative and alienated, as the weakest suffer exponentially. In Romero the vertical is dispersed, hierarchies dissolved, the dead mistaken for the living and the living for the dead. While the enjoyment of consumer consumed and the identification of consumer with commodity are common to all these movies, only in the Romero stratum is the audience made self-aware of the significance of an entertainment that 'elevate[es] the person to the level of a commodity. He surrenders to its manipulations while enjoying his alienation from himself and others ... consistent with the split between utopian and cynical elements' (Benjamin 2002: 7). In the European zombie movie cynicism mostly prevails. In Romero's work the 'utopian and cynical elements' are both present, but their synthesis (in happy ending or overwhelming pessimism) is deferred.

To enjoy the gore in a *Blind Dead* movie is to enrol in the hierarchical sadism of an elite power. To enjoy the attacks of the Romero zombie is to relish the dispersal of commodity fetishism, the consumption of the consumer by dead labour: it is to have one's flesh and eat it. The Romero zombie is one of us, the gaping crowd, while in the *Blind Dead* quartet and *The Beyond* to witness is to be rebuked and harmed. The Romero zombie's predatory wander, its hungry gaze, its attraction to the living are not dissimilar to benevolent tailing and stalking in artworks like Vito Acconci's *Following Piece* (1969) or Sophie Calle's *Suite Venitienne* (1980) where strangers were followed and documented by artists who surrendered their own volition to their unknowing 'victims'.

By the time Romero's *Dawn of the Dead* was released, North America had developed its own aesthetic urban walking; one that continues to develop, from Flux Tours of the 1970s to contemporary projects like Glowlab and e-Xplo in New York, Kate Armstrong's 2004 *Pre/Amble* festival in Vancouver, Kate Pocrass's *Mundane Journeys* (2001–) in San Francisco and Psychogeography Societies and Associations in a number of cities. Meanwhile, the European zombie movie has moved slowly, and unevenly, towards the democratic, resistant, dispersive shamble of the Romero model. Elements that were briefly on screen in *Zombie Flesh Easters* begin to dominate in Fulci's *Paura nella città dei morti viventi/The City of the Living Dead* (1980), Umberto Lenzi's *Incubo sulla città contaminate/Nightmare City* (1980) and Lamberto Bava's *Dèmoni/Demons* (1985), although Lenzi has refuted the 'zombie' label and Bava's loosed appetites on legs are ostensibly possessed rather than reanimated.

Set in a cinema screening a horror film, it would be easy to imagine that Bava's *Demons* generates its dispersal through self-conscious cinematic reference. Kim Newman described the plot as 'demonic ghouls who escape from the horror film unreeling on screen' (1988: 197). But that is wrong. The demons are released by an ancient mask – the equivalent of Romero's satellite, irrelevant and easy to miss. The movie within the movie gets the blame because it parodies the weaknesses of the movie itself. The modern setting of the cinema is infected by the gothic farrago, but de Ossorio's contempt for the modern is missing. In its place is the infection and making geographical of a dread, modern space, as pioneered by Romero.

While the US horror film found its way to the urban spaces that its aesthetic walkers had ignored, European horror initially fell back on churches, ruins, graveyards, galleons and steam trains, until finally stumbling back to the future. Just as the helicopter is key to Romero's *Dawn of the Dead*, in Lenzi's *Nightmare City* the dispersal of the horror is made clear during a helicopter rescue. Lenzi's 'nightmare' arrives by plane. European movies seemed, finally, to be initiating such geography in *28 Days Later* (Danny Boyle, 2002) with the encompassing view of an exploding petrol station lighting up an infested London (with a nod to Hitchcock's *The Birds* [1963]) followed by an early aerial shot in Zack Snyder's 2004 remake of *Dawn of the Dead* that shows a burning, ecstatic suburb laid out like a map in flames.

In Fulci's *City of the Living Dead*, the setting is a simulacrum of a non-existent USA, a Catholic Italy in 'Dunwich', a copy of a copy of a copy, a transatlantic nowhere; utopian and malleable. At one point a bar splits in two, sending its drinkers running. In Bava's *Demons* the *dérive* of the demonic spreads across the city. In its 1986 sequel, *Dèmoni 2: L'incubo ritorna/Demons 2*, the same narrative is transferred to a residential block of flats. Once the hocus-pocus of ancient curse and dental transformation has been got through, what we have is a zombie movie, feeding on the space it portrays. The demons make the familiar place of the flats strange, disrupted, questionable, possessed of ambience and unconventional possibility.

As the surrealist romances of the streets, Aragon's *Paris Peasant* (1926) and Breton's *Nadja* (1928), disperse erotic force from their objects of desire to the city itself, making nocturnal city walking rather than indoor sex the means to the erotic city, so *Demons 2* disperses bleakness from the demons to the city, a bleakness for which Long and Fulton have headed to the wilderness. Here it appears in collective domesticity, the Kierkegaardian 'dread' of these spaces expressing the scary thrill of a freedom anterior to freedom, the disturbing expanse of possibility opening up to infection. Escaping at last from historical 'text' and colonial 'supernatural' this sequel, a copy of a copy of a copy of a copy, at last suggests a sensibility akin to the modern '*dériviste*'. The European zombie film becomes geographical. This sensibility, spatial and subversive, continues to be pursued through the zombie mythos in various genres on either side of the Atlantic: in Robert Kirkman's graphic novels *The Walking Dead* and *Marvel Zombies*, in Max Brooks' handbook and 'oral history' of war with the zombies, in *Les revenants/They Came Back* (Robin Campillo, 2004) with its unexplained zombies trying to re-integrate with the living. Still not at rest, however, is a morbid 'Past', ready with its portals, past indiscretions and ruined houses to rise in movies like *The Zombie Chronicles* (Brad Sykes, 2001) or *House of the Dead* (Uwe Boll, 2003), repeating the punishment of the modern (ravers) and the opportunistic distortions of discrete geo-politics (Vietnam as bad drill). In the early twenty-first century the fracture between these tendencies is now definable far less by continent or country of production and more by international cultural politics and imagination.

In the final shot of Lamberto Bava's *Demons 2*, the survivors, having beaten the ghouls, turn their attention to the wider city (Berlin) in the anti-gothic dawn. No longer commodity-victim/commodity-consumer binaries, these living

The ordinary dead (*They Came Back*, 2004)

characters are stalking their own environments made strange, they are at home in this uncanny city. In de Ossorio's movies characters are *punished* for this sort of thing (Virginia for leaping from the train in *Tombs of the Blind Dead*), but here the urban explorer survives to enjoy the city, sensibilities changed and heightened. It is this disruption that attracts the aesthetic walker – not to walk *like* a zombie, but to walk aware of that walk, to walk in relation to the zombie. As suggested in Wrights & Sites' *A Mis-Guide To Anywhere* (2006), a book of provocations for exploring cities on foot:

> When you see others approaching, say to yourself: 'They're coming to **get** you, Barbara!'
> You are Barbara. (2006: 35)

BIBLIOGRAPHY

Aragon, L. (1994) *Paris Peasant*. Boston: Exact Change.
Baudelaire, C. (1947 [1869]) *Paris Spleen*. New York: New Directions.
Benjamin, W. (2002 [1982]) *The Arcades Project*. Cambridge, MA: Harvard University Press.
Best, A. (2003) *Occasional Sites: A London Guidebook of Missed Opportunities and Things That Aren't Always There*. London: Photographers' Gallery.
Black, A. (2000) *The Dead Walk*. Hereford, UK: Noir Publishing.
Breton, A. (1999) *Nadja*. London: Penguin Books.
Brooks, M. (2004) *The Zombie Survival Guide*. London: Duckworth.
____ (2006) *World War Z*. London: Duckworth.
Bryce, A. (ed.) (2000) *Zombie*. Liskeard: Stray Cat Publishing.
Burrell, N. J. (1995) *Knights of Terror*. Upton: Midnight Media.
Careri, F. (2002) *Walkscapes*. Barcelona: Editorial Gustavo Gili.
Debord, G. (1981) 'Introduction to A Critique of Urban Geography', in K. Knabb (ed.) *Situationist International Anthology*. Berkeley, CA: Bureau of Public Secrets.
____ (1992) *The Society of the Spectacle*. New York: Zone Books.
Gehl, J. (2003) *Life Between Buildings*. Copenhagen: Danish Architectural Press.
Hardy, P. (1993) *Horror: The Aurum Film Encyclopedia*. London: Aurum Press.
Kirkman, R. (2005) *Marvel Zombies*. New York: Marvel Publishing.
____ (2005–11) *The Walking Dead (vols. 1–15)*. Berkeley: Image Comics.
Marples, M. (1959) *Shanks's Pony: A Study of Walking*. London: J. M. Dent & Sons.
Massey, D. (2005) *For Space*. London: Sage.
Newman, K. (1988) *Nightmare Movies: A Critical History of the Horror Film, 1968–88*. London: Bloomsbury.
Pope, S. (2000) *London Walking: A Handbook for Survival*. London: Ellipsis.
Russell, J. (2005) *Book of the Dead*. Godalming: FAB Press.
Solnit, R. (2000) *Wanderlust*. New York/London: Viking Penguin.
Wrights & Sites (2006) *A Mis-Guide To Anywhere*. Exeter: Wrights & Sites.
Young, L. M. and Jackson, M (eds) (1970) *An Anthology of Chance Operations*. Second Edition. New York: George Maciunas.

ALEJANDRO AMENÁBAR AND CONTEMPORARY SPANISH HORROR

Barry Jordan

'For me, leaving something to the imagination is the essence of real horror.'
(Alejandro Amenábar, quoted in *The Washington Diplomat*,
September 2001)

'Why are you doing this to me?'
'You're a smart kid ... You figure it out.'
– *The Hitcher* (Robert Harmon, 1986)

Despite his rather limited output (three shorts and five main features), Academy Award-winner Alejandro Amenábar has managed to position himself as the new benchmark of contemporary Spanish filmmaking, at home and abroad. His work successfully combines high quality, Hollywood standard, film art with wide public appeal and strong box office performance. The remarkable and unexpected global success of his supernatural ghost story *Los otros/The Others* (2001) has also placed him at the very forefront of the contemporary Spanish genre film, especially horror (see Nguyen 2001). Until the 1990s, Spanish horror and fantasy filmmaking were generally derided as inferior, low-budget, exploitation products, of little appeal to the national demographic of 15–25-year-olds and with extremely limited export potential. This may partly explain Amenábar's resounding indifference towards native Spanish horror traditions, given his acknowledged reputation as cinephile and horror buff. Moreover, until its recent resurgence and transnational success, the term 'Spanish horror' has been largely absent from his vocabulary and almost nowhere to be found in his interviews.[1] Yet, like Pedro Almodóvar before him (who made films as if Franco had never existed), Amenábar has helped change the terms of making horror movies in Spain, as if Spanish horror did not exist.

In this chapter, I wish to explore the above proposition in part by looking at Amenábar's shorts and the ways in which they present in embryonic form many of the narrative, stylistic and thematic ingredients of his features. I also propose to comment briefly on Amenábar's relationship to the thriller and the extent to which he has helped rehabilitate a hybrid generic field in Spain which, until recently, had not enjoyed serious commercial success or critical recognition.

THE SHORTS

In order to provide a more detailed and comprehensive overview of Amenábar's 'horror work', so to speak, it is important that we engage not only with the features but also with his prize-winning, student shorts, made between 1991 and 1995, from the ages of 19 to 23. These have been seriously neglected in Amenábar scholarship hitherto, yet they constitute the crucial training ground in storytelling and film technique, support for which he found seriously deficient at university. The shorts also allowed him to road-test some of the narrative options, character types, shooting set-ups, sound palettes, performance styles, textual borrowings and so on, which fed into his main horror features. The four shorts in question are: *La cabeza/The Head* (1991), as yet unreleased, *Himenóptero/Himenopterus* (1992) and *Luna/Moon* (1994/95), made in two different formats: an original thirty-minute, black and white version on Hi8 video – on which I base my comments – and a shorter twelve-minute colour version, made on 35mm film (thanks to a film award and as yet unreleased). Amenábar made all of his shorts with his university flatmate, co-scriptwriter and regular collaborator, Mateo Gil. Already familiar with the basics of photography, it was Gil who handled the camerawork, during this period (plus some acting), while Amenábar took care of direction, editing, sound, music and various acting roles.

The shorts arguably form the crucial phase in Amenábar's apprenticeship as an autodidact, 'jack of all trades', amateur filmmaker. The films are strongly personal, autobiographical pieces (echoing Amenábar's experiences of car accidents, hitchhiking, equipment rip-offs, enclosed spaces and a childhood fascination with death). They are also heavily marked by some of his favourite Hollywood sources, such as Hitchcock's *Psycho* (1960) and *The Birds* (1963), Kubrick's *2001 – A Space Odyssey* (1969) and *The Shining* (1980), Spielberg's *Duel* (1971) and *Jaws* (1975), and Robert Harmon's *The Hitcher* (1986), among many others. Predictably perhaps, the shorts borrow but also significantly re-engineer the classic 'shock inversion' story template, where the wholesome everyday world of the Hitchcockian 'wrong man/innocent bystander' is turned upside down and whose life is catapulted into a spiralling nightmare.

LA CABEZA/THE HEAD

Amenábar describes *The Head* as 'a ghost story ... shot on VHS' (letter to the author, January 2006). Filmed largely by Gil in and around Amenábar's family bungalow, made in black and white, and at fifteeen minutes long, it concerns a young woman (Ana) whose husband (Roberto) is late home. Ana thinks she notices an intruder. But, vaguely aware that the latter might be her husband (played by Amenábar), a phone call informs her that he has just died in a car accident. On turning round, Ana sees Roberto transformed into a charred, disfigured, bleeding corpse. Startled, she reacts violently by tearing off his mangled skull, which bounces around the room and out of the window, to a Warner Bros. cartoon-style soundtrack.

The Head probably began as an experiment with a new Sanyo video camera (see Rodríguez Marchante 2002: 35). But without a script, the shoot (spread over many weekends and holidays) turned into an improvised and very untidy practice exercise in suspense and camera placement. High hopes of glittering prizes were rapidly dashed by a nightmare narrative without an ending. Unsure of how to finish it, Amenábar borrowed some gruesome, model human heads from Dream Factory, Colin Arthur's special effects studio in Madrid, where he had worked over the summer (see Rodríguez Marchante 2002: 36-7). He then added the parodic, comic, gory finale (the first and only one in his entire filmography). The film introduced a number of elements, some of which would be regularly recycled in later shorts and features: the lone, innocent figure in peril (here, fear, hysteria and victimhood are gendered feminine, with Ana recalling Angela in *Tesis* [Amenábar 1996] and Grace in *The Others*); the absent, returning male (physically damaged and transformed into a monster, like César in *Abre los ojos/Open Your Eyes* [1997], the mentally disfigured Charles in *The Others* and even the shrivelled Ramón Sampedro in *Mar adentro/The Sea Inside* [2004]); the traumatic shock of seeing the love object transformed into a monstrous 'other'; the motifs of the female vigil and the haunting, the (telephone) warning, the car crash, the use of black humour, the devices of doubling and mistaken identities, the damaged male body and female victimisation and survival (Ana neutralises the monster and survives the haunting, as do Angela and Grace). Technically, Gil also experimented with the tracking shot, but lacking a dolly he used an old tricycle (see Rodríguez Marchante 2002: 39). However, disagreements between Amenábar and Gil over the quality of their work sparked a furious quarrel and a prolonged separation, leaving the short in limbo. Undaunted, Amenábar re-edited the film (his faculty refused him use of an editing machine so he bought his own) and cleaned up the dialogue (revoicing Ana's part with help from drama student and friend Nieves Herranz). He also added a loud ticking clock to the creepy soundtrack, which he finally composed himself on his own Yamaha organ (see Rodríguez Marchante 2002: 36). In 1991, the film was entered in a competition sponsored by Spain's National Association of Amateur Filmmakers. Quite unexpectedly, having made the audience laugh and being praised for its promising sound quality, the 'short from hell' took first prize!

HIMENÓPTERO

With his self-confidence boosted by competition success (and a substantial cash prize of 300,000 pesetas), Amenábar made peace with Gil. He also bought himself a brand new video camera (a Sony V5000, with an excellent digital zoom and stereo sound) and quickly embarked on his second short, *Himenóptero*. Conceived as another black comedy, it soon developed into a rather more serious and self-reflexive commentary on suspense filmmaking, as well as a response to the rather chaotic *The Head*. Vaguely taking the form of a fake documentary or 'making of' feature, the film opens with a black screen and intertitle, which names a setting (I.B. Villa de Madrid, his old school), the month (May) and gives the precise time, 7.45 pm. The use of black screen will quickly become one of Amenábar's signature opening and closing devices. With a cast of four characters (three female students and the weird, male camera operator called Bosco, played by Amenábar), this 31-minute piece follows a group of media students over three evenings, who hide out in a school after hours to shoot a horror-thriller short, devised by the sadistic Silvia, Amenábar's screen proxy. Unfortunately, though she knows her character must show genuine fear of death, the lead player María (Nieves Herranz), refuses to take the shoot seriously and threatens to sabotage the entire project. Obsessed by achieving a 'corto decente' (decent short) and determined to punish María, Silvia arranges her real death on film, courtesy of Mónica (her co-star) and then via a pact with Bosco.

Recalling on a smaller scale the vast, geometric patterns of the Overlook Hotel in Kubrick's *The Shining*, the horror setting is a modern, brightly-lit, secondary school interior. Though comprising a series of rather anonymous classrooms, landings, passageways and corridors, Amenábar manages to conjure up (through editing and soundtrack), a labyrinth of doors and hidden spaces, all suggestive of danger. With a further spatial nod to *The Shining*, the credit sequence rolls over

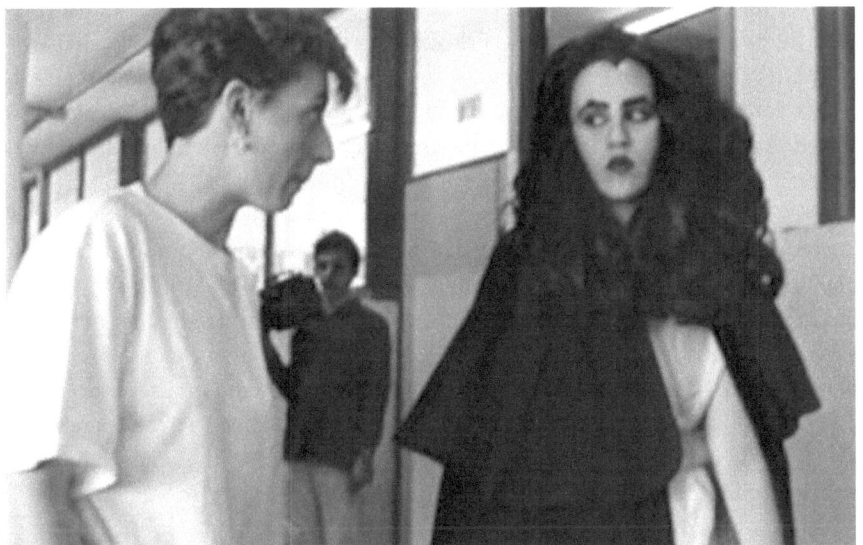

Unhappy with Monica's scene, Silvia plots how to dispose of María for real, using Bosco

the lower ground setting, the toilet/shower area, as the caretaker departs and the students emerge from hiding to set up their equipment. The opening shot is an extreme POV close-up at ground level of a wasp in its death throes (hence the film title), already dissected and then filmed by Bosco, the psychotic cameraman (with echoes of Powell's Mark Lewis and Hitchcock's Norman Bates). The film will end symmetrically, spatially and visually, with another insect close-up. Bosco's obsessive desire is to immortalise on videotape the precise moment of death; after the wasp, he practices again, filming a beetle trapped in a toilet bowl, whose drowning is cross-cut with María taking a shower after being covered in stage blood (Amenábar's homage to Hitchcock's *Psycho*). On the third and final day of shooting, with little decent footage, and fearing discovery, Mónica fails to stimulate María sufficiently for her big death scene. Silvia then calls on Bosco to terrorise María for real, using a 'plano secuencia', i.e. one long, unedited, agonising take. Yet, just as he is about to ram the stage knife into her abdomen (as happens in *Tesis*, during Angela's dream), Silvia calls him off, claiming that his (genuine) murder attempt was just a joke, a mere fiction (contradicting her earlier assertion that screen fiction ' no es un cachondeo', i.e. is no laughing matter). The film ends with the three young women in a consoling huddle on the lower stairs (curiously reminiscent of the final *pietà* in *The Others*) and with a crestfallen Bosco, denied a human sacrifice, forced to return to his wriggling insects. With its much better narrative organisation, smoother continuity editing, credible performances, clear depth of field, well-judged music track and clean sound effects, this second short did extremely well at national competitions. Among other plaudits, the film won first prize and a best director award from AICA for 1992. It also convinced director José Luis Cuerda to produce Amenábar's first feature and offer him a contract for two more, an extraordinary deal for a novice filmmaker like Amenábar.

With *Himenóptero*, the ontological boundaries between fiction and the real, reality and fantasy, playing dead and real death are effectively blurred if not dissolved. At the same time, the spectator enjoys a pleasurable, double scare: firstly, we gaze on María, as a voyeur of her own victimhood and at her genuine fear of being stabbed to death; secondly, we function as doubles for both Silvia and Bosco, as accomplices in their combined murderous voyeurism and sadistic scopophilia. Positioned behind and in front of the camera, as both voyeur and victim, the spectator enjoys the thrills and spills, confusions and vertigo of an ontological *mise-en-abyme*, which will become a trademark of Amenábar's more open, twisty, surprise endings. Also *Himenóptero* undoubtedly stands as the embryo and precursor of *Tesis* (with Bosco repeated as the villain) as well as a cautionary tale about media manipulation, screen violence and the world of the 'snuff' film, here strongly prefigured by Bosco's uncut 'long take' though not mentioned by name.

LUNA/MOON

The third short, *Moon*, ably illustrates Amenábar and Gil's combined flair for reworking genre conventions and subtly tapping into important social issues of the period. At thirty minutes, and recalling *The Hitcher*, *Fatal Attraction* (Adrian Lyne, 1987), *Thelma and Louise* (Ridley Scott, 1991) and *Basic Instinct* (Paul Verhoeven, 1992), *Moon* is a psychological thriller, shot in black and white, with dialogue recorded partly as direct sound (car interiors) and the rest overdubbed. While maintaining strong verisimilitude by way of the improvised dialogue, the film plays on reversals of gender and power relations. The threat of violence comes not from the male hitcher, but from the pick-up driver, an attractive, manipulative, psycho *femme fatale* whose name is withheld. (In the original outline, she murders her husband, puts his corpse in the car boot, and seeks a hitcher to help bury the body. This action line was dropped in favour of a female serial killer, who preys every night on a different hitcher). The short is apparently based on a real and very unpleasant incident experienced by Amenábar himself and begins and ends late at night on a lonely country road. The female driver (played by Nieves Herranz, an Amenábar regular) gives a lift to Alberto, whose car has broken down. He is a young encyclopedia salesman, played by another Amenábar regular, Eduardo Noriega, in a job that Mateo Gil had done for real. Following a stop at a service station and after intense verbal sparring, Alberto refuses to go home with the driver. Taking a detour to the nearby woods, after a quarrel, she vents her rage by shooting him in the back as he tries to flee the car. Against the moonlit sky, a further struggle in the dark is followed by the sound of two more gunshots, heard off-screen. The short closes with the same female driver, back on the road (though unseen), picking up her next victim (a brief cameo by Mateo Gil).

As Amenábar has indicated (letter to the author, January 2006), *Moon* was in large part a stylistic exercise, comprising three longish dialogue scenes, sandwiched between a prologue and epilogue. (This kind of simple dramatic structure is used in the three main horror/thriller features and constitutes a further sign of authorship). Amenábar's aim was to create suspense and tension, not through action but through a verbal duel of 'cat and mouse', ending in devastating violence. However (unlike in *Himenóptero*), he dispenses with the intrusive, voyeuristic, subjective camerawork and shoots the dialogue scenes objectively using shot/reverse-shot techniques. He also exploits the narrative possibilities of off-screen action and sound (devices consistently exploited in the features), leaving the spectator guessing as to who has shot who.

Drawing heavily upon the sadomasochistic dynamics of the hitcher movie, erotic thriller and *film noir*, the short introduces a predatory, alienated, psychotic *femme fatale* who effectively entraps a weak and indecisive young man, as the viewer's screen proxy. The piece stands as the prototype for the violent, sexualised relationship between César and Nuria in *Open Your Eyes*, as well as the basis for the car crash sequence. The female driver is also strongly reminiscent of Alex in *Fatal Attraction*, with whom she shares her loneliness, sexual obsessions, aggression, rage at rejection and unstoppable cruelty, ending in lethal violence. Yet her reasons are not clear. She appears not to be an exploited career woman fighting back against male oppression. And with little or no background, she recalls the sphinx-like, seemingly-motiveless figure of John Ryder in *The Hitcher*. Presenting her as a sadistic killer, the short suggests a troubling concern with assertive female sexuality. Moreover, in a period (the early to mid-1990s), when casual sex could be lethal, the short also seems to suggest that not all men are on the lookout for a fling. (Indeed, trapped in a potentially fatal love triangle, Alberto makes a point of ringing his girlfriend Teresa to confirm his whereabouts and his fidelity). Amenábar thus seems to have made a kind of anti-sex sex thriller; and though AIDS is not mentioned, the subliminal message is that sex may/can equal death.

Finally, as in the second short and as another signature device recycled in the features, there is also a final twist: just before the final sequence on the main road, the camera closes in on the unnamed driver's key ring. A metal plate bears the pseudonym/*nom de guerre* 'LUNA' in capitals (recalling Kane's boyhood sled and the name Rosebud, symbol of lost innocence and trigger to the retrospective narrative). *Luna* is the film title, but also a MacGuffin which is ironically echoed earlier in Alberto's dialogue, when he believes he is safely on his way home. (Oblivious to what is about to happen to him, he remarks innocently 'How beautiful the moon is', to which his antagonist replies tersely, 'How romantic'.) The name LUNA also refers to the female serial killer who works at night but above all to failed romance, alienation, sadomasochism, menace and murder. And yet, the sign fails to solve the puzzle. As with the previous short, the ending, identity and motivations of the young woman are left open, ambiguous, unresolved and a dangling tease for the audience. However, the threat posed by LUNA, whoever she is, is still active and on-going, very real and far from being contained. This lack of closure relates to genre (the cautionary tale) and to audience expectations (reminding the viewer that the serial killer is not male but female). This play with inversion prefigures the type of surprise ending we find in *The Others*, where those who appear to be ghosts are in fact real and those who appear to be living are in fact dead.

AMENÁBAR AND THE THRILLER

Amenábar's main contribution to Spanish horror arguably lies in his overcoming the great fear of the thriller in Spain. This, he says, is a tricky type of cinema which relies on intricacy of plot mechanics, delay and denial. It also requires a balance between narrative excess and strong verisimilitude in order to sustain viewer engagement. In this field, very few Spanish directors before him have found success (see Payán 2001: 40). As a student and fan of Hitchcock (the inventor of the modern film thriller), Amenábar has mastered the creation of suspense via complex plotting, restricted narration, the delay of action lines which we know are inevitable and the play of the male (and female) gazes as a prelude to sexualised violence. Like Hitchcock, he draws on black humour and jokes, and also forces his spectators to adopt the POV and inhabit the skins of often very dark, enigmatic, unsympathetic characters (Silvia and Bosco in *Himenóptero*; Bosco, Chema and even Angela in *Tesis*; César in *Open Your Eyes*; Grace in *The Others*). Unlike the Master, however, Amenábar prefers the classical 'whodunit' format of Agatha Christie, the drip feed of narrative information and the surprise ending, to which Hitchcock strongly objected.

Confused, angry, alienated, often paranoid, Amenábar's mainly young teen and 'twenty something' protagonists (Ana, María, Alberto, Angela, César, the young mother Grace) are made to suffer and given little respite, as they face overwhelming shocks and calamities in their vacuous lives. They see themselves in crisis as innocent victims of a sick, image-obsessed society, or of 'others' who would wish to occupy their living space. By their own selfishness, narcissism, bad luck or sadomasochistic drives, they are plunged into a repeating nightmare, stripped of their life-styles, comfort zones, values and consoling fictions (such as looks and religion) and forced to confront their darkest selves. Largely authors of their own misfortune, their suffering is nonetheless therapeutic, leading to a catharsis and some form of deeper understanding and self-awareness ... or so it seems. Yet nothing is quite what it seems in an Amenábar film.

His settings are typical of the thriller mode, i.e. empty buildings, lonely country lanes, gloomy shrines to video death (Chema's flat), long corridors and tunnels, evacuated city centres, labyrinths and dungeons (Bosco's garage, César's flat, Grace's mansion), high towers, haunted houses, crippled male bodies, all sites of enclosure, imprisonment, claustrophobia and vertigo. Suicide seems to be Amenábar's preferred method of coping with entrapment and madness, of exiting the nightmare of repetition, while black humour helps to deal with its paralysing effects. In formal terms, while they are designed to confuse, disorient and plunge us into the abyss, Amenábar's films increasingly demonstrate a concern with style, pattern, order and coherence. Both the shorts and the three main horror features display a strong degree of internal structural and formal integration, seen in their symmetrical beginnings and endings, the framing of the narrative with prologues and editorial epilogues, and the recycling of the investigation narrative. Also, in formal terms, Amenábar marks these films with repeated authorial signatures, including cameos, initial fade-ups from black screen, the use of off-screen voice-overs (which appear to address the audience as well as the film characters) and devices which help prefigure and summarise the story/allegory to come (for example, the storyboard-like illustrations from the children's books, at the beginning of *The Others*, where the whole narrative is set out as a series of snapshots, comprise drawings which also echo nostalgically Amenábar's own childhood reading). Overall, such extensive, internal recycling between shorts and features gives Amenábar's 'horror work' as a whole a quite striking degree of stylistic and thematic cohesion, and a strongly auteurist feel.

CONCLUSION

One of Amenábar's key achievements is to have tilted Spanish horror well away from the 'sub-producto' tradition of the 1960s and 1970s. From low-budget, potboilers and clunky pastiches of 1930s Universal and Hammer gothic camp, passing through the ironic, postmodern, gore fests of the 1990s, Amenábar has arguably installed the stylishly crafted, largely non-violent, effects-light, 'horror/thriller' hybrid as a new template for success. The international recognition of *The Others* has also helped raise levels of Hispanic co-production activity and cemented the global appeal of the supernatural ghost story, as seen in the success of Guillermo del Toro's *El espinazo del diablo/The Devil's Backbone* (2001), financed by Almodóvar's El Deseo, and more recently del Toro´s *El laberinto del fauno/Pan's Labyrinth* (2005), which cleverly integrates childhood fantasy and the horrors of Spain's Civil War. As part of the post-millenial, Latin-inflected 'new wave', del Toro's standing in Europe and the USA has also raised the external profile of Spanish genre cinema in the American market, with directors such as Jaume Balagueró, Paco Plaza, Nacho Vigalondo, Juan Antonio Bayona and so on, all now developing horror and fantasy scripts and preparing English-language products, courtesy of their American agents.

As noted above, Amenábar was discovered by José Luis Cuerda through his short *Himenóptero* and has continued this tradition of supporting younger filmmakers. His own production company (also called Himenóptero) backed Oskar Santos and his first short (the period mystery tale *El soñador/The Dreamer*, 2005), as well as his first feature *El mal ajeno/The Evil Other*, which was released in March 2010. In terms of their influence (and leaving aside the American remake of *Open Your Eyes*, entitled *Vanilla Sky*, directed by Cameron Crowe, 2001), Amenábar's first two teen thrillers are recycled in Mateo Gil's first feature, *Nadie conoce a nadie/Nobody Knows Anybody* (1999). The film is based on the lethally interactive world of computer games and role plays. Designed as a Kafkaesque *mise-en-abyme*, in its narrative outline and character relationships it is uncannily similar to *Open Your Eyes*. Amenábar's rehabilitation of the suspense thriller in Spain is also noticeable in contemporary, local examples such as *X* (Luis Marías, 2002), *Intacto* (Juan Carlos Fresnadillo, 2001), *El Segundo nombre/Second Name* (2002) and *Rec* (2007), the latter both by Paco Plaza (whose werewolf story *Romasanta* [2004] is also an intriguing, non-parodic reprise of old gothic traditions). Inspired by the template of *The Others*, we find strong Amenábarian echoes in Jaume Balagueró's *Darkness* (2002) and *Frágiles/Fragile* (2005), as well as in *Fausto 5.0* (Isidro Ortiz, Alex Ollé & Carlos Padrissa, 2001) and in Nacho Cerdá's *The Abandoned* (2006).

Perhaps the most striking recent case of Amenábar-inflected filmmaking is Juan Antonio Bayona's début feature, the mega-successful *El orfanato/The Orphanage* (2007), produced by Guillermo del Toro and starring Belén Rueda and Mabel Rivera, who both played major roles in Amenábar's *Mar adentro/The Sea Inside* (2004). As Spain's Oscar candidate for Best Foreign Film of 2007, *The Orphanage* seemed uniquely tailored to the liberal-left outlook of Academy members. It came replete with universally resonant 'social issues': the care of abandoned children with special needs (and incurable diseases), a mother's search for her missing son, the limits of maternal sacrifice, children and parents coping with loss and death, good and bad mothering, scientific as opposed to faith-based forms of sleuthing, and so on. There were also many echoes of *The Others*: cute kids, ghost story, the haunted house, buried crimes, repressed guilt, confronting the past, séance scene with wacky medium (a cameo by Geraldine Chaplin), allegories of faith, allusions to Peter Pan, suffering as a route to self-awareness, defence of the family, no child left behind, twist ending, and so on. Almost a remake, deeply sentimental and rather overwhelmed by its sound design, such promising cases remind us of just how high Amenábar has set the bar for contemporary Spanish horror.

NOTE

1 For example, see the index in Rodríguez Marchante (2002), which is dominated by the names of Anglo-American directors.

BIBLIOGRAPHY

Aguilar, C. (ed.) (2005) *Cine fantástico y de terror español, 1984-2004*. San Sebastián: Donostia Kultura, Semana de Cine Fantástico y de Terror de San Sebastián.
Faulkner, S. (2004) *Literary Adaptations in Spanish Cinema*. London: Támesis.
Jancovich, M., A. Lázaro Reboll, J. Stringer and A. Willis (eds), *Defining Cult Movies: The Cultural Politics of Oppositional Taste*. Manchester: Manchester University Press.
Kinder, M. (1993) *Blood Cinema: The Reconstruction of National Identity in Spain*. Berkeley: University of California Press.
Nguyen, K. N. (2001), 'Thriller Maestro. Spanish Prodigy Amenábar invades America with *The Others*', on-line. Available HTTP: http://www.washdiplomat.com/01-95/b5_09_01 (Accessed 27 September 2007).
Payán, M. J. (2001) *El cine español actual*. Madrid: Ediciones JC.
Rodríguez Marchante, O. (2002) *Amenábar: Vocación de intriga*. Madrid: Páginas de Espuma.
Triana-Toribio, N. (2003) *Spanish National Cinema*. London: Routledge.
Willis, A. (2003) 'Spanish horror and the flight from art cinema 1963–73', in M. Jancovich, A. Lázaro Reboll, J. Stringer and A. Willis (eds), *Defining Cult Movies: The Cultural Politics of Oppositional Taste*, Manchester: Manchester University Press, 71–83.

ITALIAN HORROR CINEMA

ITALIAN HORROR CINEMA

Patricia Allmer, Emily Brick and David Huxley

In the post-war period Italy has been probably the most prolific producer of horror films in Europe, establishing a tradition of directors such as Mario Bava, Dario Argento and Lucio Fulci, all of whom have become identified with the horror genre and had international success in the field. Because of the infrastructure established in the silent period and the massive Cinecitta studios in Rome (founded in 1937), Italy has had an efficient factory system which moved through a whole series of popular generic cycles, including farcical comedies (1948–54) and peplum ('sword and sandal') films (1958–64). Although Christopher Frayling (1981) claims that a cycle of horror films only lasted from 1959 to 1963, in fact it was much longer lasting. Arguably starting in 1957 with Riccardo Freda's *I vampiri/The Vampires* it has continued well into the twenty-first-century with, for example, Dario Argento's *La terza madre/The Mother of Tears* (2007). Of course, it is possible to argue that there are sub-generic differences which divide these horror films into shorter, self contained cycles. The series of '*mondo*' films, which contained loosely connected actual and faked footage of gore and shocking scenes, is arguably very different from Mario Bava's gothic horror films of the 1960s. It is certainly the case that *mondo* films were then considered beneath contempt, even for those writers who were generally enthusiastic about horror film. Thus Carlos Clarens, writing in defence of Tod Browning's shocking 1932 American film *Freaks* comments that, 'If the film were no more than a tour of a teratological universe, it would be as gratuitous and voyeuristic as the worst of *Mondo Cane*' (1971: 106). Yet some thirty years later in a book devoted to this genre Mark Goodall could describe the film as 'beautifully crafted, mesmerizing and unique' (2006: 8). Bava has not had to wait so long for critical approval. Clarens is somewhat ambiguous about the quality of Bava's work, but says of *Black Sunday* (1961) 'the quality of the visual narrative was superb' (1971: 229) and he describes the work of Bava's mentor Riccardo Freda as creating 'lovingly wrought miniatures, the handiwork of a careless, but undoubtedly talented, minor master' (1971: 228).

After Bava, critical opinion became even more divided as greater violence and more visceral horror began to appear in Italian films. Bava is credited with founding one of these new, more violent sub-genres, the *giallo*, with *La ragazza che sapeva troppo/Evil Eye* (1963). *Gialli* were named after yellow-fronted thriller novels, but in the process of their adaptation the intense visual emphasis placed on the nature of the murders in these films locate them solidly in a horror aesthetic. By the time that *giallos* were beginning to decline in the second half of the 1970s two further, interrelated sub-genres appeared with Lucio Fulci's *Zombi 2/Zombie Flesh Eaters* (1979) and Ruggero Deodato's *Cannibal Holocaust* (1980). Both gave rise to violent sub-genres, and Fulci, inspired by George Romero's seminal American film *Night of the Living Dead* (1968) in particular went on to be identified with the zombie film. Deodato's film, with its *mondo* overtones and plentiful gore, succeeded in being banned in many parts of Europe.

Mark Goodall's chapter here deals with the zombie film, in particular Bruno Mattei's *Inferno dei morti viventi/Zombie Creeping Flesh* (1982). He reassesses the current cultural standing of the Italian zombie cycle in relation to this heavily-criticised example, and examines the extent to which the cannibalism in the film can be seen as a metaphor for European political concerns about poverty in the Third World. Anna Powell's chapter deals with probably the most famous of Italian horror directors, Dario Argento. Powell sets Argento's work, in particular *Suspiria* (1977), in the context of Gilles Deleuze's theories of the aesthetic sensorium, relating them to Argento's use of heightened, saturated colour and sensory horror. The two chapters therefore bring together an analysis of one of the most respected of Italian horror directors and a discussion of a sub-genre which is still one of the most controversial in Italian cinema.

BIBLIOGRAPHY

Clarens, C. (1971) *Horror Movies: An Illustrated Survey*. London: Panther.
Frayling, C. (1981) *Spaghetti Westerns: Cowboys and Europeans from Karl May to Sergio Leone*. London: Routledge.
Goodall, M. (2006) *Sweet and Savage: The World Through the Shockumentary Film Lens*. London: Headpress.

LIVE ATE:
GLOBAL CATASTROPHE AND THE POLITICS AND POETICS OF THE ITALIAN ZOMBIE FILM

Mark Goodall

The present work relationships, as well as the relationships between people – social, political, and economic – are still basically cannibalistic. [...] Cannibalism has merely institutionalized itself, cleverly disguised itself. The new heroes, still looking for a collective consciousness, try to devour those who devour us.

– Joaquim Pedro de Andrade (in Johnson and Stam 1995: 82--3)

Some time ago, I was reading a story about the whirlwind genocide that occurred in Rwanda in 1994 when I began to think of the Italian/Spanish horror film *Inferno dei morti viventi/Zombie Creeping Flesh* (Bruno Mattei, 1981). Even by postmodern standards of irony this is a fairly preposterous juxtaposition, yet it is not perhaps as ridiculous as it first seems. The article I was reading, from the *Guardian* newspaper, was a reaction to the recently issued film *Hotel Rwanda* (Terry George, 2004) which aims to chart, with typical Hollywood manoeuvring, the attempt by one man to salvage some compassionate humanity from the cruel actions of others. We encounter such atrocities with disquieting frequency; in this instance it was the brutality of the slaughter of one tribal people by another (see Freedland 2005). The article clearly then evoked the art of film as a powerful political tool, capable of rendering 'real world' events with an enduring emotional punch. Secondly, the piece alerted those of us in the West to act immediately, as we did not in Rwanda, in order to stop the same thing happening in a contemporary site of atrocity, the Darfur region of Sudan. The film *Hotel Rwanda* has a stark message: we should have done more, then. The newspaper article also has a message: we must do more *now*. Bruno Mattei's *Zombie Creeping Flesh*, the film that I freely associated with these modern horrors and will now discuss, has a message too: if we do not feed the Third World, then they will come and feed on us. Is it possible that something as incredulous and inept as a European zombie film, an artefact that enjoys a status lowly even by the standards of cult film studies, teach us anything – outside of knowing irony and paracinematic discourse (see Sconce 1995) – about global politics? It is this question and the peculiar and haunting relationships associated with it that I want to examine in this chapter.

CANNIBAL CULTURES

'He devours their intestines, when their bodies are charged with magic.'
— Egyptian Cannibal Hymn (quoted in Rothenberg 1985: 149)

Cultural theorists are familiar with the idea that 'low' cultural materials, of which zombie films (especially *Italian* zombie films) are arguably a prime example, can teach us many things. In Italy, where the graphic zombie film arguably was invented, the distinction between high and low culture has arguably never been as marked as it is in Anglo-Saxon cultures and cultural 'contradictions' are common (the work of Olivier Toscani, for example, can be critical of the fashion industry and at the same time exist within that industry). Italy is a country where the modern and the postmodern, according to Carlo Antonelli and Peppino Ortoleva (1999), were aggressively materialised through popular art (the films of Dino Risi promoted the new morality while Italian film composers, classically trained, write music for genre cinema including horror and soft porn). Critics Kim Newman (1986) and John Martin (1996) have in their own way defended the cultural credibility of Italian horror films in light of the constant criticism these films received from British reviewers. Newman's piece in particular 'Twenty Years in Another Town: The History of Italian Exploitation', occurring as it did in a journal (*Monthly Film Bulletin*) that seemed most offended by Italian genre traditions, is particularly striking: 'the best examples of most Italian imitation cycles are surprisingly sophisticated mixtures of imitation, pastiche, parody, deconstruction, reinterpretation and operatic inflation' (1986: 20) he notes. It is also worth recalling that Italian film industry workers were very 'well trained' (ibid.): Lucio Fulci for example began his career at the Centro Sperimentale di Cinematografia under the tutelage of Luchino Visconti alongside Michelangelo Antonioni and Nanni Loy. Recently Brian Yuzna observed that 'in the next century film historians will discuss the *giallo* (Italian thrillers) as pure cinema' (2002: 24); certainly the heightened, visceral power of the Italian horror sensibility overcomes any conventional desire for plot, narrative, character. The work of Mario Bava and Dario Argento (as this collection demonstrates) is now credible academic subject matter.

Despite the reputation *Zombie Creeping Flesh* has for being one of the 'worst horror films ever made' (Slater 2002: 179) such analysis misses the point of the Italian horror experience which is almost totally visceral – Yuzna's 'pure cinema'. The notion scriptwriter Claudio Fragasso had to represent hunger in the Third World through the living dead merely echoes (albeit crudely) more 'serious' attempts at metaphorical experimentation (for example Pier Paolo Pasolini's *Porcile/Pigsty* [1969] and Joaquim Pedro de Andrade's *Macunaíma* [1969]) and even earlier literary movements where the metaphor of cannibalism was used as a political device (*Macunaíma* began as a 1928 novel by Mário de Andrade; the 1969 film version is an anthropophagist reading of the book). The Brazilian *antropofagia* movement developed a critique of late capitalism and disabused distinctions between the primitive/backward and the bourgeois/modern, instead promoting a celebration of Brazilian primitive culture and identity that could be viewed as positive. The 'anthropophagy' movement was modernist, forward-looking and revolutionary in tone: an 'authentic native tradition as well as a key metaphor for cultural independence' (Stam 2005: 320). But this revolution was also 'carnivalesque' (Stam notes the grossness of *Macunaíma*'s Rabelaisian imagery, 2005: 331–3) and in a similar, if crudely perverted and sometimes reactionary sense, the Italian zombie/cannibal film suggests an ecological concern with the damage caused by capitalistic activity and the effect this rampant globalising 'progress' – an encroachment of technology into the natural world – has on indigenous peoples. These films use popular cultural forms to express 'ideas' and 'issues', most notably a critique where the barbarism of the developed techno-world is crueller than that of so-called 'native cannibalism'. The Italian zombie film also famously reflects an obsession with the decaying and the rotting, echoing perhaps the medieval naturalist liberal heresy (informed by Indian cosmology) of Domencio Scandella, which proposed that the origins of the world did not exist in Holy miracles but instead began through putrefaction – a primordial cheese from which worm-like men were born. In the sixteenth century Scandella became fascinated by a book relating the travels of Sir John Mandeville which included accounts of 'islands inhabited by cannibals' (actually the land mass of Dondun) and offered particularly lurid testimonies to the gruesome rituals performed in these sites. In the same way that Scandella, fatally – he was later executed – confused, interpreted and revised the images and ideas of such texts, the vivid imagination of the Italian filmmaker delivers its own 'transposed and remoulded' vision of ritual practices and anthropologic discovery (Ginzburg 1980: 47). Films in the classic zombie tradition vigorously exhibit this 'aggressive distortion of the text' (ibid.): the emergence of a political/anthropological dialogue from the crude matter and decay, whilst at the same time revelling in the often perverse travels of white men. In the same way that historian Carlo Ginzburg recovered the story of Scandella as a valuable record of mediaeval 'popular culture', and thus deconstructed hierarchies of thought, it is possible that now we can view the low arts of the Italian genre film as offering some insight and inspiration, and read their thrilling viscerality against still prevailing notions of taste, quality and status.

ITALIAN ZOMBIE FILMS

Much has already been written about the Italian zombie film, most of it trite and non-critical, honing in on the violence and special effects achievements and the spectacularity of the subgenre, obsessed with image, anecdote and fragmentation. The artistry of the Italian zombie film is in no doubt and as noted above, the practitioners of the genre were effectively trained and often experimental in their approach (Fulci once described it as 'Artaudian' [see Palmieri and Mistretta 1996: 60). A film such as Fulci's *E tu vivrai nel terrore – L'aldilà/The Beyond* (1981) is famous for its gore but perhaps less regarded for the intriguing and disturbing *mise-en-scene* and use of avant-garde music that create a fabulous atmosphere, in the absence of a particularly coherent narrative (the *Monthly Film Bulletin* review typically dwelt on the 'lack of any consistent convention' [Pulleine 1981: 243]). *Zombi 2/Zombie Flesh Eaters* (Lucio Fulci, 1979) contains a 'promisingly gruesome' sequence and has passed into legend as one of the despised 'video nasties', while Umberto Lenzi's *Mangiati vivi!/Eaten Alive* (1980) was described on release as 'grotesque' (Pulleine 1981: 251). These films are all concerned with the infection of the developed world by the primitive and savage other and either the descent of civilised Westerners once they are immersed in the Third World; or the battle to stave off the devouring of Western landscapes by a mysterious and pernicious diseased corpus. One irony of these cinematic attacks on the commodification of life under consumer capitalism is that in terms of gender representation Italian zombie films exhibit their own reification of sexuality through what Marilyn French calls a 'cannibalistic male psyche' (1992: 166). But that is perhaps another essay.

I have chosen to discuss a film often dismissed even within this canon as worthless (yes, the discussion of zombie films has its hierarchies too!). Yet my remarks on *Zombie Creeping Flesh* set aside any assumptions of cultural worth or subcultural credibility rather serving to illuminate some of the largely ignored aspects of the film that locate it within a particular Italian cinematic tradition. Zombie films, for obvious generic reasons, are usually tracked back to the Italian horror and *giallo* cycles. But for me this tradition equally begins, as we shall see, in the documentary form of the Italian *mondo* film.

MONDO DECOMPOSIZIONE: *ZOMBIE CREEPING FLESH*

Zombie Creeping Flesh, an Italian/Spanish production was released in 1981. The director was credited as Vincent Dawn, a pseudonym for Bruno Mattei. The pulsating electronic progressive-rock score was composed by Goblin, Dario Argento's favourite musicians. In 1984 in the UK the film was included on the Director of Public Prosecutions list of 'video nasties', thus gaining instant cult status. The film, however, is poorly regarded (John Martin described it as a film that could have been 'directed by a five-year old' [1993: 171]) and is often overlooked in studies of zombie and cannibal films (for example, Brottman 1997). It has become infamous due to a sequence where the principal female character is attacked by a zombie who inserts its hand in her mouth and pushes her eyeballs out of their sockets, and the film's renown is based if anything on this sequence. *Zombie Creeping Flesh* opens at a chemical plant in New Guinea, the Hope Centre, and the notion of contamination of an earthly paradise by technological progress (albeit conceived, it seems, to aid an underdeveloped nation) is evoked by the use of an ugly blue filter and ominous electronic music. The Centre is supposedly developing innovative ways of feeding the starving population. It is revealed at the end of the film that in fact the plant was devising a chemical gas that caused natives to eat each other – a rather drastic measure to solve global overpopulation. A thrown-together team of commandos link up with a reporter and cinejournalist to then embark on a dangerous mission to find the truth about what caused the workers to become cannibalistic zombies. It turns out that the commando crew were dispatched to suppress the truth about the Centre.

The director of the film, Mattei, was already associated with the Italian documentary tradition through his films *Sesso Perverso, Mondo Violento/Libidomania 2* (1980) and *Sesso Perverso/Sexual Aberration* (1981), good examples of a trend in the late 1970s and early 1980s for a sexually explicit documentary, or 'shockumentary', style known since as the *mondo* film. The *mondo* film developed in the 1960s as a sensational form of long travelogue energised by a sneering narration, violent contrasts of scenario and early forms of full-colour sexploitation. The first true *mondo* film was Gualtiero Jacopetti, Franco Prosperi and Paulo Cavaras's *Mondo Cane* (1963), a global box-office smash which, with its *National Geographic* style montage of pseudo-ethnographic attractions and haunting lush musical score inaugurated the subgenre. Hundreds of copies of this film ensued and *mondo* became a generic term, as well as a commonly despised phenomenon (see Goodall 2006 for a detailed study of the *mondo* film). In such films Mattei had already developed a tendency for inserting what has been described as 'stock footage' into his 'documentary' accounts of primitive ritual and practices. In fact often these sequences, rather than being licensed news, reportage or actuality footage, were usually sections retrieved from other *mondo* films. This dubious practice arguably reached its zenith, often with unintentional comical overtones, in *Zombie Creeping Flesh* (more radical applications of the technique of inserting 'real' footage into drama – Fukasaku's *Battle Royale II* (2003) for example – are by the way completely lacking in this type of film [see Sharrett 2005: xiii]).

The first occurrence of this sampling technique is as footage glimpsed in an old news broadcast of 'frightened natives' of New Guinea made by reporter and protagonist Lia Rousseau, documenting early fears about something going wrong on the island. Secondly, the footage appears as an establishing backdrop crudely cut into the commando squad's arrival in the jungle where shots of natives' rowing boats and exotic wildlife clips are utilised. Footage of ritual dancing, piles of corpses and bones, animal disembowelling, and a rotting, partially embalmed corpse is then intercut with scenes of a ludicrous 'primitivised' Lia (complete with painted face and, naturally, naked breasts) entering their domain. This editing is very badly done and it is striking that the *mondo* footage and Mattei's footage are clearly of different film stock. Often the shot perspective is contradictory and mismatched. Following this there is a sequence where a TV news cameraman, Max, stumbles upon a tribal cannibalistic ritual as a maggoty corpse is picked at and nibbled by a grieving relative. Max looks on in horror and disbelief ... but then steels himself, ensuring that he captures the entire scenario on film. All of the above documentary scenes where lifted from a little-known yet enthralling and frequently disturbing Japanese/Italian *mondo* film made in 1974 by Akira Ide, *Nuova Guinea del Isola dei Cannibali/Guinea Ama*. This film, in focusing on the momentous changes occurring in the South Pacific island between the 'primitive' and 'modern' worlds (including the territory's independence from the governance of the United Kingdom), mines a characteristically binary oppositional *mondo* approach. The dramatic and violent tensions between the old and the new were, for *mondo* directors, always cinematically irresistible; these films drew on a carnivalesque tradition of satirical documentary that exists also in earlier films such as Jean Vigo's *A Propos de Nice* (1930). But there are also elements in the presentation of Ide's film that clearly echo the horror tradition. Many of the gorier moments are dwelt upon or reinterpreted (i.e. the 'suspended corpse' of Ide's film comes to life and attacks the crew for dramatic effect in *Zombie Creeping Flesh*) or eerily slowed down.

The title sequence is notable for its terror tropes of maggot-infested skulls, crimson blood-dripping text and pounding musical underscore. Under Mattei's tactics, already appalling sequences are 'cannibalised' from the *mondo* canon not just literally, as above, but also figuratively and *Zombie Creeping Flesh* in certain deceitful anthropological/documentary moments reworks some of the key *mondo* aesthetics. The notion of a Western camera capturing, voyeuristically for

The suspended corpse (*Guinea Ama*, 1974)

entertainment, the powerful rituals of the non-West mimics the tendency for *mondo* films to exhibit this style. *Mondo* films in fact made a virtue of blurring the boundaries between what was real and what was staged. Even very famous and iconic global incidents could be restaged for the film, for example the ritual suicide of Vietnamese monks (see Kerekes and Slater 1995: 115–18). It is precisely this attribute that concerned critics faced with reviewing the films as documentaries as they emerged in the 1960s and 1970s. As a form of unsophisticated critique this is also a partial reworking of Ruggero Deodato's earlier *Cannibal Holocaust* (1979), a film that despite its reputation as a disgusting example of Euro-sleaze offers a clever, even critical, denunciation of the morally ambiguous *mondo* film methods. Not long after Mattei's film was released Antonio Climati and Mario Morra, themselves pioneers of the 1960s 'classic' *mondo* films, made *Natura contro* (1988) which developed the theme of dangerous exploration into 'zombie/cannibal' territory further. This film was even re-titled *Cannibal Holocaust 2* to cash in on Deodato's work. Meanwhile Franco Prosperi, another original *mondo* pioneer, in his film *Belve Feroci/Wild Beasts* (1983) occupied a similar terrain. In this film the contamination of the environment by chemical negligence leads to the animal population becoming crazed and murderous after imbibing polluted water. Parallels with recent panics over livestock contaminated by chemical leakage are not hard to make. In addition to narrative similarities and overlaps, the framing of *mondo*, where filming from helicopters is reinvented from a practical necessity into a cinematic style, and present in all of the above *mondo* and pseudo-*mondo* films, is regularly exploited in the Italian Zombie film (see *Cannibal Holocaust*, *Zombi 3/Zombie Flesh Eaters 2* [Lucio Fulci, 1988] and so on). The ominous view of a helicopter circling over unknown, deadly terrain has penetrated deeply into the zombie/cannibal cinematic imagination.

Although reviews of *Zombie Creeping Flesh* at the time of its release dismissed any subversive sub-text as being 'buried in an orgy of flesh-chewing and vomiting as well as dialogue that beggars belief' (Jenkins 1982: 229), the film offers some indicators of how the history of Italian genre cinema has integrated socio-political issues. In addition to offering kinetic, visceral violence, the Italian zombie film often draws on contemporaneous concerns, and for its artistry has always drawn on a variety of textual sources. *Mondo* directors were often trained as marine biologists or natural scientists and the ecological concerns are tangible in both Italian shockumentary and eco-horror cinema (examples of films with broader environmental concerns and scientific scepticisms include Fulci's *Zombie Flesh Eaters*, Umberto Lenzi's *Incubo sulla città contaminate/Nightmare City* [1980] and Mario Girolami's *Zombie Holocaust* [1980]).

Returning to the news article on Rwanda that began this discussion another unlikely parallel between the reportage of history and the trash of the zombie film emerges. The author of the piece condemns the United Nations for its 'debating society response' inaction, a mocking criticism that materialises also in Mattei's film during a comical UN-style debate on the activities in New Guinea. 'Genuine' footage of New Guinea natives debating a new constitution and protesting their rights on the streets, taken from Ide's film, are again coarsely combined with a staged security council scenario, a terribly acted, sparsely attended debate with much hurling of paper and hysterical verbal abuse. A supposed New Guinea UN representative bitterly accuses the world: 'You have brought on the apocalypse. You have launched the beginning of the end. Brother eats brother; mothers devour their offspring in a chain of foul slaughter until nothing will remain but the earth soaked in putrefying flesh!' In the same way that the speaker's pleas are dismissed by the chair in this instance ('We'll continue tomorrow your Excellency. Goodnight.'), demands for UN action on the Khartoum government and its Janjaweed militia have been similarly ineffectual in the real world.

CONCLUSION

As has been demonstrated, *Zombie Creeping Flesh* is a far from classic example of what is actually a rich Italian horror tradition. There is little point in debating its cinematic strengths and weaknesses in any depth here; there are many 'better' horror films (and in any case some work on this is already available: see Martin 1993 and Slater 2002). The film is in many ways an example, quite literally, of 'rotting European culture' (Stam 1989: 124). While the always prescient eco-catastrophe theme of the film may be echoed in recent zombie film offerings (such as Romero's *Land of the Dead* [2005]) there is little evidence today that this film has profoundly influenced or will influence generic filmmaking practice (although these films can always be subjected to critical revision). That said its concern with ways of seeing the 'Third World' as political/ecological metaphor and the examination of the complicit role of cinejournalism and mass media in world affairs is entirely contemporary, possibly even radical. Robert Stam reminds us that the carnivalesque 'turns conventional aesthetics on its head in order to locate a new popular, convulsive beauty, one that dares to reveal the grotesquerie of the powerful and the latent beauty of the "vulgar"' (2005: 363). If the Italian zombie film wallows in sensationalism it merely reflects a literary and 'scientific' tradition stretching back centuries which also dwelt on the shocking aspects of a 'ubiquitous' anthropophagy (see Arens 1979: 165). The horrific images displayed in the zombie film are now available on television networks and the internet and reports appear in the media telling of 'zombie computers' (see Markoff 2007) and of deadly strains of malaria-'zombism' that regardless of their reliability keep the man-eating myth alive. Fear is growing, at an increasingly populist level, of the contamination of the Third World, of global ecological catastrophe, and of the destructive forces of a rampant consumerism. Bruce Parry's prime-time anthropology adventure series *Tribe*, for example, ended with a stark warning from the threatened Penan tribe of Malaysia that 'we need the forest to live but so do you' (BBC2, 2007) (while aesthetically the pounding music and the deadly precision of weapons such as the blowdart employed by hunter-gatherers in Parry's programmes also recall the lurking horrors of zombie/cannibal jungle films, at least for those who have watched too many of them). 'When the creeping dead devour the living flesh', the tagline of *Zombie Creeping Flesh*, describes a symbiotic relationship. We can only seek refuge from the cannibal zombies of our own 'conspicuous consumption' for so long (see Kilgour 1998: 241).

The unevenness of the *mondo* and zombie genres (and of the places where these genres coalesce); the tensions between (after Ginzburg) a learned culture and a popular culture cannot obscure what remain salient geopolitical concerns. And the warnings of Jacopetti and Prosperi's classic *mondo* film *Africa Addio* (1966) (where Rwandan genocide was reported forty years ago, complete with dreadful visions of mutilation, mass-murder and putrification) restated horrifically, if clumsily, via Mattei's rather inept horror œuvre, have tragically yet to be heeded.

BIBLIOGRAPHY

Antonelli, C. and P. Ortoleva (1999) 'The Italian Way to Modernity', in G. Malossi (ed.) *Volare: The Icon of Italy in Global Pop Culture*. New York: Monacelli Press, 66–75.

Arens, W. (1979) *The Man-eating Myth*. Oxford: Oxford University Press.
Brottman, M. (1997) *Meat is Murder!: An Illustrated Guide to Cannibal Culture*. London: Creation.
Cambodian Troops Quarantine Quan'sul. On-line. Available HTTP: http://65.127.62/south_asia/4483241.stm.htm (1 September 2006).
Freedland, J. (2005) 'How to stop Hotel Darfur', *The Guardian*, March 30th. On-line. Available HTTP:http://www.guardian.co.uk/Columists/Column/0,,1448006,00.html (23 January 2006).
French, M. (1992) *The War Against Women*. London: Penguin.
Ginzburg, C. (1980) *The Cheese and the Worms: The Cosmos of a Sixteenth-century Miller*. London: Routledge and Kegan Paul.
Goodall, M. (2006) *Sweet and Savage: The World Through the Shockumentary Film Lens*. London: Headpress.
Jenkins, S. (1982) Review of '*Inferno dei morti-viventi (Zombie Creeping Flesh)*', *Monthly Film Bulletin*, 49: 585, 229.
Johnson, R. and R. Stam (eds) (1995) *Brazilian Cinema*. New York: Columbia University Press.
Kerekes, D. and D. Slater (1995) *Killing for Culture: An Illustrated History of Death Film from Mondo to Snuff*. London: Creation.
Kilgour, M. 'The Function of Cannibalism at the Present Time', in F. Barker, P. Hulme and M. Iversen (eds) (1998) *Cannibalism and the Colonial World*. Cambridge: Cambridge University Press, 238–59.
Markoff, J. (2007) 'Attack of the Zombie Computers', *The New York Times*. On-line. Available HTTP: http://www.nytimes.com/2007/01/07/technology/07net.html?_r=1&oref=slogin (30 December 2007).
Martin, J. (1993) *The Seduction of the Gullible: The Curious History of the British 'Video Nasties' Phenomenon*. Nottingham: Procrustes Press.
_____ (1996) 'The Critics Who Knew Too Little', in L. Palmieri and G. Mistretta (eds) *Spaghetti Nightmares*. Florida: Fantasma Books, 160–1.
Newman, K. (1986) 'Thirty Years in Another Town: The History of Italian Exploitation', *Monthly Film Bulletin*, 53: 624, 20–4.
Palmieri, L. and G. Mistretta (eds) *Spaghetti Nightmares*. Florida: Fantasma Books.
Pulleine, T. (1981) Review of '*E tu vivrai nel terrore! L'Aldila (The Beyond)*', *Monthly Film Bulletin*, 48: 575, 243.
_____ (1981) Review of '*Mangiati vivi dai cannibali (Eaten Alive)*', in *Monthly Film Bulletin*, 48: 575, 251.
Rothenburg, J. (1985) *Technicians of the Sacred*. Berkeley, CA: University of California Press.
Sconce, J. (1995) 'Trashing the Academy: Taste, Excess and an Emerging Politics of Cinematic Style', *Screen*, 36: 4, 371–93.
Sharrett, C. (2005) 'Preface', in J. McRoy, *Japanese Horror Cinema*. Edinburgh: Edinburgh University Press, xi–xiv.
Slater, J. (2002) *Eaten Alive!: Italian Cannibal and Zombie Movies*. London: Plexus.
Stam, R. (1989) *Subversive Pleasures: Bakhtin, Cultural Criticism and Film*. Baltimore: Johns Hopkins University Press.
_____ (2005) *Literature Through Film: Realism, Magic and the Art of Adaptation*. Oxford: Blackwell.
Yuzna, B. (2002) 'Italian Zombies', in J. Slater, *Eaten Alive!: Italian Cannibal and Zombie Movies*. London: Plexus, 24–5.

A TOUCH OF TERROR:
DARIO ARGENTO AND DELEUZE'S CINEMATIC SENSORIUM

Anna Powell

'Whether through words, colours, sounds or stone, art is the language of sensations. Art does not have opinions.' (Deleuze and Guattari 1991: 196)

Dario Argento, the maker of gore-splattered *gialli*, and Gilles Deleuze, the philosopher of molecular becoming at first appear to have little in common. Deleuze's own taste in films reflected the Parisian *cinéaste* canon of his habitus and he was deeply suspicious of certain 'mass' forms, particularly the 'bad cinema' of explicit violence and sex (Deleuze in Flaxman 2000: 367). Produced by forces of 'gratuitous cruelty and organised ineptitude', he claims, bad cinema 'travels through lower-brain circuits' (ibid.). On reading Deleuze's work more closely, however, European horror film motifs appear as a strand in his thought not overtly acknowledged.

Deleuze explores European cinema's more philosophical and psychological work and its extreme phenomena: hallucination, madness, the visions of the dying, nightmare and dream (see Deleuze 1989: 55). He focuses specifically on classic expressionist and surrealist works such as *The Cabinet of Doctor Caligari* (Robert Wiene, 1920) and *Vampyr* (Carl-Theodor Dreyer, 1932) not as horror films *per se* but as tools to think through the aesthetics of light and dark and their terrifying metaphysics.

Deleuze acknowledges the aesthetic force of Italian horror film in one brief reference to Mario Bava's work as an impulse-image. Yet his insights are not limited by his own canon but come to us ready for active extension by further application. In the following brief encounter with *Suspiria* (1977), *Inferno* (1980) and *Phantom of the Opera* (1998) and other Argento films I will argue that Deleuze's insights can be used to rethink both these and the broader cinematic sensorium of horror.

THE CINEMATIC SENSORIUM

A Deleuzian approach to film looks elsewhere than plot and theme. Its focus is on stylistic affects as they impact upon screen and viewer, viscera and brain as a continuum. Specific cinematic devices fuel Deleuze's philosophical speculations, including *mise-en-scène*, camera movement and editing. In *Cinema 2: The Time-Image* (1989) he identifies three types of images: opsigns, sonsigns and tactisigns. These unextended images do not develop into plot action and cannot be processed as narrative components. I argue that Argento's work, although overtly generic, is filled with such images that work to unravel clear storylines and psychologically plausible characters.

Argento's work, with its perversely erotic plot content, has attracted the kind of psychoanalytic readings usually applied to the horror genre (see Mendik 2000, 2003; Schneider 2004). Although they provide useful theorisations of overt psychosexual themes and symbols, I will contest them here. Deleuze's critique consistently refutes the symbolic 'archaeology' of psychoanalysis. As Steven Shaviro provocatively contends, semiotic and psychoanalytic approaches to film want to normalise or 'oedipalise' historically specific devices of mechanical reproduction and their corresponding obsession with the scopic regime.

Deleuze instead asserts a cinema of sensation via 'affect, excitation, stimulation and repression, pleasure and pain, shock and habit' (Shaviro 1993: 27). Shaviro argues that vision is grounded 'in the rhythms and delays of an ungraspable temporality, and in the materiality of the agitated flesh' (1993: 45). Instead of reading horror film through abjection like the Kristevan Barbara Creed, he aligns it with the viewer's position in a more celebratory way (see Creed 1993). With specific reference to Argento's films, Shaviro feels 'powerless not to see' footage which compels him into a 'forced, ecstatic abjection before the image' (1993: 49).

When watching material extreme in style as well as content, the spectator's optic nerves and auditory membranes struggle to process fragmented and overloaded data. As perceptual frameworks are undermined, we slide into a molecular assemblage with the body of the film. Made of images, like our thoughts themselves, on-screen affects and percepts hook into the sensorium as the film gets into our bloodstream by viral infection. It continues to live in our embodied minds as memories that can be recalled into the present as coloured and living images with corresponding sensations.

Film viewing involves the eye, and much more than the eye as a distanced, controlling gaze. It is a mental encounter with images made through the viscera. On-screen images are, in one sense, non-material simulacra, yet the viewer encounters them corporeally. They stimulate the neuronal networks with biologically quantifiable affects: increased pace of heartbeat and breathing, genital arousal and goose-bumps. For Gilles Deleuze and Félix Guattari, such encounters operate by *mimesis* that both copies and materially connects objects together. Slumped in our cinema seat, or at home in front of the TV screen, our customary body maps can potentially become bodies-without-organs, a concept I will return to later.

Working overtly on sight and sound, films simulate other senses via haptic engagement and synaesthesia, although smell and taste often depend on verbal description or characters' reaction shots. By watching characters touch objects and each other on screen, we sense the affect of sensation on the skin's surface, and experience visceral responses of our own. The engaged viewer recalls memories of tactility, recreates the corresponding corporeal affect and 'feels' it direct.

Deleuze and Guattari present art as the language of sensation, 'composed of percepts, affects, and blocs of sensation that take the place of language' (1984: 176). By this apparent refutation of symbolic content, they advocate looking elsewhere, beyond ideological/semiotic equations or representations. Yet art does more than just reproduce the sensory stimulus in the organ. It sets up 'a being of the sensory, a being of sensation, on an anorganic plane of composition' (Deleuze and Guattari 1991: 302), as part of a more radical and potentially micropolitical process. Virtual becoming potentialises actual change. Specifically, Deleuze and Guattari assert that 'sensation is pure contemplation, for it is through contemplation that one contracts, contemplating oneself to the extent that one contemplates the elements from which one originates. Contemplating is creating, the mystery of passive creation, sensation [is a kind of] self-enjoyment' (1991: 212). So how might cinematic sensations operate via the colour, sound and texture of Argento's films?

SENSATIONAL COLOUR: SPECTRAL HORROR

'[Colour] immediately renders a force visible' (Deleuze 2003: 151)

Argento offers a Poe-esque sensorial palette of forces designed to frighten and arouse. Densely saturated blues and reds, with subsidiary purple and gold, are used most frequently, either singly or in combination, to overpower the eye's cognitive capacities. These lurid colours lack nuance and assault the sensorium with their perverse mimicry of the Disney cartoon spectrum (see Shulte-Sasse 2002).

Red predominates as a variety of vibrant shades, from pink to deep crimson.

In *Suspiria*, red is first glimpsed on an anonymous woman at the airport when American dance student Suzy Bannion (Jessica Harper) arrives. Red light invades Suzy's cab and tints the rain to the colour of blood. She next sees red on a terrified student fleeing the ancient Freiburg Dance Academy. The academy still honours the *fin-de-siècle* tastes of its undead witch queen Helene Marcos. Its sanguine exterior and the claustrophobic opulence of interior sets function as a Deleuzian 'pure description of world which replaces the situation' and emanates an oppressive atmosphere of surveillance that blurs logical thought and saps will (Deleuze 1989: 63).

For Deleuze, film colour is used in a dream-like way not limited to an oneiric symbol system. He explains that 'colour is dream, not because the dream is in colour, but because colours ... are given a highly absorbent, almost devouring value' which we must struggle against to avoid 'losing ourselves and being snatched away' (ibid.). As in the paintings of Francis Bacon, colour 'immediately renders a force visible' (Deleuze 2003: 151). In the world of Argento's film, colour forces are vampiric tools for the coven to drain their victims' life.

Solid scarlet coats the outer walls of this house of blood, spreading inside via wallpaper and drapes in an expressive series: décor, wine, nail varnish, lipstick as well as its most potent source, human blood. Arterial red is complimented by venous blue with which it alternates by means of velvet curtains and wallpaper as well as lighting. Blue shades range from indigo to purple, at times shifting to sickly green. This Technicolor palette vibrates in us intensively, oppressing but at the same time arousing us. It drains the strength of the good characters by absorbing their life-energy and glowing brighter, yet it is challenged by Suzy's pure white.

In *Inferno* likewise, blues and reds are heavily saturated in and around the sinister apartment block, running into a rich purple where they blend. The 'very strange bittersweet smell' noted by Rose (Irene Miracle), is perhaps their scent correspondence, and makes Mark (Leigh McCloskey) gag when he smells it neat, seeping from a ventilation shaft. The predominance of blue and red pipes, tubes and water channels work as a kind of architectural venous system conveying poison from the centre of the building's system and drawing the victims' life-force into it as vampiric sustenance.

Despite the distinctions of painting and film, Deleuze's insights on Bacon's colouration are relevant to a study of cinematic colour. Painters apply colour to static canvases, mobilising virtual movement and energy in the space constrained by the frame. Deleuze considers the complex relations of colour regimes and their tonal harmonies (2003: 151). His imagery of spatialising energy expresses natural dynamics in 'the shores of vivid colours and the flows of broken colours' (2003: 142). Such vibrant interrelations are expressed in different ways by colour film.

For Deleuze, colour is a qualitative force and he elides both these terms as 'colour-force'. The crux of Deleuzian colourism is the affective vibrational perception of intensive force (Deleuze 2003: 160). The sensorial affect of colours works through the speed of their light vibrations. He presents colour as a stimulus and modulator of the 'colouring sensation' (2003: 112). Tonal relations have a tactile as well as a visual dimension.

The characterisation of colours as 'warm' or 'cool' is based on their spectral complementarity. Modulation of intensity or saturation is determined by relations of colours to their ground on canvas or within the film frame. The frame delimits the content of the shot, but the colours themselves are already in vibrational motion. Intensive, on-the-spot motion combines with the more extensive movements of camera, characters and editing to unlock the virtual forces of affect.

The intensive quality of Argento's colour is made overt in *Phantom of the Opera*. It reaches a particularly affective climax in the *dénouement* scene, in which the Phantom/Eric is killed. It begins with a camera glide through the sparkling blue-tinged facets of the crystal chandelier down onto the stage where the diva Christine (Asia Argento) sings. The deep blue of the Phantom's (Julian Sands) cavern is given a supernatural quality in some late sequences. Within the blue light and black shadow a ghostly red glow appears. Its intensity drains the natural colour from Christine's anguished face as her fiancée rows her away from the dying Eric. The technical quality of this enhanced affect perhaps results from push-processing the film, digital colour optimisation or post-processing solarisation. The most Deleuzian possibility here would be machinic automatism. In this case, the enhanced colour effect would have been an unintentional technical blip caused by burning cine film onto DVD. Colour affects us as an optical sensation. Our whole body is caught up in the affects of colours as we vibrate in unison with them.

Vision is an organic conduit between inside and out. It operates as reflected and refracted light waves stimulate the retinal contractions and pass through the eye. In Argento's horror films, eyes are insistently present as organs. They are delicate 'soft machines', easily torn from their sockets in *Inferno* and *Terror at the Opera/Opera* (1987). There is much symbolic play with eyes and blindness in *Suspiria* via Suzy's wide-open eyes and the blindness of Daniel the pianist (Flavio Bucci).

Via Deleuze, I assert the eye as a pivotal cog in the whole cinematic sensorium. Vision mobilises at least two senses. Deleuze describes its capacity to mix with other sensory properties and its subsequent expansion of perceptual scope. Rather than the optical separatism of those theories of the gaze inspired by Laura Mulvey (1975), Deleuze argues that film, like painting 'gives us eyes all over: in the ear, in the stomach, in the lungs' and that the spectator's eye itself is a 'polyvalent and transitory organ' (2003: 52). In *Terror at the Opera*, psychotic police inspector Alan Santini (Urbano Barberini) fixes razor spikes beneath the eye-sockets of diva Betty (Cristina Marsillach), forcing her eyes wide open to witness his murders. In images of optical tactility like these, Argento's aesthetics forcibly extend vision to incorporate the sensation of touch.

TACTISIGNS

Argento evokes the tactile impact of both natural and occult phenomena. As well as terrifying sights and sounds, his films compel us to encounter affectively repulsive textures, such as the wet stickiness of human blood or the squidginess of maggots. Rather than Julia Kristeva's (1982) symbolic identification of the abject as matter out of place, my focus is on the sensorial impact of repellent stimuli.

In Argento's films, elaborate pursuit, torture and murder produce tactisigns to excruciating degrees. Inflicted by mostly invisible torturers, their affective potency is increased by the lack of any distancing subject/object split. This is further intensified by extreme close-up. Knife blades dominate the screen as they gash into flesh, and internal organs are torn loose and exposed. When Sara, one of *Suspiria*'s victims, believes she has escaped, she falls into a bed of wire coils. They clutch and slice her, trapping her further as she struggles. She dies an agonising death by tactility, cut to shreds by metal wires then strangled.

Animal-life is a key source of tactile horror. In *Suspiria*, a swarm of maggots invade the dormitories, touching the sensitive skin of the undressed dancers. Three fat white maggots squirm between the teeth of Suzy's comb, and her fingers lift one up. Thousands of maggots land in their hair and squirm on the floor and the girls are compelled to squash them with shoes or naked feet. The use of close-up intensifies the viewer's virtual sensation of slime, squirming larvae and viscous texture.

In *Phantom of the Opera*, the tactile property of rats is foregrounded more than their narrative function. This obsessive textural focus ranges from the rat-catchers' mincing them in the blades of their sweeper truck and squeezing blood from their chopped-off tails, to the Phantom's stroking of their fur and erotic rapport with

Death by touch: Sara is shredded (*Suspiria*, 1977)

the rodents that rove under his clothes and on his naked flesh.

Deleuze's work analyses the relationship of touch and sight, interconnected in the digital, the manual and the haptic. The digital marks subordination of hand to eye, but the optical retains depth, contour and relief. The manual reverses hand/eye relation. Formless space and restless motion exceeds the eye's capacity and dismantles the purely optical. The most significant relation between hand and eye is haptic. Including distinctive elements of touch, the haptic elides the visual and the tactile in the 'tactile-optical function' (Deleuze 2003: 151).

The 'tactisign' is 'a touching which is specific to the gaze' (1989: 12). Not an extensive act of the hand, it is the intensive sensation of touch 'on condition that the hand relinquishes it's prehensile and motor functions to content itself with a pure touching' (ibid.). In other words, we haptically produce our own virtual sensation of touch as in the sticky, thickening texture of blood, the dripping wetness of rainwater or the soft smothering quality of velvet walls. More overtly, we feel with fingers the dancers' fingers searching hair for maggots or the ripping of the dressmaker's flesh by scissors in *Terror at the Opera*. As well as colour, light and touch, I want to offer a few Deleuzian pointers to the films' powerful battery of electronic sounds.

SONSIGNS

In Argento's dubbed films, the effect of lip-sync glitches, voices by other actors and the stilted formality of dialogue shift emphasis away from linguistic signification to other sonic affects. The rare silences also have ominous intent. Our ears are assaulted by sounds from the piercing clarity of sopranos and orchestral music to a barrage of synthesised electronic effects, so that the listener's vibrating aural nerves become part of the noise assemblage.

Tweeters, clangs and enhanced echoes are used to powerful effect. In a particularly Sadeian scene from *Suspiria*, Daniel is led across a vast, empty square by his guide dog. The dark space is filled with an ominous silence broken by the hollow tapping of the man's cane and the panting of the dog's breath. The animal's sudden burst of aggression is impelled both by sourceless winged shadows that sweep across the square and by rustles, squeaks and reverberations that madden the aural nerves. Like the viewer, Daniel is only able to feel and hear the forces that assail him, and is savaged by the possessed dog that tears out his throat.

Sound techniques with an exaggerated, hyper-real echo are deployed as affective devices. The electronic chords and discords of the rock band Goblin create a rich sound texture in *Suspiria*. Whirring, whispering, sawing and hollow booming without any diegetic source grate on the spectator's hearing mechanisms and stimulate anxiety, as in the jarring electronic chords before the first murder we witness that sound like the twittering of bats. The tapping and thudding of ballet dancers' shoes resonates with a hollow echo on the floorboards and the thumping and slapping of *schuhplattler* dancers swells to an infernal volume. In *Inferno*, the natural sounds of wind and rain are electronically enhanced by Keith Emerson's synthesiser to convey their force of supernatural threat, a literal 'witches' wind' both outside and within the sinister apartment block.

Female singing voices in *Terror at the Opera* and *Phantom of the Opera* are crystal-clear, with a hollow tonal quality that stands out in isolation from the broader sound mix. Even when the opera diva sings in one spot, she moves dynamically by the sonsign vibrations and modulations of her voice. For Deleuze and Guattari, music has a special status in relation to becoming.

Patricia Pisters usefully contrasts psychoanalytic perspectives on sound with those of Deleuze and Guattari. For them, she suggests, 'sound has nothing to do with castration anxiety, jouissance, or an encounter with the Real', but is a potent catalyst for molecular becomings (2003: 188). For Deleuze, sound is a more potent force of deterritorialisation than sight, because, as sound becomes more refined 'it tends to dissolve and connects with other elements easily in a machinic way' (ibid.). The sound quality of a song exceeds the signification of its lyrics.

Dubbing means that the actress lip-syncs lyrics supposed to come from her heart, rendering their sincerity doubtful. Pisters reminds us that in psychoanalytic film theory (see Silverman 1988), the female singing voice is seen in 'a negative (lethal) although fascinating way' and specifically, the opera diva's voice functions as a classic Lacanian *objet petit a* (2003: 197). Deleuze and Guattari's interest lies elsewhere, in the 'machining' function of voice in the assemblage.

What Pisters calls the 'lulling' lover's refrain acts to territorialise the loved one's sexuality. But the diva's showpiece improvisations have a deterritorialising function and serve as an opening opening to forces of chaos. When Christine sings to the Phantom's organ notes, her over-shrill dissonances are screams of desire. Deleuze gives the improvisations of the *ritornello* a metaphysical quality. He connects this sound, made 'at the limits of language' with the singularity retained by a soul 'when it takes to the open road' at the limits of the body that produces it (1998a: 187).

Sound waves travel though us and work strongly on the sensorium, bypassing the cerebral cortex and mainlining into our central nervous system, a process exacerbated by the extreme sensory bombardment of horror. Deleuze's work on post-World War II European cinema mentions the 'pure' sonsign. Like its corresponding opsigns, sound serves to cancel 'ordinary sensory-motor links' and is not necessarily connected to motor extension (1989: 62). Pure sound situations break from the narrative drive of the movement/action image to offer the more philosophical kind of cinema of 'pure contemplation' (1989: 6).

Suspiria's *dénouement* is a typically flamboyant sensory showpiece. Suzy enters the hidden chambers of the coven via its magic art nouveau key, a blue-coloured metal iris in a wall frieze. She accidentally knocks over a glass peacock ornament, which encapsulates the film's colour scheme in miniature (see Shulte-Sasse 2002). When Suzy pierces Marcos, the amorphous, shadowy witch-queen, with a triangular shard of glass, she forces her to materialise in the partial form of organs without a body. Her mouth, eyes and hands, each one a sensory tool hideously bloated, appear from the dark in isolation to perceive and at the same time terrify her assailant. Electronically-mixed slowed-down sound is used to deepen and distort Marcos's voice. In a finale of heat and colour, the red academy is finally burned down in a conflagration of scarlet flames. This hellish red is repeated in *Inferno* when the apartment block is similarly engulfed.

The aggressively expanded sensorium of Argento's films demand bodily responses. Yet the nature of this affected body is problematised by Deleuze and Guattari's concept of the body without organs. I would like to close this brief study with a fuller consideration of the relevance of this term to the films.

ARGENTO'S BODIES WITHOUT ORGANS

Argento's serial killers leave the screen strewn with literal bodies without organs. Yet it is important to clarify that these are not necessarily Deleuze and Guattari's bodies-without-organs. Here, Argento's films present us with a conundrum. For Deleuze and Guattari, the body-without-organs is not used in its obvious meaning of an eviscerated corpse. Their focus is not 'organs without bodies, or the fragmented body', but a 'body-without-organs, animated by various intensive movements' in process of becoming (1988: 171). Yet although the killers' graphically dismembered victims are literal bodies-without-organs, it is the style of these films that mobilises a powerful series of intensive affects via the cinematic sensorium.

Deleuze and Guattari's body-without-organs, with its 'poles, zones, thresholds and gradients ... traversed by a powerful, nonorganic vitality' is figured geographically (Deleuze 1998b: 131). In a Gothic move, Argento extends *élan vital* to the nonorganic locales of the murders, as buildings, corridors and rooms are impregnated with the force of the hero/heroine's fear and the victims' anguish and pain.

Obviously, Argento's films also affect the spectator's own neurological body via their excessively sanguine *mise-en-scène*. As well as saturated colour of blues, purples and reds and the disorienting flicker of catastrophe curve reflections, the sensory palette includes opulent and repulsive textures and intensive sounds of heartbeats, footsteps, and nerve-grating electronic noise. Deleuze and Guattari's description of the smooth space as a body-without-organs can be applied to the screened films of Argento. Instead of being an organisation, they argue, perception is 'based on symptoms and evaluations rather than measures and properties. That is why smooth space is occupied by intensities, wind and noise, forces, and sonorous and tactile qualities' (1988: 479). Drawing on their theories my chapter remaps Argento's cinematic sensorium as a body-without-organs.

Deleuzian horror films set out to threaten the wholeness of body and mind, transforming the embodied mind of the spectator as well as bodies on screen. Like the buildings, the entire films are themselves Deleuzian bodies-without-organs, a shifting assemblage of image/forces on physical and mental planes. Viewer and film interlock in a machinic assemblage of movement-image as we undergo the deterritorialisation of an 'intensive voyage' (Deleuze and Guattari 1984: 319).

The 'Cinema' books are part of Deleuze's wider philosophical project to assert that 'the brain is the screen', and to validate his interpretation of Henri Bergson's view of the universe as metacinema (see Deleuze 2000: 366). European horror films like Argento's are, I suggest, productive of embodied thought both during and after the encounter. We think as well as feel films directly on our nerve-endings, 'inside' with affects and ideas and 'outside' as we are bombarded with perceptions. Through the senses, cinema is capable of inducing perceptual thoughts of a philosophical kind on the nature of time, space and motion as well as offering a self-reflexive exploration of perception itself.

Through the cinematic sensorium, the films of Argento may arouse us erotically, make us feel sick or move us to tears. Nevertheless, the perceptual continuum between actual and virtual always retains a gap or interval. Here, in the interstice between sensuous engagement and conceptual reflection, Deleuze and Guattari offer us a set of tools to begin rethinking the European horror film.

BIBLIOGRAPHY

Castricano, J. (2002) 'For the Love of Smoke and Mirrors: Dario Argento's *Inferno*', *Kino–Eye*, 2, June 10. On-line. Available HTTP: http://www.kinoeye.org/02/11/castricano11.php (6 August 2007).
Creed, B. (1993) *The Monstrous Feminine: Women in the Horror Film*. Manchester: Manchester University Press.
Deleuze, G. (1989) *Cinema 2: The Time-Image*. Trans. H. Tomlinson and R. Galeta. London: Athlone.
_____ (1998a) 'Bartleby; or the Formula', in *Essays Critical and Clinical*. Trans. D. W. Smith and M. A. Greco. London and New York: Verso, 68–90.
_____ (1998b) 'To Have Done with Judgement', in *Essays Critical and Clinical*. Trans. D. W. Smith and M. A. Greco. London and New York: Verso, 126–36.
_____ (2000) 'The Brain is the Screen', in G. A. Flaxman (ed.) *The Brain is the Screen: Deleuze and the Philosophy of Cinema*. Minnesota: University of Minnesota Press. 365–75.
_____ (2003) *Francis Bacon: The Logic of Sensation*. Trans. D. W. Smith. London: Continuum.
Deleuze, G. and F. Guattari (1984) *Anti-Oedipus: Capitalism and Schizophrenia*. Trans. R. Hurley, M. Seem and H. R. Lane. London: Athlone.
_____ (1988) *A Thousand Plateaus: Capitalism and Schizophrenia*. Trans. Brian Massumi. London: Athlone.
_____ (1991) *What is Philosophy?* Trans. G. Burchill and H. Tomlinson. London: Verso.

Flaxman G. A. (ed.) (2000) *The Brain is the Screen: Deleuze and the Philosophy of Cinema*. Minnesota: University of Minnesota Press.

Kristeva, J. (1982) *Powers of Horror: An Essay on Abjection*. Trans. L. S. Roudiez. New York: Columbia University Press.

Mendik, X. (2000) *Tenebre/Tenebrae*. London: Flicks Books.

_____ (2003) *Dario Argento*. On-line. Available HTTP: http://www.sensesofcinema.com/contents/directors/03/argento.html (7 August 2007).

Mulvey, L. (1975) 'Visual Pleasure and Narrative Cinema', *Screen*, 16: 3, 6–18.

Pisters, P. (2003) *The Matrix of Visual Culture: Working with Deleuze in Film Theory*. Stanford, CA: Stanford University Press.

Schneider, S. J. (2004) *Horror Film and Psychoanalysis: Freud's Worst Nightmare*. Cambridge: Cambridge University Press.

Shaviro, S. (1993) *The Cinematic Body*. Minneapolis: University of Minnesota Press.

Shulte-Sasse, L. (2002) '*Suspiria*: The "Mother" of All Horror Movies', *Kino–Eye*, 2: 11, 10 June. On-line. Available HTTP: http://www.kinoeye.org/02/11/schultesasse11.php (27 August 2007).

Silverman, K. (1988) *The Acoustic Mirror: The Female Voice in Psychoanalysis and Cinema*. Bloomington, IN: Indiana University Press.

GERMAN AND NORTHERN EUROPEAN HORROR CINEMA

GERMAN AND NORTHERN EUROPEAN HORROR CINEMA

Patricia Allmer, Emily Brick and David Huxley

The history of the horror film in Germany is a chequered one. The early flowering of silent 'expressionist' films, in particular *The Golem* (Paul Wegener and Henrik Galeen, 1915), *Das Kabinett des Dr Caligari/The Cabinet of Dr Caligari* (Robert Wiene, 1920) and *Nosferatu* (F. W. Murnau, 1922) is taken to be crucial in the formation of horror cinema and a discussion of these films forms the opening section of almost every historical overview of the genre. However after the 1920s there seems to be no subsequent coherent horror tradition. Part of the reason for this appears to be obvious – the changing political climate in Germany meant that there had been no tradition of 'degenerate' horror production coming out of the Nazi era and so many practitioners had moved to Hollywood that it could be argued that German horror film relocated to America, with German influence surfacing in the Universal horror films of the 1930s. Initially German directors such as Murnau had moved to Hollywood, lured by the possibilities it promised in terms of opportunities and finance, whereas later *émigrés* such as Fritz Lang and Robert Siodmak moved to escape the Nazi regime.

The few sporadic horror films released in the immediate aftermath of World War II were, perhaps understandably, not well received. This is despite the fact that films like Fritz Böttger's *Ein Toter Hing im Netz/Horrors of Spider Island* (1959) were no worse than many other cheap 'B' picture horror films being produced at that time. Steffen Hantke has argued that part of the problem has been 'a lack of generic self awareness' in German film but adds 'fans know very well that some great horror films have been coming out of Germany for the last fifty odd years' (2007: xv, viii). Nevertheless the fact remains that there is no large consistent body of horror film production in post-war Germany (or other parts of Northern Europe). This was certainly not due to a lack of infrastructure as in 1911 UFA had founded the Babelsberg Studios, which grew into one of the largest film production facilities in the world. Possibly some changes in post-war national characteristics and sensibilities could account for this lack of horror production.

Certainly Lotte Eisner's judgement of the German character, originally written in 1952, seems to be a gross oversimplification, not supported by the facts of the immediate post-war period: 'The weird pleasure the Germans take in evoking horror can perhaps be ascribed to the excessive and very Germanic desire to submit to discipline, together with a certain proneness to sadism' (1969: 95).

A successful trend was created with a series of thrillers beginning with *Der Frosch mit der Maske/Fellowship of the Frog* (Harald Reinl, 1959) which are often seen as proto-horror films. Based on the novels of British writer Edgar Wallace and christened '*krimis*', the increasing violence and emphasis on murder scenes in these films throughout the 1960s certainly place them within a broad definition of the horror film. Reinl's *Die Schlangengrube und das Pendel/The Blood Demon* (1967) is clearly a more traditional gothic horror, with Christopher Lee starring as Count Regula, the 'blood demon' of the title. However in 1979 there was a major, big-budget German horror production when the respected director Werner Herzog returned to the origins of German horror cinema with the production of a new version of Murnau's *Nosferatu*. Not strictly a remake, Herzog's version, starring Klaus Kinski as the vampire, was widely regarded as being successful in achieving Herzog's stated aim of 'building a bridge to the expressionist era' (Badley 2007: 60).

But it was a series of largely underground, maverick directors who began a more sustained revival of German horror cinema. In 1974 hardcore pornography was legalised in Germany; this had the duel effect of damaging the market for softcore exploitation films which had proliferated since the 1960s and at the same time opening the way for filmmakers to address more extreme and taboo subject matter through the vehicle of the horror film. It was not until 1987 that this new potential freedom was exercised in full with Andreas Schnaas's *Violent Shit* (1989), a low-budget splatter film which looked like an updated version of Hershell Gordon Lewis's American gore films of the 1960s, and spawned a number of similar sequels. These new directors were able to take advantage of new technology, video equipment and cheap lightweight cameras.

The most famous of them, Jörg Buttgereit, produced four feature films, beginning with *Nekromantik* in 1987, all of which dealt with a combination of elements including necrophilia, mutilation, grave robbing and torture in a graphic, sometimes *cinéma vérité* style. The morbid fascination and unrelenting vision of Buttgereit caused censorship problems even in the comparatively liberal climate of 1980s West Germany (see Stevenson 1991). This extreme low-budget tradition has continued with controversial directors such as Uwe Boll and Timo Rose, with the former's video-game inspired films leading to an online petition requesting him to desist from filmmaking altogether. There have also been some internationally successful larger-budget productions, including Stefan Ruzowitzky's *Anatomie/Anatomy* (2000) and the Austrian director, Michael Haneke's *Funny Games* (1997). Whilst the former film fits into a tradition of 'medical horrors' *Funny Games* and

Haneke's subsequent films have caused controversy with an unusual combination of extreme violence and subversion of genre expectations which Thomas Elsaesser has described as 'disturbingly post-modern' (1999: 10). Haneke's films tie in with and continue art movements in Austria, such as the Viennese Actionists, which tried to shake up radically an ongoing complacency in relation to the Nazi regime, particularly strongly anchored in and enforced by the bourgeoisie.

Mark Jancovich's chapter discusses the career of German *émigré* Robert Siodmak and examines the way in which his Hollywood output was seen as 'chillers' or 'thrillers' by contemporary critics. Jancovich demonstates the way in which these films have been retrospectively appropriated into the *noir* canon and problematises generic definitions of the horror film. Samuel Umland's chapter demonstrates the sharedness of history between Germany and Sweden and examines the shadow cast by the Nazi era, comparing Fritz Lang's *Testament of Dr Mabuse* (1933) and Ingmar Bergman's *Das Schlangenei/The Serpent's Egg* (1977). Catherine Wheatley's chapter deals exclusively with Michael Haneke. It focuses in particular on *Funny Games* and *Benny's Video* (1992) and the way in which, through these films, Haneke examines the breakdown of bourgeois society into increasingly violent, uncontrollable behaviour.

BIBLIOGRAPHY

Badley, L. (2007) 'Kinski's Nosferatu, and the Myths of Authorship', in S. Hantke (ed.) *Caligari's Heirs: The German Cinema of Fear after 1945*. Lanham: Scarecrow Press, 57–78.
Eisner, L. (1969) *The Haunted Screen*. Berkeley, CA: University of California Press.
Elsaesser, T. (1999) 'German Cinema in the 1990s', in *The BFI Companion to the German Cinema*. London: British Film Institute, 3–16.
Hantke, S. (ed.) (2007) *Caligari's Heirs: The German Cinema of Fear after 1945*. Lanham: Scarecrow Press.
Stevenson, J. (1991) 'Sex, Death, Animal Porno and Lesbian Vampires: Censorship and the Cinema in Germany: One Story', in *Shock Express*. London: Titan Books, 53–9.

'A FORMER DIRECTOR OF GERMAN HORROR FILM':
HORROR, EUROPEAN CINEMA AND THE CRITICAL RECEPTION OF ROBERT SIODMAK'S HOLLYWOOD CAREER

Mark Jancovich

Although Robert Siodmak is best known today as the director of a number of *film noir* classics, particularly *Phantom Lady* (1944) and *The Killers* (1946), in the mid-1940s, when he made these films, he was known primarily as a director of horror films, and was marketed by Universal as 'Robert "Goose Bumps" Siodmak' (see Greco 1999: 24). Indeed, it is often acknowledged that *film noir* is a retrospective term applied to films by critics of later periods, and not a term that was used to classify these films in the original contexts of their production, mediation or consumption (see Naremore 1998). Furthermore, as I have argued elsewhere, many of these films were originally identified as horror films and, while the thriller and the horror film are seen as quite separate categories today, they were virtually indistinguishable categories during the 1940s.

One sign of this close association between the thriller and the horror film was their association with directors strongly connected with German cinema. For example, 1944–45 saw the release of four films that are seen as representing the consolidation of *film noir*, all four of which were directed by *émigré* directors associated with German cinema (Fritz Lang, *Woman in the Window*; Otto Preminger, *Laura*; Robert Siodmak, *Phantom Lady*; and Billy Wilder, *Double Indemnity*), and each of these films were identified as horror on their original release in the United States. In its review of *Phantom Lady*, the *New York Times* even explained this association when it referred to Siodmak as 'a former director of German horror films' (Crowther 1944a). In other words, German cinema was seen as having a strong affinity with horror materials, which explains why these émigré directors were put to work on horror-related materials as the 1940s horror cycle gained momentum after the success of Jacques Tourneur's *Cat People* in 1942 (see Snelson 2009). However, it is important to remember that this association with horror was largely a matter of the industry's perception of German cinema and the directors associated with it, and many of these directors had no prior connection with the German expressionist cinema. As Lutz Koepnick points out, 'when considering the ways in which exile film workers may have imported Weimar sensibilities to Hollywood, acts of performative repetition and unforeseen redress clearly outnumbered instance of direct transfer' (2003: 85; see also Koepnick 2002), and he cites the example of Siodmak, whose 'directorship prior to Hollywood had showed no expressionist predilections whatsoever' (ibid.).

Robert Siodmak will also provide the focus for this chapter, which will examine the critical reception of his films to explore the ways in which they were understood generically. If, as we have already seen, their status as horror films were strongly associated with Siodmak's supposed status as 'a former director of German horror films', this chapter will also suggest that the supposedly Germanic qualities of these films raised a number of anxieties about the boundaries between art and entertainment. In other words, films that were simply defined as entertainment were often viewed more positively than those that were seen as too 'arty', and hence as 'pretentious' horror films.

On his arrival in Hollywood in the 1940s, the industry seems to have had little sense of what to do with Siodmak, but he eventually proved lucky with *Son of Dracula* (1943), which he directed for Universal. The film did not receive good notices, and the *New York Times* claimed that it 'is often as unintentionally funny as it is chilling' (A.W. 1943: 16). None the less, it earned him a contract with Universal and established an identity for him as a director.

Siodmak's next film, *Phantom Lady*, was therefore described as the latest of his 'superior chillers' (Winsten 1944a), and as 'a killer-diller of a horror yarn', which confirmed that Loew's Criterion, where it was being shown, was 'the place for horror fans this week' (Creelman 1944). Furthermore, it was in relation to *Phantom Lady* that the *New York Times* made the above-mentioned claim that Siodmak was 'a former director of German horror films', a term that it used interchangeably with the phrase 'German psychological films'. The film was also associated with Hitchcock through its producer, Joan Harrison, 'who was associated with producer-director Alfred Hitchcock for eight years as secretary, reader and scripter' (Crowther 1944a). As a result, the *New York Times* wished that it 'could recommend [the film] as a perfect combination of the styles of the eminent Mr. Hitchcock and the old German psychological films, for that is what it tries very hard to be. It is full of light and shadow, of macabre atmosphere, of sharply realistic faces and dramatic injections of sound' (ibid.). However, the review is ultimately unconvinced by the collaboration.

While the film is seen as a classic example of *film noir* today, it was also strongly associated with the paranoid woman's film during the 1940s, through its strong female lead, who acts as an 'amateur detective to unravel a strange murder' (Walt. 1944), and it is claimed that the 'whole story is the girl's quest' (Cook 1944). It is even suggested that there is a shift 'about half way through the movie when the audience is let in on' the identity of the killer and that, through this shift, the story changes from a whodunnit so that the heroine finds herself under threat from an unreadable 'neurotic' killer (Crowther 1944a), a situation that replicated a central feature of the paranoid woman's film.

However, while many critics praised the film, others were more wary. For example, James Agee felt that 'the film is being talked about too excitedly' (1944: 261). Similarly, the *New York Times* relished the prospect of a collaboration between Siodmak and Harrison, which promised 'something severe and unrelenting, drenched in creeping morbidity and gloom', but ultimately took exception to the film's narrative, which was claimed to lack a 'plausible, reasonable plot' (Crowther 1944a). While it is 'studiously constructed for its weird and disturbing effects', the film is condemned on the grounds that 'sensation is specious without reason' but that 'reason is what this picture lacks'. Given that the *New York Times* review of Siodmak's *The Spiral Staircase* (1945) would later praise the film as a 'shocker plain and simple' (T.M.P. 1946a), as a film that never attempted to offer anything more than mere visceral thrills, it would seem that its objection to the sensationalism of *Phantom Lady* was more due to the film's ambitions. While the *New York Times* did not object to the lack of a plausible plot in films that had no pretensions to be anything other than entertaining fantasies, it is probably the association with Hitchcock, and with the German psychological horror films, that were a problem in the case of *Phantom Lady*.

For all the *New York Times*' criticisms, *Phantom Lady* was a commercial success and it established Siodmak's image as an important film director. His next picture was therefore 'a spectacular production, screened in glorious Technicolor and staged in the grand Hollywood manner' (O'Connor 1944). However, if *Phantom Lady* was accused of aiming too high, this next production, *Cobra Woman* (1944), was seen as aiming too low. It was also far from being a straight horror film, and was described as one that will probably please 'those who like fantastic films of adventure' (ibid.). However, the association with horror was still present, partly through the presence of Lon Chaney Jr, Universal's key horror star in the period, and through its title, which evoked an association with the cycle of female monster movies that followed the phenomenal success of *Cat People* in 1942 (see Snelson 2009). The reviews also picked up on this association so that *Hollywood Reporter* claimed that the film combines 'two formulas that have coined fortunes for Universal. Into the lush, tropical backgrounds where Maria Montez is accustomed to distort herself in eye-watering Technicolor, a definite note of horror is strongly injected' (Anon. 1944: 4). Similarly, the *New York Post* argued that Universal's 'next South Sea picture' should feature 'Bela Lugosi, quite mad and scientific ... just to make it complete' (Winsten 1944b).

However, *Cobra Woman*'s key feature was presumed to be its sex appeal. For the *New York Newspaper PM*, this was a film of 'lissom legs, thinly clad breasts and sizzling jungle love-making' that is recommended with 'one long, low whistle' (McManus 1944). However, while it was largely dismissed as a rather ridiculous affair, in which 'the intelligence level of the whole thing is that of the chimpanzee' that appears within it (Crowther 1944b), there is little sense of concern expressed about the film and it is even claimed that audiences that 'go in the right frame of mind ... might find amusement in the absurdities of the plot and in the antics of Montez, Hall and company' (Cameron 1944).

If *Cobra Woman* was a pleasantly absurd romp, *Christmas Holiday* was seen as a depressing and sordid venture despite the presence of another 'pathological killer' (Barnes 1944). For the *New York Times*, the film's problem was not so much its seedy subject matter but rather its failure to tackle this subject matter directly. It is therefore described as the story of a young soldier that 'falls in with a melancholy "hostess" in a questionable New Orleans "club" and becomes the grave and sympathetic listener to this young lady's tale of woe' (Crowther 1944c). In other words, for the *New York Times*, the 'hostess' is clearly a prostitute and that the 'club' is clearly a brothel but the film's problem is that, due to the restrictions of the Production Code, it does not admit this. The review also objects to the presence of Deanna Durbin in the picture and it claims that 'it is really grotesque and outlandish what they've done to Miss Durbin in this film. Imagine a sweet young school girl performing the role of Sadie Thompson in "Rain"!' (ibid.).

The Suspect (1945), however, was generally seen as both a return to form, and a return to more straightforward horror. This 'engrossing psychological thrillodrama' (Thirer 1945) was claimed to be part of the 'cycle' of horror films that included '*Laura, Double Indemnity*, most of *The Woman in the Window* and other recent excellences along the same line' (Cook 1945). Furthermore, it was claimed that the film featured 'some horrifying moments, and some moments of terror' (Creelman 1945), moments that were generally attributed to Siodmak, who was by this time claimed to be 'one of our leading specialists in these pictures' (Cook 1945). As a result, *Time* claimed that it was 'directed to the last gasp and shudder by Robert Siodmak [who] developed his talent for terror in the great studios of pre-Hitler Germany' (Anon. 1945a). Manny Farber also made the association with German expressionism and claimed that in comparison with Fritz Lang's *The Woman in the Window* and *Ministry of Fear* (both 1944) and *Hangover Square* (John Brahm, 1945), '*The Suspect* is my favorite ... because it has tried to create character and to rework its ideas – which have been done before by Hitchcock, von Stroheim and pre-Nazi German movies – with the most vivacity' (1945: 296). Again, he also identifies these as horror films claiming that they 'wish to scare the audience and keep it in a constant state of horror', although he also claims that they are a little heavy-handed. They 'pulverize you with anxiety' and are 'overloaded with scare devices' (ibid.).

Siodmak's next collaboration with Joan Harrison was yet another classic *noir* that was seen as horror on its release, *The Strange Affair of Uncle Harry* (1945), an adaptation of 'Thomas Job's horror play' (Cameron 1945). Like *The Woman in the Window*, this film featured a twist at the ending in which its principal character awakes to find that the majority of the film has been a literal and not just a metaphorical 'nightmare'; and like the Lang film, this ending was greeted with derision by reviewers. Archer Winsten (1945) claimed that this supposed 'twist' left him 'more outraged than surprised', while others used it as an excuse to attack the Production Code: 'The ending and the circumstances of censorship and prissiness which obviously dictated it, should have the effect of plaguing the Hays Office out of its high moral collar and into something more comfortable for all of us' (McManus 1945). However, it was not just the ending that was subject to censorship but also the central tension between its main characters, so that the film's 'hints of psychological incest ... are so arranged that you can take or leave them' (Anon. 1945b).

As a result, responses to the film were ambivalent or uncertain. The *New York Post* claims that the film's topic is an 'unpleasant business' but conceded that its filmmakers handled it with 'a fair degree of integrity' (Winsten 1945). Similarly, James Agee (1945) claimed that Siodmak and Harrison should be 'thanked for so intelligently casting, specifying, and bringing to life this generally superior movie'. Conversely, the *New York Times* described it as a 'drab and monotonous succession of routine episodes', featuring uncharacteristically 'slow and stiff' direction from Siodmak, and a number of roles that are 'badly miscast' (Crowther 1945a). However, its main complaint seems to be directed to the Hays Office, which is seen as responsible for the film's lack of purpose: 'This business – compelled by the Hays Office – of having murderers dream their crimes is becoming extremely aggravating' (ibid.). Thus, while the *New York PM* declared it a 'shocking murder story' (McManus 1945), the *New York Daily News* complained that its 'horror and suspense are watered down and the sardonically bitter ending of the play has been sacrificed to a typical Hollywood happy outcome' (Cameron 1945). In this way, complaints about the ending further accentuated its identification as a horror story so that the *New York Journal-American* observed: 'One would think that after years of providing "Frankensteins," "Draculas" and all those other mystery, horror and gangster pictures, Hollywood would figure that the average filmgoer can take a murder story straight' (Pelswick 1945).

Similarly, Siodmak's *The Killers*, an adaptation of a short story by Ernest

Hemingway, was also associated with the horror genre, with the *New York Times* describing it as a 'fearful and fatalistic tale', that is not only 'morbid' but features 'a pretty cruel and complicated plot in which a youthful but broken-down prizefighter treads a perilous path to ruin' (Crowther 1946). Similarly, Agee (1946a) referred to it as a 'brilliant, frightening story', while *Time* referred to the original Hemingway tale as 'a masterpiece of terror by suggestion' and claimed that this 'sinister classic has now been blown up ... into a full length movie' (Anon. 1946). Furthermore, while the *New York Times* did not see it as a major film, its economy and lack of pretension were identified as being its key virtues, with Siodmak being praised for his 'restrained direction', which gives the film a 'tempo [that] is slow and metronomic', a tempo that 'makes for less excitement' but works to intensify the 'suspense' (Crowther 1946).

James Agee (1946a) also championed the film and used it to attack those 'people who think of themselves as serious-minded and progressive [but] thoroughly disapprove of crime melodramas'. For Agee, these people 'feel that movies should be devoted, rather, to more elevated themes' and they 'seem not to remember or not to care that in Germany, a few years ago, movies had to be constructive; stories of crime, and of troubled marriage, for instance, were strictly forbidden'; he therefore praises the film for its 'energy' and its 'attention to form and detail', qualities that make it better 'to watch than the bracing, informative, constructive films which are the only kind these progressives would allow, if they were given half a chance' (ibid.). Manny Farber went even further:

> Though there is a cheapness about *The Killers* that reminds you of five-and-ten jewellery, its scenes of sadism and menacing action have been formed and filled with a vitality all too rare in current movies. It is a production that is suspense-ridden and exciting down to tiny details in the background. The stolid documentary style; the gaudy melodramatic flavour; the artiness (most noticeable in the way scenes are sculpted in dark and light) are largely due to Robert Siodmak, who has made German movies as well as Universal thrillers. (1946: 415)

Once again, Siodmak is identified as a director with a pedigree in the German expressionist cinema.

Furthermore, while contemporary accounts present this film as a *noir* classic, featuring both a hard-boiled detective plot and an impressive *femme fatale*, Kitty Collins, the reviews of the period give a quite different sense of the film. The detective plot is largely seen as a mere device for expanding the original story, so that the film is described as 'movie melodrama, pieced out as a mystery' (Crowther 1946). Similarly, while Kitty is referred to as 'a siren of no mean proportions [who] completely befouls [the hero's] career', there is no sense that there is anything particularly novel about her presence or that she is representative of some broader trend; instead, it is the hero that intrigued reviewers and he was described as 'a victim of love misdirected' (ibid.). If critics in the 1940s showed little awareness of the *femme fatale* as she is understood today, they were acutely aware of another figure, the attractive but potentially deadly husband of the paranoid woman's film, and there is a suggestion that the relationship between Kitty and Swede, the prize fighting hero, was understood as a reversal of the gender dynamics seen as typical of the paranoid woman's film. This sense is also conveyed by Farber's (1946) review, which clearly saw the male victim, rather than the female temptress, as the key innovation of the film: 'Swede is a fascinating, unstereotyped movie tough. He has a dreamy, peaceful, introspective air that dissociates him from everything earthy'.

Indeed, it is notable that in 1946, when *The Killers* was released, Siodmak also released two other thrillers, *The Spiral Staircase* and *The Dark Mirror*, both of which were 'woman's films'. *The Spiral Staircase* was a classic paranoid woman's film in which a 'psychopathic killer' menaces 'a mute serving-girl' (T.M.P. 1946a), and most critics were highly positive about the film. *Variety* claimed that 'Director Robert Siodmak has retained a feeling for terror throughout the film by smart photography, camera angles and sudden shifts of camera emphasis' (Bron. 1946). Similarly, the *New York Times* praised the film as 'a shocker plain and simple' that had 'drawn on practically every device known to produce goose pimples' (T.M.P. 1946a). Furthermore, while it claims that Siodmak makes it clear that he is 'at no time striving for narrative subtlety', this is not meant as a criticism. On the contrary, it is stressed that, 'even when you are conscious that the tension is being built up by obvious trickery, the effect is nonetheless telling', and that 'the film is likely to scare the daylights out of most of its audiences'; in other words, the film is praised as effective visceral entertainment that has few pretensions and simply works on 'the time-tested theory that moviegoers are seldom more satisfied than when a film causes them to experience cold chills' (ibid.).

However, if the *New York Times* praised *The Spiral Staircase*, it found *The Dark Mirror* to be a lamentable production that operated as little more than a vanity project for Olivia de Havilland, who 'has been tempted by the lure of playing against herself' (T.M.P. 1946b). In this film, de Havilland plays identical twins, one of whom is 'a knife wielding paranoiac killer' (Anon. 1946), and the casting of de Havilland was particularly significant given that she was not only a star of woman's films but also the sister of the key star of the paranoid woman's films, Joan Fontaine. Furthermore, given the well-publicised tensions between de Havilland and Fontaine, those involved in the production would have been well aware that the film would be seen as a commentary on their relationship. However, if the dual roles were meant to demonstrate her range as an actress, reviews clearly differed over her success in the role. On the one hand, James Agee observed that de Havilland 'has long been one of the prettiest woman in movies; lately she has started to act, as well' (1946b: 536). On the other, the *New York Times* complained that 'for the life of us we never were sure when she was being Ruth, the good sister, and Terry, the evil one. Or, was it the other way around?' (T.M.P. 1946b). As a result, despite her ambitions, it stated that 'Miss de Havilland does nothing in *The Dark Mirror* that will add to her stature as an actress.'

Furthermore, when the film was praised, it was often due to its association with Siodmak, 'who makes a fairly regular habit of getting his name associated with slick first-rate thrillers' (Anon. 1946), while complaints were directed at the film's scriptwriter and producer, Nunnally Johnson, who is said to have failed to 'resolve his puzzle in a satisfying manner' but to have simply resorted to 'a bit of trickery which is no credit to his craftsmanship' (T.M.P. 1946b).

Unfortunately, having established his reputation as a horror specialist, Siodmak made an unsuccessful attempt to demonstrate his range as a director with *Time Out of Mind* (1947) and, by the time he returned to the materials for which he was known in Hollywood, fashions had changed and the horror cycle of the 1940s was largely over. Furthermore, while many of its features, particularly the figure of the psychotic killer, were still a vital element of Hollywood production, these features were now associated with a cycle of realist crime thrillers, a cycle that was increasingly understood as being distinct from, rather than a part of, the horror genre. As a result, although Siodmak made a number of important thrillers in the late 1940s and early 1950s, particularly *Cry of the City* (1948), *Criss Cross* (1949) and *The File on Thelma Jordon* (1950), he was no longer seen as a specialist in terror but rather as one of a series of thriller directors. By the early 1950s, then, he was disillusioned with Hollywood and returned to Germany, and only came back to Hollywood to make the ill-fated *Custer of the West* (1967) (for an account of Siodmak's post-war work in Germany, see Koepnick 2002). In this way, the reception of Siodmak's 1940s Hollywood films demonstrates the ways in which the category of horror incorporated films now seen as thrillers, *film noir* and examples of the woman's film, but it also illustrates that German cinema and its directors were strongly associated with horror, an association on which directors such as Siodmak capitalised in their pursuit of a Hollywood career.

BIBLIOGRAPHY

A. W. (1943) 'At the Rialto', *New York Times*, 6 November, 16.
Agee, J (1944) 'Films', *The Nation*, 26 February, 261–2.
_____ (1945) 'Films', *The Nation*, 25 August, 189–90.
_____ (1946a) 'Films' *The Nation*, 14 September, 305–6.
_____ (1946b) 'Films', *The Nation*, 9 November, 536–7.
Anon. (1944) 'Cobra Woman Exciting Hit!', *Hollywood Reporter*, 21 April, 4.
_____ (1945a) 'The New Pictures', *Time*, 5 February.
_____ (1945b) 'The New Pictures', *Time*, 27 August.

_____ (1946) 'The New Pictures', *Time*, 21 October.
Barnes, H. (1944) 'Christmas Holiday', *New York Herald Tribune*, June 29.
Bron. (1946) 'Film Reviews', *Variety*, 9 January, 79.
Cameron, K. (1944) 'Maria Montez in Technicolor On Criterion Theatre Screen', *New York Daily News*, 18 May.
_____ (1945) '"Uncle Harry" Now Playing at Criterion', *New York Daily News*, 24 August.
Cook, A. (1944) 'Franchot Tone a Villain in Macabre Phantom Lady', *New York World-Telegram*, 18 February.
_____ (1945) '"The Suspect" is Pleasant and Thrilling Entertainment', *New York World-Telegram*, 31 January.
Creelman, E. (1944) '"Phantom Lady," Horror Thriller About Some Murders and a Charming Maniac', *New York Sun*, 18 February.
_____ (1945) 'Charles Laughton is "The Suspect"', *New York Sun*, 1 February.
Crowther, B. (1944a) '"Phantom Lady," a Melodrama of Weird Effects, With Ella Raines and Franchot Tone, Has Premiere at Loew's State', *New York Times*, 18 February.
_____ (1944b) 'Snakebite Remedy', *New York Times*, 18 May.
_____ (1944c) '"Christmas Holiday," Presenting Deanna Durbin in Serious and Emotional Role, Supported by Gene Kelly, Opens at Criterion', *New York Times*, 29 June.
_____ (1945a) '"Uncle Harry," Taken from the Stage Melodrama, Stars George Sanders, Geraldine Fitzgerald at the Criterion', *New York Times*, August 24.
_____ (1945b) 'Deanna Durbin Plays Part of Debutante Heroine in "Lady on a Train," Universal Film Now at the Criterion', *New York Times*, 15 September.
_____ (1946) '"The Killers"', *New York Times*, 29 August, 1946, 24.
Farber, M. (1945) 'Crime Does Pay', *The New Republic*, 26 February, 296.
_____ (1946) 'Caper of the Week', *The New Republic*, 30 September, 415–6.
Greco, J. (1999) *The File on Robert Siodmak in Hollywood: 1941–1951*. Parkland: Dissertation.com.
Jancovich, Mark (2009) '"Thrills and Chills": Horror, the Woman's Film and the Origins of Film Noir', *New Review of Film and Television*, 7: 2, 157–71.
Koepnick, L. (2002) *The Dark Mirror: German Cinema Between Hitler and Hollywood*. Berkeley, CA: University of California Press.
_____ (2003) 'Doubling the Double: Robert Siodmak in Hollywood', *New German Critique*, 89, 81–104.
McManus, J. T. (1944) 'Sarongs Don't Make a Right', *New York Newspaper PM*, 18 May.
_____ (1945) 'Good Up to the Last Drop', *New York Newspaper PM*, 24 August.
Naremore, J. (1998) *More than Night: Film Noir in its Contexts*. Berkley, CA: University of California Press.
O'Connor, J. (1944) 'Jungle Film at the Criterion', *New York Journal-American*, 18 May.
Pelswick, R. (1945) '"Uncle Harry" at Criterion', *New York Journal-American*, 24 August.
Snelson, T. (2009) *Horror on the Home Front: The Female Monster Cycle, World War Two and Historical Reception Studies*, unpublished PhD thesis, University of East Anglia.
T.M.P. (1946a) 'At the Palace', *New York Times*, 7 February, 35.
_____ (1946b) 'The Dark Mirror', *New York Times*, 19 October, 15.
Thirer, I. (1945) '"The Suspect"', *New York Post*, 1 February.
Walt. (1944) 'Film Reviews', *Variety*, 26 January, 12
Winsten, A. (1944a) '"Phantom Lady' Opens at Loew's State and Met. – A Chiller-Diller', *New York Post*, February 18.
_____ (1944b) 'Animal Kingdom Congregates in "Cobra Woman" at Criterion', *New York Post*, 18 May.
_____ (1945) '"Strange Affair Uncle Harry" Opens at Loew's Criterion', *New York Post*, 24 August.

WORLD OF BLOOD AND FIRE:
LANG, MABUSE, AND BERGMAN'S *THE SERPENT'S EGG*

Samuel J. Umland

'Nothing works properly except fear.'

– Inspector Lohmann, *The Serpent's Egg*

MABUSE'S BERLIN

Although Ingmar Bergman's *Das Schlangenei/The Serpent's Egg* (1977) is not a film especially admired by the critics or even by the director himself, who considered it an 'embarrassing failure' (Bergman 1988: 73), at least one critic – Peter Cowie – has noticed the relationship between Bergman's film and the work of Fritz Lang. Cowie has observed, quite correctly, that *The Serpent's Egg* 'pays homage to Fritz Lang both covertly and overtly' (1982: 314). However, I shall not argue that *The Serpent's Egg* is an homage to Fritz Lang – an homage being analogous to the citation of another's work. Rather, my thesis is that Bergman's film represents a misreading of Fritz Lang's *Das Testament des Dr Mabuse/The Testament of Dr Mabuse* (1933). A misreading is different from an homage. By way of analogy, a misreading means that one's work has been ghost-written by an unsigned and unnamed author. But *The Serpent's Egg* represents a peculiar kind of misreading, because it is a misreading that was encouraged and promulgated by Lang himself.

We now know that Lang largely rewrote his personal history in order to encourage a widespread misreading of *The Testament of Dr Mabuse* as a courageously anti-Nazi film and an allegory of the rise of Adolf Hitler. One might say that Bergman, colloquially speaking, swallowed the bait. However, the extent of Lang's fabrication was not known in 1976, the year in which Bergman made *The Serpent's Egg* – and the last year, coincidentally, of Lang's life. The title of Bergman's film is taken from a line in William Shakespeare's *Julius Caesar*[1] and is used by Bergman as a metaphor for Nazism *in utero*. (What lies in Germany's future is 'like a serpent's egg. Through the thin membranes, you can clearly discern the already perfect reptile.') The inspiration to make *The Serpent's Egg* an allegory of the rise of Nazism was *The Testament of Dr Mabuse*, but since the film was made in 1976, and not in 1932 as was Lang's film, Bergman could not claim to have had the prescience Lang claimed he had, and so its power as a prescient allegory is vitiated: *The Serpent's Egg* is an allegory devoid of the earlier film's putative prophetic insight.

As a teenager, Bergman witnessed first-hand the power of Nazi spectacle, but his memoirs detailing his relationship to Nazism are not rife with fabrication and embellishment of the actual facts, in contrast to Lang's accounts of his relationship to the Nazis. The crucial difference between the two men is that Bergman had no desire to manipulate his public image the way Lang did. For instance, Lang often told the story of a meeting he had with Adolf Hitler's minister of propaganda, Joseph Goebbels, but there's not one shred of evidence indicating this meeting ever took place. As David Kalat observes, 'The story of his confrontation with Goebbels has become a key point in Fritz Lang's largely dubious personal history, the proof of his stalwart anti-Nazism. In turn, generations of film critics have hailed *The Testament of Dr Mabuse* as the first motion picture to address the evils of Hitler' (2001: 70). Since the sale of Lang's passport to the Stiftung Deutsche Kinemathek in Berlin some years ago, however, we now know that Lang left Germany months after his alleged meeting with Goebbels, not, as he later averred, the very night following his meeting. Thus it was Lang himself who invented the myth that the film is an anti-Nazi allegory. Through his transformation of *The Testament of Dr Mabuse* into an anti-Nazi parable ('This film meant to show Hitler's terror methods as in a parable' [Eisner 1976: 129], he said in 1943), Lang unwittingly demonstrated the validity of what Walter Benjamin said about allegory: 'Any person, object, any relationship can mean absolutely anything else' (1977: 175). In effect, Lang did with his film precisely the same thing that Robert Ray says Douglas Sirk, in a series of interviews he gave in the early 1970s, did with the Universal melodramas he had directed in the 1950s. By claiming his Universal melodramas (for example, *Magnificent Obsession* [1954]) were, in fact, subversive, satirical parodies of the

Hollywood melodrama, Sirk had extended Marcel Duchamp's readymades tactic, for Sirk had remotivated found objects that were his own work without modifying or 'correcting' them in any way. (The closest comparison would be to Duchamp's remotivated *Mona Lisa* ['Shaved'] [1965], which leaves the original untouched but depends on Duchamp's previous modification, the goateed *L.H.O.O.Q.* [1919]) (Ray 2001: 59). Lang's remotivated *Testament of Dr Mabuse* became the template for *The Serpent's Egg*, with its self-conscious allegorising of the rise of Nazi Germany.

The relationship between Bergman and Lang is not just one of artistic influence, but also one of biographical enigmas, linked to the early years of the Third Reich. Not especially interested in aggrandising his public image, Bergman admitted in his 1987 autobiography, *The Magic Lantern*, that he had Nazi sympathies during World War II. He says that during the summer he turned sixteen years old – that is, 1934 – he went to Nazi Germany for six weeks as an *Austauschkind*, an exchange student. He would celebrate his sixteenth birthday there, with a German pastor's family in the small town of Haina, 'halfway between Weimar and Eisenach' (Bergman 1988: 119). His friend, Hannes, 'seemed to have been cut out of a National-Socialist propaganda broadsheet, blond, tall and blue-eyed, with a fresh smile [...]. After a while, Hannes suggested I should go with him to school and listen in on the lessons [...]. The subject was Religious Knowledge, but Hitler's *Mein Kampf* lay on the desks' (1988: 120).

Bergman also reveals that while in Germany that summer his host family invited him to attend a Nazi Party rally held in Weimar, where he witnessed all the hoopla from a location near the saluting platform. Remembering himself as a youth listening to *Der Führer's* speech, he admits becoming caught up in the excitement, captivated by the rally's extraordinary spectacle: 'I shouted like everyone else, held out my arm like everyone else, howled like everyone else and loved it like everyone else' (1988: 123). On his birthday (14 July) he was given by the family a present consisting of a photograph of Adolf Hitler: 'Hannes hung it up above my bed so that "I would always have the man before my eyes", so that I should learn to love him in the same way as Hannes [...] loved him. I loved him too. For many years, I was on Hitler's side, delighted by his successes and saddened by his defeats' (ibid.). When the truth of the extermination camps finally emerged, Bergman says that he was 'overcome with despair, and my self-contempt, already a severe burden, accelerated beyond the borders of endurance' (1988: 124).

And so the biographies of Bergman and Lang, inextricably intertwined with the early years of the Third Reich of 1933–34, are, perhaps improbably, bound together, as are their two films. But where Bergman, writing with a certain degree of shame and self-loathing, fully admitted his fascination with Adolf Hitler and Nazism, Lang, in contrast, occluded his past, fabricating his indignant response to the rise of the Nazis and arguing for *The Testament of Dr Mabuse*'s prescient anticipation of Nazi criminality. As we have seen, Lang claimed that Joseph Goebbels offered him the prestigious post of head of German film under the Third

Reich. Lang – of course – refused. As several biographers and scholars have noted, Goebbels' detailed diary makes no mention of any such meeting with Lang. And in fact, Lang never referred to the alleged meeting with Goebbels until roughly a decade later, when he was then making films in America and in the context of promoting his anti-Nazi film, *Hangmen Also Die!* (1943). *The Testament of Dr Mabuse* had just opened in America, some ten years after it was completed, 'and Lang was eager for it to be received as the anti-fascist parable he had crafted it to be' (Kalat 2001: 67). At the opening of the film in New York in 1943, Lang told the audience, 'The slogans and beliefs of the Third Reich were placed in the mouths of criminals' (quoted in Eisner 1976: 129). Certainly Lang was doing nothing different than any other Hollywood studio director at the time – promoting his film – but he repeated the story about his film being an anti-Nazi allegory long after, perhaps so many times he actually came to believe it himself.

When Bergman saw *The Testament of Dr Mabuse* is uncertain, but definitely not in Germany the summer of 1934 when he was an *Austauschkind*. It is well-known that it was censored by the Nazis (not because they perceived it as an anti-Nazi allegory, but because the film's conclusion robbed the authorities of their proper role in bringing a criminal to justice). The film premiered not in Germany but in Budapest, Hungary, in April 1933; it was not shown in Germany until 1951. Perhaps Bergman saw it in Sweden during the war, or possibly around 1951 after its restoration and re-release, or conceivably in 1973, when the fully-restored version was first shown in the United States and elsewhere.

I should stress that Bergman does not refer to *The Testament of Dr Mabuse* in any of his published writings regarding *The Serpent's Egg*. By his own account, the idea for *The Serpent's Egg* was hatched in November 1975: 'During the previous summer I had read Joachim Fest's biography of Adolf Hitler [1973]', and he was haunted by Fest's characterisation of Weimar Germany as having 'a grotesque quality to reality' (Bergman 1994: 191). To give shape to the film forming in his imagination, he returned to ideas that he had used in earlier films: he drew from *Tystnaden/The Silence* (1962), about three tourists (two women and a small boy) stranded in a foreign, war-ravaged city, and from *Riten/The Ritual* (filmed 1967, released 1969), about three internationally famous performance artists called before a judge for an inquiry. He writes: 'I wanted to reactivate my old idea of the two trapeze artists who are stranded because the third member of their act has died. They have been left in a war-ravaged city. Their accelerating decline was to be interlaced with the destruction of the city' (1994: 190). He invoked Shakespeare by means of the film's title because Shakespeare's later plays exhibit a preoccupation with 'the break between a world of order, with laws of ethics and social norms, and total collapse, an irresistible chaos that suddenly breaks into a regulated reality and annihilates it' (1994: 194). This latter insight – the ontological collapse of quotidian reality – suggests the way *The Serpent's Egg* is a horror film. While Bergman made only one overt horror film, *Vargtimmen/Hour of the Wolf*

(1968), features of the horror film appear in *Ansiktet/The Magician* (1958), *Såsom i en spegel/Through a Glass Darkly* (1960), *Persona* (1966) and *Aus dem Leben der Marionetten/From the Life of the Marionettes* (1981).

Bergman made *The Serpent's Egg* in Munich, where he had settled following his much-publicised departure from Sweden in April 1976. As is well known, on 30 January 1976, Bergman was arrested on suspicion of tax fraud. As a result of the trauma of the event, he suffered a nervous breakdown and was taken to the psychiatric ward of the Karolinska Hospital, spending weeks there. His reaction to his arrest eventually turned into anger, and in late April 1976 he left Sweden. He eventually settled in Munich, where he spent the next several years. *The Serpent's Egg* was filmed at the city's Bavaria Studios, October–December 1976.

Munich was Adolf Hitler's home for many years, and the city where his failed 'Beer Hall Putsch' occurred on 8–9 November 1923. *The Serpent's Egg* is set in Berlin during the five days leading up to the failed *putsch*. Hitler is alluded to on three occasions, twice by Inspector Bauer (Gert Fröbe, who had played Commissioner Kras in the last of the Mabuse films directed by Lang, *Die 1,000 Augen des Dr Mabuse/The 1,000 Eyes of Dr Mabuse* [1960]), the third and last time near the end of the film, which concludes two days after Hitler's failed *putsch*.

Hence the villains are not Nazis; Nazi Germany exists, figuratively, only *in utero*. Like that of *The Testament of Dr Mabuse*, *The Serpent Egg*'s setting is Weimar Germany, not Nazi Germany, and the inhabitants of Berlin are depicted as perverse and decadent. To lift a phrase from Lang's film, the Berlin of *The Serpent's Egg* is an 'empire of crime.' Bergman's workbook contained the following quotation from Fest's biography of Hitler: 'The inflation lent a grotesque quality to reality and crushed not only people's incentive to accept the reigning order but also their feeling for permanency in general and made them accustom themselves to living in an impossible atmosphere' (quoted in Bergman 1994: 191). Within this miasma, crime is rampant and several bizarre murders have occurred in the month preceding the film's opening sequence, that takes place on the evening of 3 November 1923.

The film's villain is a master criminal, a sinister, Mabuse-like character named Hans Vergérus (Heinz Bennent), a scientist engaged in cruel experiments with human subjects, using the benign front of St Anna's Clinic as the place to conduct them. The surname Vergérus holds a special place in Bergman's films, denoting an emotionally cold, artistically unimaginative type. Characters named Vergérus appear in *The Magician*, *En passion/The Passion of Anna* (1968), *Beröringen/The Touch* (1970) and in *Fanny och Alexander/Fanny and Alexander* (1982/83). In this latter film the name is explicitly linked to a sinister figure, Bishop Edvard Vergérus. Additionally, the name Hans has at least two connotations: Hannes was the name of the German boy who loved Hitler, with whom the young Bergman, as an exchange student, spent six weeks in 1934. Hans is also the name of the child murderer in Lang's *M* (1931). It is worth remembering that in Bergman's one overt horror film, *Hour of the Wolf*, the protagonist, Johan Borg, admits to his wife of having murdered a boy some years earlier: the name Hans, in German as in Swedish, is short for Johannes (John).

LANG'S EGG, BERGMAN'S TESTAMENT

Nobody could fight his way through here, even with a message from a dead man.

– Franz Kafka (1976: 244)

There are messages received from dead persons on two occasions in *The Serpent's Egg*. The first message is a suicide note left by Abel Rosenberg's (David Carradine) brother Max (Hans Eichler), consisting of a scrawled, handwritten message of which only a single fragment is legible: 'There's poisoning going on.' Fritz Lang had used the device of the suicide note, as the initial hermeneutic puzzle, to open *The Big Heat* (1953). The second is also a suicide note – characterised by Inspector Bauer as he presents it to Abel as 'a very strange letter, totally muddled' – left behind by a woman Abel recognises but barely knows. The woman's anguished letter says that she 'had been frightened to death' and that 'the pain was unbearable.' Messages in *The Serpent's Egg* do not proliferate to the degree they do in *The Testament of Dr Mabuse*, but the messages are equally as oracular.

It so happens that the woman's suicide is one of seven mysterious deaths in and around a particular neighborhood in Berlin – the neighborhood where Abel Rosenberg shared an apartment with his brother Max – that have occurred, according to Inspector Bauer, in the city in the past month. So amid the chaos of a labyrinthine Berlin, in the midst of a society teetering on the edge of anarchy, a possible serial killer is running amok. 'Nothing works properly except fear,' utters Inspector Bauer, but he might just as easily said, 'except terror.' Superficially, the murders invoke the Berlin of Lang's *M*, but the perpetrator of the crimes is not a serial killer like Hans Beckert. The allusion to *M* is intentional nonetheless, as at one point Inspector Bauer orders Abel to sit down while he writes a letter to 'Inspector Lohmann', Lohmann the detective appearing both in *M* and *The Testament of Dr Mabuse*, both times played by Otto Wernicke, to whom Gert Fröbe bears a passing resemblance.

In *M* the murderer is a distinct, morally culpable individual named Hans Beckert, but in *The Serpent's Egg*, as in *The Testament of Dr Mabuse*, the situation regarding moral culpability is altogether more ambiguous. In the latter, the writings of the inscrutably silent, hypergraphic Dr Mabuse are collected, studied and internalised by Professor Dr Baum. One might suspect, therefore, that Hans Vergérus is more closely analogous to *The Testament of Dr Mabuse*'s Dr Baum than Dr Mabuse himself, but like Mabuse, Vergérus is the *author* ('mastermind') of crimes, not their actual perpetrator. The seven murders (as well as other crimes we learn about later) are *authored* by Hans Vergérus, the demiurgic puppet master/Mabuse figure, but not carried out by him. Indeed, the actual perpetrators remain anonymous, although Abel's brother Max, Vergérus reveals, may have been guilty of the rape and murder of his own fiancée, while under the influence of an anguish-producing drug, 'Thanatoxin.'

Hence Hans Vergérus, like Dr Mabuse, is the author of crime, the 'master' criminal and demiurge, what Tom Gunning refers to as the 'grand enunciator' (2000: 89). It is for this very reason, incidentally, that it was rather easy for Lang to allegorise *The Testament of Dr Mabuse* and draw an analogy between Dr Mabuse and Adolf Hitler, and also why an anonymously authored crime of the sort Mabuse and Vergérus instigate is so easily assimilable under the category 'terrorism.'

The use of poison gas – invisible, odourless – is a powerful mechanism of terror, says Dr Mabuse in one of his writings. One of Dr Baum's associates, having accidentally knocked a pile of Mabuse-authored papers to the floor of Baum's office, comes across a page in which Mabuse discusses both the effectiveness and ease of use of glass bulbs filled with gas to incite public panic. Later in the film, of course, Dr Baum, for similarly terroristic reasons, will spectacularly blow up a gas factory.

While the use of poison gas in the Nazi extermination camps is an unavoidable association, Vergérus's use of toxic gas, like his use of the drug 'Thanatoxin,' is merely one of an array of stimuli he deploys to elicit responses, if entirely

Abel Rosenberg (David Carradine, left) faces the Dr Mabuse-like demiurge and master criminal of *The Serpent's Egg*, Hans Vergérus (Heinz Bennett, right)

unpredictable, in his human subjects. Like any good Hegelian, Vergérus transforms an epistemological limitation into a positive ontological condition. Vergérus sets the stage, introduces the variable, and then observes the behavioural outcome, recording it on film. The fact that Vergérus stages – arranges the *mise-en-scène* – and then surreptitiously records the resulting action by means of a motion picture camera, links the power of Vergérus to that of the movie director: he functions as Bergman's self-reflexive *doppelgänger*, a demiurge manipulating a world of his own making. Vergérus is also, obviously, linked to surveillance, just as Dr Mabuse is linked to surveillance in both *The Testament of Dr Mabuse* and *The 1,000 Eyes of Dr Mabuse*.[2]

The film's self-reflexivity encourages us to expect authorial self-inscription, and indeed Bergman has done just that, linking Abel and Vergérus through a boyhood past. When he was a boy, says Abel to his brother's former wife, Manuela (Liv Ullman), he would spend the summers with his family in Amalfi. It was in Amalfi as a boy that he first met Hans Vergérus. Everyone thought Vergérus a bit strange but a genius nonetheless. He admits that as boys he and Vergérus once 'caught a cat and tied it down. Hans cut it open. It was still alive. He let me see how its heart beat.' He tells Manuela he ran into Vergérus again about ten years ago while travelling with the circus, then at the cabaret the other day. What Abel doesn't know, however, is that Manuela has slept with Vergérus on several occasions, information which she discreetly chooses to withhold. Both Abel and Manuela, therefore, are irrevocably linked to Vergérus, one through the shame of boyhood cruelty, the other through financial need; Abel through the act of vivisection, Manuela through the act of sex.

It is impossible not to perceive Hans Vergérus as a sort of Josef Mengele-like figure, and therefore monstrous, but it is also impossible to deny Vergérus's keen interest in vision and seeing, as both are essential to his profession, medical science. Vergérus is associated with vision when he is first introduced in the film, the moment when he (again) bumps into his boyhood acquaintance Abel Rosenberg. Vergérus is standing to the side of the cabaret stage watching the performance when Abel emerges from Manuela's dressing room. Vergérus says to him, 'It's funny seeing everything from the side like this.' Seeing, in the form of empirical observation, is behind his boyhood act of vivisection. While we are to infer that Vergérus was deeply sadistic from the start, vivisection has long been controversial. Beginning in the eighteenth century, with Henry Baker's vivisection of frogs, during which 'the skin of the belly was slit from the anus to the throat and stretched with fish hooks in front of the microscope' (Stafford 1997: 181) in order to demonstrate the circulation of blood, moralists have raised the aesthetic issue of the proper exhibition of empirical observations. Barbara Stafford also points out that when microscopy became a scientific enterprise in the eighteenth century, moral concerns quickly came into conflict with 'exploratory curiosity' (1997: 180). The campaign opposing vivisection became the leading *cause célèbre* of the day, led by moralists outraged by the cruelty perpetrated on animals under the name of scientific observation. She writes:

> Lurking beneath the surface of various attempts to make scientific training graphic and attractive was the much broader polemic concerning the right or wrong presentation of information. Long before the onset of nineteenth-century positivism, arguments were mustered for severing enjoyable watching from exacting observation. This dichotomy was promoted by the rise of the logocentric critic as rational censor, external to the inferior sensory field of inquiry being judged. (Ibid.)

Following Stafford's argument, the logocentric critic within us, incapable of resolving the tension between voyeurism (seeing as pleasure) and exacting observation (seeing as knowledge) that largely informs Vergérus's speech in the penultimate sequence of the film, condemns him for the visual recording of his experiments, while at the same time finding it impossible to challenge the conclusions he has drawn from them. In his transition from scientist to nihilistic prophet, during which he anticipates the rise of the Nazis in allegorical form through his invocation of the serpent's egg as the avatar of imminent historical catastrophe,[3] Vergérus claims to be ahead of his time, asserting that the knowledge of human behaviour and psychology that is the fruit of his experiments will be used by future social technicians in order to manipulate entire nations, large masses. He tells Abel that once this inevitable 'revolution' occurs, 'our world will go down in blood and fire.' He says, 'The old society, Abel, was based on extremely Romantic ideas of Man's goodness. It was all very complicated since the ideas didn't match the reality. The new society will be based on a realistic assessment of Man's potentials and limitations.' Interestingly, Vergérus's declaration seems like a virtual paraphrase of positivist philosophy as outlined by Auguste Comte, whose reductive method required the elimination of 'theological' or 'metaphysical' questions because they were in effect unanswerable:

> As long as individual minds are not unanimously agreed upon a certain number of general ideas of forming a common social doctrine ... nations will necessarily remain in an essentially revolutionary state [...]. [T]he actual confusion of men's minds is at bottom due to the simultaneous employment of three radically incompatible philosophies – the theological, the metaphysical, and the positive. It is quite clear that, if any one of these three philosophies really obtained a complete and universal preponderance, a fixed social order would result. (1970: 28–9)

Since Comte considered positive philosophy as 'the only solid basis of ... social organisation' – Vergérus calls 'realistic' – he therefore urged for its adoption.

But Vergérus the positivist does not triumph. He is merely a demiurge. The inadvertent poisoning of Manuela, apparently unintended by Vergérus, reveals how he, like Dr Mabuse, seemingly in complete control of his creation, is actually an inept demigod unable to control it. As Gunning has observed, 'Lang's authors, whether master criminals or obsessed painters, architects and novelists, all are undone by their own creations' (2000: 477). So, too, is Hans Vergérus who, in his final moment before his imminent arrest, bites on a cyanide capsule while studying himself in a mirror, empirical observer to the last.

But Vergérus's *selbsmort* is not the final catastrophe. Inspector Bauer manages to find Abel a job in a circus and suggests he accept it. Abel acquiesces, but on the way to the train station he escapes his police escort. The final sequence of the film reveals Abel rushing *somewhere* through a heavily trafficked Berlin street, while the narrator informs us he was never seen again. The implication is that the effacement of identity is the inevitable condition of modernity, inevitably looping us back like a Möbius strip to the first images of the film, black-and-white footage (as in a newsreel) consisting of a drab, anonymous space filled with a restless mass of people – men, women and children – slowly walking toward some unknown, unanticipated future catastrophe, uncomfortably crowded together shoulder-to-shoulder, trudging silently, united only by their despair. One thinks of Walter Benjamin's 'Theses on the Philosophy of History' and his reading of Paul Klee's painting *Angelus Novus* (1920), but rather than 'the angel of history,' it is *our* face that is 'turned toward the past,' toward the wreckage piled upon wreckage, and it is we who are driven 'irresistibly ... into the future' to which *our* back is turned, while the pile of debris before us grows ever skyward (Benjamin 1969: 257–8).

POSTSCRIPT

On 2 August 1976, about eight weeks before filming of *The Serpent's Egg* began in Munich, Fritz Lang died in Los Angeles, California at the age of 85. The *auteur* died, but like Dr Mabuse, his creations thrived. They have lived on, but have been subjected to countless aberrant misreadings.

NOTES

1 The reference to the serpent's egg occurs in *Julius Caesar* II, i (ll. 28–34) and is spoken by Brutus of Caesar:
   And since the quarrel
   Will bear no colour for the thing he is,
   Fashion it thus: that what he is, augmented,
   Would run to these and these extremities.
   And therefore think him as a serpent's egg –

>   Which, hatched, would as his kind grow mischievous –
>   And kill him in the shell.

2   See Crary (1996) for a discussion of Mabuse and surveillance.
3   Vergérus's image of the outline of the perfect reptile coiled within the serpent's egg, used to allegorise incipient Nazism (allegory the privileged form of all true modernists) is an instance of what Slavoj Žižek calls 'the parallax Real': 'In a first move, the Real is the impossible hard core which we cannot confront directly, but only through the lenses of a multitude of symbolic fictions, virtual formations. In a second move, this very hard core is purely virtual, actually non-existent, an X which can be reconstructed only retroactively, from the multitude of symbolic formations which are "all that there actually is"' (2006: 12).

BIBLIOGRAPHY

Benjamin, W. (1969) 'Theses on the Philosophy of History', in *Illuminations*. Trans. Harry Zohn. New York: Schocken.

_____ (1977) *The Origin of German Tragic Drama*. Trans. J. Osborne. London: New Left Books.

Bergman, I. (1977) *The Serpent's Egg: A Film*. Trans. A. Blair. New York: Pantheon.

_____ (1988) *The Magic Lantern: An Autobiography*. Trans. J. Tate. New York: Viking.

_____ (1994) *Images: My Life in Film*. Trans. M. Ruuth. New York: Arcade.

Comte, A. (1970) *Introduction to Positive Philosophy*. Trans. F. Ferré. Indianapolis: Bobbs-Merrill.

Cowie, P. (1982) *Ingmar Bergman: A Critical Biography*. New York: Scribner.

Crary, J. (1996) 'Dr. Mabuse and Mr. Edison', in Ed. R. Ferguson, *Art and Film Since 1945: Hall of Mirrors*. Los Angeles: Museum of Contemporary Art, 262–79.

Eisner, L. H. (1976) *Fritz Lang*. London: Secker and Warburg.

Gunning, T. (2000) *The Films of Fritz Lang: Allegories of Vision and Modernity*. London: British Film Institute.

Kafka, F. (1976) 'The Great Wall of China', in Ed. N. Glatzer, *Franz Kafka: The Complete Stories*. New York: Schocken, 235–48.

Kalat, D. (2001) *The Strange Case of Dr. Mabuse: A Study of the Twelve Films and Five Novels*. Jefferson, NC: McFarland.

Ray, R. B. (2001) *How a Film Theory Got Lost and Other Mysteries of Cultural Studies*. Bloomington, IN: Indiana University Press.

Stafford, B. M. (1997) *Good Looking: Essays on the Virtue of Images*. Cambridge, MA: MIT Press.

Žižek, S. (2006) *The Parallax View*. Cambridge, MA: MIT Press.

'LE CINÉASTE D'HORREUR ORDINAIRE':
MICHAEL HANEKE AND THE HORRORS OF EVERYDAY EXISTENCE

Catherine Wheatley

The climate of [my] films derives from an experience that is familiar to us all, cold indifference, breakdown in communication, and the increasing violence in the immediate living space of each one of us. I can't get the suspicion out of my mind, that it is this civil war that is close to desperation, rather than the spectacular one that is all too often seen on the television; that renders people helpless, baffled, afraid and – in the true sense of the words – murderously aggressive.
– Michael Haneke, press notes to Der Siebente Kontinent/The Seventh Continent (1989)

A television presenter receives gruesome drawings, seeming portents of a violent future. A young boy slaughters a schoolmate to 'see how it feels'. A family are held hostage, tortured and killed, one by one, by a pair of mirthful psychopaths. Another family arrive at their woodland cabin to discover hostile locals awaiting them...

Such are the premises of *Caché/Hidden* (2005), *Benny's Video* (1992), *Funny Games* (1997) and *Le Temps du Loup/The Time of the Wolf* (2001) – four of the ten feature films produced by Austrian filmmaker Michael Haneke over the course of his career. Thus summarised, they bear a striking resemblance to the plots of horror films ranging from *The Hills Have Eyes* (Wes Craven, 1997; Alexandre Aja, 2006) to more recent works such as *Ringu/The Ring* (Hideo Nakata, 2000; Gore Verbinski, 2002) and *Hostel* (Eli Roth, 2005). The director's 1997 *Funny Games* (remade in English in 2007 and released under the same title), in which a family are taken hostage in their home, tortured and murdered, is perhaps the most easily appropriated of Haneke's films for a generic reading, with Robin Wood (2004), for example, claiming that 'its relationship to the horror becomes apparent quite early on'. But to categorise Haneke's other works as 'horror films' in any general sense of the term would be highly problematic – not to mention grossly misleading. As readers familiar with his work will be aware, the precise, minimalist aesthetic and rigorously controlled scenes of everyday alienation that typify his films have, at first glance, little in common with the excesses generally held to typify the genre.[1] Nonetheless, close attention to Haneke's earlier work, *Benny's Video*, reveals that this film draws heavily on the coding of realist horrors such as *Henry: Portrait of a Serial Killer* (John McNaughton, 1990), as delineated by Cynthia Freeland (1995). Moreover, if Haneke's entire œuvre is concerned with the ways in which the politesse and social niceties of the European middle-classes masks a climate of alienation and disaffection – within which lurks the horror of the everyday, then although not immediately recognisable as horror narratives, films such as *Der Siebente Kontinent/The Seventh Continent* (1989), *71 Fragmente einer Chronologie des Zufalls/71 Fragments of a Chronology of Chance* (1989) and *Hidden* can be seen to succeed 'by creating terror and unease, both promising and withholding the spectacle of violence' (Freeland 1995: 128). In what follows I shall examine how this sense of terror and unease is created through Haneke's deployment of a modernist self-reflexivity that forces the spectator to consider his or her own relationship to the events on screen: by extending his use of the conventions of the realist horror film throughout his work Haneke is able to situate the horrific within the contemporary – a society of which the spectator is forced to acknowledge s/he is part.

REALIST HORROR: *BENNY'S VIDEO*

In her 1995 article, 'Realist Horror', Cynthia Freeland delineates the features that distinguish films such as *Psycho* (Alfred Hitchcock, 1960), *Peeping Tom* (Michael Powell, 1960) and *The Silence of the Lambs* (Jonathan Demme, 1991), from other sub-genres of horror. Taking Noël Carroll's concept of 'art-horror' – the distanced emotional response to a representation – as a touchpoint (see Carroll 1990: 179–82), Freeland argues that realist horror falls outside the perimeters of theories which depend on the fictitious nature of the monsters at the centre of horror for their affect. If art-horror posits that horror can be at once repellent and enjoyable precisely because its monsters, although scary, 'do not threaten us directly', since we are 'protected by knowing they are fictional' (Freeland 1995: 127), then realist horror offers a different experience, since the monsters it depicts, often taken from real life, are a long way from the werewolves, vampires and other beings 'not believed to exist according to contemporary science' (Carroll 1990: 38). Where such entities fascinate because they violate our conceptual categories, the villains of realist horror are possible beings, more often than not 'ordinary' men, whose actions are easily explained with recourse to childhood trauma and sexual repression – often detailed at the film's close.

Realist horror problematises classical approaches to the genre, Freeland claims, by thwarting the initial assumption that we can draw a clear distinction between artistic assumptions and reality. In this respect, it should be noted that the sub-genre posits a peculiarly symbiotic relationship between fictional and news stories. In our contemporary media culture, 'realistic elements from news stories are easily, commonly, and quickly integrated into new feature film plots' and that conversely, 'fictitious characters (like Hannibal Lecter) are alluded to in presenting or describing real ones (like Jeffrey Dahmer)' (Freeland 1995: 134). Consequently, plots in realist horror reflect real-life acts of violence: occurring randomly they are presented to us, via the nightly news broadcast, in terms of spectacle and aftermath. On the spectator's part, our reaction to these fictional events is no longer any different to that we might experience upon switching on our television sets to see footage of the latest atrocity: 'like the news, realist horror evokes real, albeit paradoxical reactions: at the same it is both emotionally flattening (familiar, formulaic, and predictable in showcasing violence), and disturbing (immediate, real, gruesome, random)' (ibid.). As evidence of these claims, Freeland cites the example of *Henry: Portrait of a Serial Killer*. McNaughton's film offers no audience identification figure. It consistently withholds spectacle, consigning violence for the most part to the off-screen space and focusing instead on its consequences. The plot, in as much as we can speak of one, is flat and fragmentary, and offers no righting of wrongs at its *dénouement*. Psychology is minimally sketched as little explanation is offered for the characters' actions – and those we are given are so contradictory as to render them meaningless. *Henry: Portrait of a Serial Killer* violates the usual rules of both the horror in general and the slasher in particular.

This is not to say that realist horror withholds violence altogether, rather that the violence it does present tends to be somewhat arbitrary, and rather matter-of-fact. Inasmuch, one might be tempted to pronounce a negative verdict on its audience effect: to condemn it as one of the many systems of images that flatten our experience of the world, rendering all events equal and turning even horrific disasters into simulacra, as Jean Baudrillard would have it. However, Freeland attempts to invert such negative conceptions by pointing to the extreme self-reflexivity of many of the films that make up the sub-genre, which encourage the audience in its critical awareness of its own spectacle (1995: 139). In *Henry: Portrait of a Serial Killer*, for example, what appears to be the filmic portrayal of the protagonist and an accomplice, Otis, committing a murder, is in fact revealed to be a diegetic videotape, which we are watching alongside the killers. 'Naturally', Freeland claims, 'this prompts audience unrest and questions' (ibid.) – although she admits that such questions are often left unpursued.

Benny's Video exhibits many of the features that Freeland claims are characteristic of realist horror: the film is based on a real-life incident; presented in an observational, episodic manner; it offers no narrative closure or ultimate justice and the *spectacle* of violence is replaced with the *spectre* of violence. That is, the film's central event, teenager Benny's murder of a young girl, constitutes only a ten-minute section of Haneke's film, and with the exception of the opening slaughter, it is the sole act of violence that the film offers. Since Benny has positioned the camera on a tripod, the action is captured obliquely: the victim drops out of the frame upon being shot, and the spectacle of her bloody death is replaced with glimpses of Benny as he lurches in and out of the shot. There is no clear picture of what is happening, and only the soundtrack of the victim's screams is typical of classic horror's excesses. The event, which one would expect to form the climax of the narrative, takes place within the film's first thirty minutes. Henceforth, with the murder consigned to the off-screen space and its bloody aftermath swiftly cleaned up, the second half of the film focuses on the response of the film's characters to the crime.

In the wake of the murder, Benny is shown compulsively playing and replaying the tape. Eventually he confesses his crime to his parents, but his admission entails no request for forgiveness, it is simply a statement of fact. Like Henry's deadpan explanations of how to evade detection, his attitude to the act of killing disturbs through its lack of emotion. But Benny is not even given to us as a sexy anti-hero to be admired for his guile, cunning or Nietzschean nihilism. He is no Henry, nor is he a Hannibal Lecter figure – rather he is a pallid, passive, gawky teen – who when asked by his father why he did it, can only respond 'to see how it feels'. The implication is that the teenager suffers a failure of feeling, of engagement with 'reality'. He is, in Haneke's terms 'emotionally frozen', and the film provides us with sufficient incidental detail to suggest that his perception has come to be mediated by the technology with which he is surrounded. As Brigitte Peucker has pointed out, for Benny, 'visual discernment takes place chiefly through a video camera, and the sounds of television and rock CDs form an aural space that envelops him' (2000: 178). The images which surround him include not only the choreographed violence of action movies but also the restrained, 'normalising' television reportage of scenes of death in Bosnia, in which images of carnage are accompanied by voices of commentators carefully trained to exclude all emotion, thus rendering a sanitised version of the real precisely where the spectator has come to believe he has access to its immediacy. In this context, his confession appears to echo the calm detachment of a news commentator, his compulsive replaying and rewinding of the video cassette is at once an attempt to reduce and deflate through its overpresence the murder's shock value, and an attempt to gain a purchase on the reality of the act he has committed.

Benny, it seems, can only understand life through a lens. Haneke emphasises this point by repeatedly calling into question the boundary between the ongoing diegetic video and the so-called 'reality' of the film narrative, and at various junctures, the spectator is only retrospectively made aware that the footage he has been watching is actually part of Benny's video (as opposed to Haneke's film).

For their part, Benny's parents, Anna and George, respond to the crime with unmitigated efficiency, dismembering the body for easy disposal and whisking Benny off to Egypt, where he is instructed to create a video diary which will, if necessary, serve as media-friendly evidence of his 'normality'. There are few tears, no raised voices, and certainly no attempt to examine the causes or implications of Benny's behaviour. And it is perhaps in Anna and George's genteel erasure of the murder in order to retain social acceptance and prestige that the film's true horror lies. Certainly, Anna and George's lack of panic or petrification is as indicative of a climate of disaffection as their son's murderous behaviour is reflective of a loss of connection to the real, and their implication in the crime serves to underline the fact that Benny's action is the perhaps inevitable consequence of a way of life. Given his parents' behaviour, it is little wonder that Benny needs to see how 'it' feels. Discussing this point, Christopher Sharrett comments that 'although George surely has more affect than his son, his crimes are far more horrible ... [his] cold, calculated act of butchery ... refocuses the narrative: the affectless present embodied in Benny is the legacy of Western civilisation' (2006: 12).

A HORROR OF CIVILISATION

Benny's Video is, then, not a 'horror of personality', as Charles Derry would have it, in which violence and horror is explained in terms of a psychotic or evil individual (1977: 18). Rather it is what we might call a 'horror of civilisation', and the villain of the piece is no more Benny than the culture which can give birth to him. This society exists by its own highly codified ways of behaviour and rules of engagement, rules dominated by the twin gods of money and media. As Robert Yates points out in his review of the film for *Sight and Sound*, it is a world in which 'communication has been replaced by consumption' (1993: 42). If the film is replete with cine-televisual imagery, it is also shot through with the imagery of commerce: there are repeated shots of money changing hands, and of the accoutrements of capitalism, such as luxurious living rooms and sports cars. We even see Benny dine in a McDonalds.

The murderous violence of *Funny Games* can similarly be understood to be a consequence of the Western consumer lifestyle. The film's opening scenes emphasise the affluence of the Schöber family home, in which they will be held hostage and tortured by two anonymous young men, in a series of close-ups of their designer shoes, expensive golf-clubs, mobile phones and mountains of food. These objects will be turned against them over the course of the film's narrative as objects of dispute and attack, just as their elegant home will become their prison, the security gates and double locks intended to keep intruders out serving instead to trap the inhabitants within its confines.

It is telling that the Schöbers' veneer of politeness masks an attitude of mistrust and hostility. When the strangers come calling – ostensibly to borrow some eggs – matriarch Anna is obliging but hardly gracious. She is loathe to give away more than the minimum, despite the fact that we have already been shown an abundantly stocked fridge, and when 'Peter' and 'Paul' push the issue she quickly becomes hostile, demanding that they leave and roughly manhandling them. If her shoving of the two boys is not the film's first act of violence, then the open-handed slap that her husband George delivers to one of the intruders shortly afterwards is. The ordeal that the family subsequently undergo is thus initiated not by the 'villains' of the piece, but the victims. Like Henry and Benny, Peter and Paul are recognisable as human beings (rather than Carroll's monsters, although as Robin Wood [2004] has pointed out this rewind scene hints at the 'supernatural'), but once more their motives are so diverse as to be rendered obsolete: they give varying versions of the psychological traumas that led them to commit these acts, and any suspicion that the crime might be sexually motivated is rendered defunct by their dismissal of Anna's naked body as a mere joke. Wood reads their opacity as 'suggesting that our civilisation, by dehumanising our inhabitants, intrinsically produces psychopaths who therefore require no further explanation' (ibid.). An alternative to this view might be that, their fictional status so clearly foregrounded, the characters of Peter and Paul become the literal embodiments of the way in which the cine-televisual medium has invaded our homes and our minds. Whichever one of these readings we accept, the fact is that these 'characters' are reduced to mere ciphers for the violence already present within the Schöbers' environment.

Haneke's films are filled with citizens who have barricaded themselves into their middle-class milieus, shutting themselves off from the outside world. In *Hidden*, too, the Laurent family take refuge behind the walls of their own home. Elizabeth Ezra and Jane Sillars point out that the film consistently reinforces the fact that the couple's stylish house is in many ways a gated fortress: shots of its exterior puts its vertical barred windows centre frame; horizontal bars cut across shots; the clanging of the iron gate rings out on the soundtrack (2007: 216). Even when the outside world intrudes upon their carcereal existence in the form of television news broadcasts, their response is to blithely ignore it – as indeed is ours. In the film's most self-conscious scene, in which television presenter Georges and

MICHAEL HANEKE AND THE HORRORS OF EVERYDAY EXISTENCE

The televisual simulacrum (*Hidden*, 2005)

his wife Anne discuss the whereabouts of the young son while news of the Iraq War blasts from the widescreen TV in the centre of the frame, the conventions of the suspense thriller which Haneke draws upon compel viewers to shut out news of the outside world in order to focus on the apparent domestic crisis. As Ezra and Sillars put it, 'The ease with which we fail to identify with (or even notice) real events, and the insistence we place on Georges and Anne ... underscores the film's apparently perverse but ultimately effective interrogation of what John Berger famously called "ways of seeing"' (2007: 218).

But perhaps the most poignant visualisation of this profound alienation comes in the opening scenes of *71 Fragments of a Chronology of Chance*. After several extreme close-ups of a saloon car in a car-wash, the film cuts to inside and holds a long take (under the credits) from the back seat looking out of the front window as a family of three – who we will later learn are father George, mother Anna and daughter Eva – sit in silence; when the credits have rolled and the wash has finished, the car drives away past an oversized, exotic tourist advert for Australia which will recur in attenuated forms throughout the film. Based on a news story about a family opting for collective suicide rather than continuing in the present alienated world, the film takes numerous deceptive turns as we expect the members of the Schöber family, who go through daily life in a set of rote behaviours, to leave for the promised utopia of rural Australia, since this advert, shot in much brighter colours than the body of the film and transformed into a moving landscape, appears at regular intervals throughout the film. However, the film's climax, which lasts some thirty minutes, sees the family systematically destroy their home and possessions before taking their own lives. It is divided into three sections, of which the first two chronicle a series of episodes, or moments, in the family's life, and this opening segment both sketches in notions of automatism and alienation and simultaneously lays out both the dialectical style of the film's intrinsic norms – long-take master shots and more rapidly-cut close-ups – and its particular manner of usage – to convey both fragmentation and stasis: the disjointed aimlessness of contemporary, lived reality. It also provides, as Adam Bingham puts it, 'a microcosmic metaphor for the family: trapped in a car/cage [if not of their own design, then at least of their own purchasing], moving slowly, silently and mechanically through their lives' (2006).

Yet again, what is horrific about the family's final act of self-immolation is not the act itself, which takes place once more outside the periphery of the image, but the painstaking care and logic with which it is carried out. The final third of the film documents the systematic destruction of the family's belongings as ultimately, both life (in the form of Eva's pet goldfish) and its means (hard cash) are flushed down the toilet. Brian Murphy has written of the horror film that its capacity for being enjoyed depends precisely on the perpetuity of certain rules and tenets to which all monster movies adhere, claiming that, 'horror's never-never land is bearable because it is so entirely rational' (1972: 34), but for Haneke, the horrific resides not in a fantasy 'never-never land' inhabited by werewolves, vampires or zombies – rather it is to be found in an all too real Neverland, the Jackson ranch that appears on a diegetic television screen at the end of *71 Fragments of a Chronology of Chance*. It resides in the lurking possibility of child abuse, random violence, war, all packaged neatly by the nightly news bulletin, sanitised and explained away. It is precisely because it is so rational that *The Seventh Continent*'s violence is almost unbearable: here, suicide is given as the logical response to the ongoing disaffection that characterises life in the Western world. To quote Richard Combs, 'lives lived without connection must disappear into a black hole of their own making' (2002: 28).

INVERTED IDEOLOGY

In some ways, Haneke's films can be seen as the Europeanisation of a genre which has often stressed that the essence of the horrific lies within human relationships and the collapse of a false social order of which we are in great denial. As Stephen Snyder argues in relation to *The Texas Chainsaw Massacre, Burnt Offerings* (Dan Curtis, 1976), *Halloween* (John Carpenter, 1978) and *The Shining* (Stanley Kubrick, 1980), 'the notion of ... (middle-class) life as tantamount to the world of horror has been mushrooming' (1982: 4). This location of horror in the home is symptomatic of a 'network of anxieties ... often realised in terms of the troubling insatiateness which underlies the structure of American family life' (ibid.). Snyder identifies in the American 'collective psyche', a 'leisure culture, syndrome' (1982: 5), in which 'traditional masculine values of conquest coupled to a mindless consumerism, 'threaten to unhinge "our sanity:' (1982: 4). Tony Williams (1980/81) takes this argument further, seeing the family as a key institution for the production of individuals in the social roles required for the perpetuation of the (patriarchal) state and therefore itself an instrument of repression and supported by other apparatuses of oppression, the church, the police and so on. The source of horror, then, is not so much in the family's economic role but in the monstrous reactions that inevitably erupt against its repressiveness when fantasy attempts to obliterate what cannot be changed by political means. The Vietnam War, for example, simply provides the opportunity for a re-enactment of the monstrous fantasies engendered within the heart of the repressive patriarchal family.

If it is a characteristic of many recent accounts of the realist horror film to explain the genre in terms of a specifically American crisis of conscience, Haneke's films suggest that the global spread of capitalist culture carries its associated horrors alongside it. But if we are to see the films as thus continuing a tradition of cultural critique, we must note the pivotal break that Haneke forges in making explicit what is merely implicit in the vast majority of American genre films (both studio-produced and independent). For while realist horrors such as *Henry: Portrait of a Serial Killer* can be read 'against the grain' as critiques of the contemporary society of the spectacle, Cynthia Freeland concedes they can more readily be seen to 'perpetuate a climate of fear and random violence where anyone is a potential victim', at the same time as sending out 'the comforting message that we are safe because the violence is, at the moment, striking someone else':

> The emphasis on pessimism and powerlessness in realist horror ... obscures the truth about factors that produce a climate of violence: racism; inequities in education, health care, social and economic status, and political power; urban blight and flight; drug use; and gun laws. So instead of the horror prompting action and resistance, it works to produce passivity and legitimise current social arrangements. (1995: 138)

Within Haneke's films, however, far from striking elsewhere (and thereby placing the spectator at a remove from its implications) violence strikes us with the same force as it does the onscreen characters.[2] For the films expand upon a modernist self-reflexivity familiar from – although by no means exclusive to – realist horror. Deploying devices such as the diegetic screen, the troubling of the image status, the long-take and the extreme close-up, the inexplicability of the action and the aperture of narrative, Haneke's films consistently foreground their status as construct, and as such, the product of their author. Unlike the images on the Laurents' television screen, they cannot be dismissed or ignored, since they refuse to be neatly packaged away, easily explained, made digestible. Rather, they demand the spectator's attention – and they demand that the spectator consider his or her own relationship to them. Watching Haneke's films, we all too often become aware of ourselves sitting in the auditorium, experiencing horror – and this in turn provokes a secondary moment of revulsion, as we realise that the events on screen are not so far removed from the world in which we live as we would like to think.

Describing the narrative events of *Hidden*, Ezra and Sillars write that 'in a world where turning a blind eye has become an art [the film] explores the ways in which being made to look – and to think – can be experienced as forms of terror' (2007: 215). One might argue that the narrative events of *Hidden* analogise the spectatorial situation for the viewer of Haneke's films: like Georges, we are brought to a realisation of the horrors of our own existence largely through the power of horrifying images. But terror, John S. Nelson has claimed, preempts escape, it prevents hope: 'Terror radicalises anxiety. It projects death or degradation as immanent possibilities from action. Therefore terror disables you from action. It diminishes personal movement into mere behaviour' (2006: 184–85). It is precisely this stasis that Haneke's films depict within the narrative. If the terrors of everyday life, of bombs, of bullies, of monsters or murderers, petrifies us, Haneke's films see us likewise stalled, unable to move or act, as a result of the ubiquity of the image and our 'willing surrender of life to the products of the fantasy industry' (in *71 Fragments of a Chronology of Chance*, a TV report on the 'Third PC Expo', at Vienna's Trade Fair Center declares that, 'Frenetic images and fantasy worlds are still market leaders'). His films, far from obscuring the causes of violence in society, adding to a climate of fear in which anyone can be a sudden victim, suggest the ways in which we contribute to a society which paralyses us, thus thrusting us into a position of responsibility. Precisely what we should do with this responsibility is a question left unanswered by Haneke. What is clear is that continuing indifference is the most horrific response one can offer to our contemporary predicament.

NOTES

1   For a concise account of the relationship of excess to horror, see Williams 1991. Elsewhere, I have argued for viewing Haneke's films as heavily predicated on generic formulae – and have made a claim for viewing the marketing of his films as a key tool in creating expectations that the films themselves compound – and then undermine, to devastating effect. It is outside the limits of this chapter to expound on this point here. However, I would like to raise the point that a case for reading Haneke's *Funny Games* as a legitimate contribution to the horror genre could be made – and that the promotional materials for the film would easily lend support to such a view. See Wheatley 2008.
2   Consider, for example, Peter Bradshaw's response to *The Piano Teacher*, upon seeing it screened at the 2001 Cannes Film Festival: 'At the premiere of Michael Haneke's last film but one, *Funny Games* – that intensely bewildering orgy of off-camera violence – audiences started staggering out after about 20 minutes, offended, revolted, or maybe just winded. At the Cannes unveiling of *The Piano Teacher* this year, I like to think we crossed the finishing

line in better shape. We were just numbly silent, twitchily uncertain of when to speak. Only one person was in tears. I was reasonably calm, but I think I remember leaving the auditorium on my hands and knees.' (2001: 16–17)

BIBLIOGRAPHY

Bingham, A. (2006) 'Modern Times: Notes towards a Reading of Michael Haneke's *71 Fragments of a Chronology of Chance*'. On-line. Available HTTP: http://www.sensesofcinema.com/contents/cteq/05/34/71_fragments.html (18 June 2006).
Bradshaw, P. (2001) 'Now Wash Your Hands' (review of *La Pianiste*), *The Guardian*, Section 2, 9th November, 16-17.
Carroll, N. (1990) *The Philosophy of Horror*. New York and London: Routledge.
Combs, R. (2002) 'Living in Never-Never Land: Michael Haneke Continues the Search For a New European Cinema', *Film Comment* 38: 2, 26–8.
Derry, C. (1977) *Dark Dreams: A Psychological History of the Modern Horror Film*. London: Thomas Yoseloff.
Ezra, E. and J. Sillars (2007) '*Hidden* in Plain Sight: Bringing Terror Home', *Screen* 48: 2, 215–21.
Freeland, C. (1995) 'Realist Horror', in C. Freeland and T. E. Wartenberg (eds) *Philosophy and Film*. London and New York: Routledge, 126–42.
Murphy, B. (1972) 'Monster Movies: They Came From Beneath the 1950s', *Journal of Popular Film and Television*, 1: 1, 31–4.
Nelson, J. S. (2006) 'Four Forms of Terrorism: Horror, Dystopia, Thriller and Noir', in E. Ezra and T. Rowden (eds) *Transnational Cinema: The Reader*. London and New York: Routledge, 181–95.
Peucker, B. (2000) 'Fragmentation and the Real: Michael Haneke's Family Trilogy,' in W. Riemer (ed.) *After Postmodernism: Austrian Film and Literature in Transition*. Riverside, CA: Ariadne Press, 176–87.
Sharrett, C. (2006) 'Michael Haneke and the Discontents of European Culture', *Framework*, 47: 2, Fall, 6–16.
Snyder, S. (1982) 'Family Life and Leisure Culture in *The Shining*', *Film Criticism* 7: 1, 4–13.
Wheatley, C. (2008) *The Films of Michael Haneke*. Oxford: Berghahn.
Williams, L. (1991) 'Film Bodies: Gender, Genre and Excess', *Film Comment*, 44: 4, 2–13.
Williams, T. (1980/81) 'American Cinema in the 70s: Family Horror', *Movie*, 27/28, 117–26.
Wood, R. (2004) 'What Lies Beneath', in W. Rothman and S. J. Schneider (eds) *Freud's Worst Nightmares*. Cambridge: Cambridge University Press, pp. xiii–xviii. On-line. Available HTTP: http://www.sensesofcinema.com/contents/01/15/horror_beneath.html (2 January 2007).
Yates, R. (1993) Review of 'Benny's Video', *Sight and Sound*, 3: 9, September, 41–2.

EASTERN EUROPEAN AND TURKISH
HORROR CINEMA

EASTERN EUROPEAN AND TURKISH HORROR CINEMA

Patricia Allmer, Emily Brick and David Huxley

This section covers what could loosely be termed 'non-Western' Europe, incorporating the Central and Eastern regions as well as Turkey, which sits on the boundaries of Europe and North Africa. The term 'Eastern Europe' refers to the Soviet-influenced Eastern Bloc countries, grouped together by similar political and economic systems. In 1945, Winston Churchill stated that 'an *iron curtain* has descended across the Continent'[1] splitting off Poland, East Germany, Hungary, Czechoslovakia, Yugoslavia, Romania and Bulgaria. Europe was divided until the fall of the Berlin Wall in 1989 when Germany reunified. The Soviet Union dissolved in 1991 and many borders were redrawn.[2] In terms of film production the former Eastern Bloc countries have developed separate independent national cinemas although many films discussed in this section are cross-country productions. Whilst there is work on individual national cinema, such as Romania and Russia (Stojanova 2005 and Wolf 2005) and Jan Švankmajer and the Czech Republic (Uhde 2005), there is however an absence of work on Eastern European horror cinema as a whole.

Eastern Europe's most obvious legacy to horror is Dracula. The myth which is so prevalent in Western horror cinema has two origins – the figure of Vlad Tepes (1431–76), and the vampire superstition which is present throughout Romania, Hungary and Slovakia, with myths of 'so many species of bloodsucking, flesh-eating and sexually disturbing creatures of the night, disruptive of harvest, livestock and family life' (Stojanova 2005: 221). These two sources morphed into the vampire tradition which saturates many national horror cinemas but is absent in Eastern European horror where the real 'Dracula' is generally represented as a heroic figure. Likewise, the Elizabeth Báthory myth, in which she bathed in the blood of young girls to keep her youth, has also been appropriated in Western horror cinema, from predatory lesbian vampires to its re-enactment in *Hostel II* (Eli Roth, 2007). *Bathory* (2008), a joint Czech/Slovak film directed by Juraj Jakubisko, instead presents the myth as the story of a tragic heroine within the context of a love story, rather than a monster in a horror film.

Although 'horror' film production or reception is still not widely established in Eastern Europe, it is increasingly being used as the setting for Western horror. In *Severance* (Christopher Smith, 2006), a group of English office workers go on a team-building weekend to the Hungarian mountains where they are ambushed, terrorised and murdered by ex-soldiers driven to cannibalism by the horrors of war. Within the *mise-en-scène* of films such as this one, the East/West axis forms the same dynamic as the urban/rural axis of American horror. *Hostel* (Eli Roth, 2005) and *Hostel II* both position Eastern Europe as the unknown, uncivilised other, although within these particular films the violence is enacted by outsiders and American imperialism is located as the source of violence.

Christina Stojanova's chapter here examines the representation of Eastern Europe within horror cinema in terms of Western constructions of the Eastern Bloc as a dark monstrous other, and the way that horror develops as a genre within these national cinemas utilising local myths and motifs. This chapter covers Slovakia, Yugoslavia, the Balkans, Hungary, Romania and Bulgaria and concludes with the development of horror motifs within recent Russian horror cinema. Stojanova explores the political nature of horror film, specifically the influence of Communism on representations of the West, and in the way that the East represents itself as a place of horror.

Patricia Allmer's chapter examines the ways in which the body horror of *Taxidermia* (György Pálfi, 2006) is grounded in the social and political history of Hungary. The notion of what constitutes a 'horror film' is, however, very different across audiences and while films may be perceived externally as horror, they are not read as such by Eastern European audiences. *Taxidermia* itself was described by Channel 4 as 'horror' for its UK screening, but is not referred to as a horror film anywhere on its own website, or in Hungarian reviews. The grotesque and surrealist aesthetics which characterise *Taxidermia* locate the text firmly against a background of high art rather than the popular/trash culture usually associated with horror.

Similarly, Turkey has a very different history and cultural landscape to the West as well as a different history of film production. The first Turkish film widely recognised as 'horror' was *Drakula Instanbul'da/Dracula in Instanbul* (Mehmet Muhtar, 1953). Until this point the absence of horror film was a symptom of an absence of film production in general, but although other genres took off as the industry developed, horror was lacking in Turkish cinema. From 2000 onwards, a sudden boom occurred, which is discussed here. Kaya Özkaracalar's chapter examines the recent surge in Turkish horror cinema, providing an overview of its history and of the contemporary boom. From the early modern period when much of Europe was governed by the Holy Roman Empire, Turkey, as part of the Islamic Ottoman Empire, has been separated from Europe on religious grounds. The key difference between Turkey and the rest of Europe is still one of religion.

Horror cinema often relies heavily on religious iconography and frameworks of meaning to present notions of good and evil. This chapter focuses on the way in which Turkish horror films adapt and remake existing texts in relation to Islamic motifs.

NOTES

1   Winston Churchill, 'Sinews of Peace' address March 5, 1946, Westminster College, Fulton, Missouri.
2   The ending of the Soviet Union led to social, economic and political independence for Latvia, Lithuania, Estonia, Ukraine and Belarus. Czechoslovakia separated into the Czech Republic and Slovakia. Yugolavia separated into Croatia, Slovenia, Bosnia and Herzegovina, Macedonia and Yugoslavia/Serbia and Montenegro (which later split into Serbia, Montenegro and Kosovo).

BIBLIOGRAPHY

Stojanova, C. (2005) 'Phenomenology of Horror in Romanian Cinema', in S. J. Schneider and T. Williams (eds) *Horror International*. Detroit, MI: Wayne State University Press, pp. 220–34.
Uhde, J. (2005) 'Implicit Horror in the Films of Jan Švankmajer', in S. J. Schneider and T. Williams (eds) *Horror International*. Detroit, MI: Wayne State University Press, pp. 259–72.
Wolf, J. (2005) 'Russian Cinema and Horror', in S. J. Schneider and T. Williams (eds) *Horror International*. Detroit, MI: Wayne State University Press, pp. 336–58.

NOTES

A GAZE FROM HELL:
EASTERN EUROPEAN HORROR CINEMA REVISITED

Christina Stojanova

In his book *Horror: A Thematic History of Fiction and Film* (2002) Darryl Jones quotes John Carpenter's 'somewhat crude', but useful division of all horror narratives into two groups: 'left-wing' or 'Frankensteinian', and 'right-wing' or 'Draculean'. In the former, Carpenter says, 'the source of threat is within [...] that which we have to fear is located within ourselves, in the human mind ... and in the human body'. The latter interprets 'the threat [as coming] from without, something other, alien and external to humanity ... and against which we must guard if we can' (quoted in Jones 2002: 146).

In light of Carpenter's proposition, the subject of the first part of this chapter is the 'right-wing' horror of Western genre cinema, where Eastern Europe is construed as a continuous source of dread from without, a site of an abject, horrifying Other. This 'outsourcing' of evil way out East could be tracked down to Bram Stoker's *Dracula* (1897), which put Transylvania and vampirism on the map of modern Western European imagination at the end of the nineteenth century. This part also discusses briefly the symbiotic relationship between the Western subject and the Eastern object of the gaze with regard to the development of the horror genre. The second part deals with 'left-wing' horror narratives of recent art and genre films from Eastern Europe, where evil is imagined from within its ground zero, so to speak, and as fluctuating between object and subject of the gaze. This chapter also builds on my previous research on the phenomenology of Romanian cinematic horror (Stojanova 2005) and on the evolution of Soviet and Russian horror films (Stojanova 2004).

FEAR WEST OF THE EAST

It is the face of our own shadow that glowers at us across the Iron Curtain.
– C. G. Jung, *Man and His Symbols* (1993, v. 18: 85)

Stoker's classic, drawing on tensions between the modernised, 'civilised West' and the 'primitive Eastern Europe', designates the fault lines of their ongoing cultural, social and ideological discrepancies in a myriad of films, horror or otherwise. This archetypal clash could be 'understood in psychoanalytical (Jungian) terms as stemming from ... representation [of Eastern Europe] as the West's "shadow", revealing the hidden or repressed contents of the Western collective unconscious, which becomes manifest in the popular ... texts' as displaced symbolic projections (Stojanova 2005: 221). In other words, from a Western point of view, Eastern Europe is seen as its sinister *doppelgänger*, harbouring people who seem 'like us' but are uncannily different, like Count Dracula. To quote Slavoj Žižek, the 'Balkans (or "the not-quite-so European East"), signify ... timeless space onto which the West projects its phantasmatic content' (quoted in Galt 2006: 135). Dracula and his copious cinematic progeny were a mass media device for safely defusing the pent-up horrors of death and the supernatural, and the frustrations of sexuality from the late nineteenth and the first half of the twentieth century.

In a similar fashion, the terror of nuclear apocalypse, identified with Eastern Europe during the Cold War, was fertile for the evolution of the Hollywood horror thriller and its most successful spin-off, the science fiction film. Their 'right-wing' narratives articulated a cathartic release from the ubiquitous Red Scare by displacing the East/West stand-off onto the symbolic plane of victorious confrontation against the fantastic 'other coming to get "us"' (Jones 2002: 146). As Linda Badley has aptly put it, 'in myth, art, and pop culture [the fantastic] functions as a rite of defilement in which the subject ... loses its boundaries in encounter with the Other, until the reflex of horror re-establishes them. The most primitive of languages, horror simultaneously alters identity and proclaims the subject's reality' (1995: 36).

After the collapse of Communism in the late 1980s, the West became privy to the atrocities suffered by Eastern Europeans at the hands of totalitarian regimes. The revelations of routine victimisation and psychological trauma on a large social scale, however, failed to inspire Western imagination as Dracula or the threat of nuclear holocaust did. What captured Western imagination was the abject materiality of the disintegration of Yugoslavia as it coincided with the ongoing process of demythologisation of cinematic horror. The symbolic and 'mythical projections of evil were no longer believable or necessary' as 'the monsters of the id were demystified and dissected, latent psychosexual contents have become manifest, [and] subtext has become text' (Badley 1995: 10, 13).

The Yugoslav wars overlapped with the intensification of globalisation, which fostered the political and economic arrogance of the West as an island of reason amidst an unfathomable sea of needs and passions, but also with its paranoid fears of defilement. The graphic representation of the Balkan atrocities generated a lot of controversy surrounding the way the horror stories should be told: from within or from without. A case in point is the vehement debate about Emir Kusturica's *Bila jednom jedna zemlja/Underground* (1995), and the Balkanist discourse it has allegedly internalised.[1] In other words, the film was accused of telling the story from without, perpetuating the Othering of Eastern Europe as a source of evil.

This accusation, while highly contested with regard to *Underground*, could be laid at the door-step of *Les fleurs d'Harrison/Harrison's Flowers* (Elie Chouraqui, 2000), whose story evolves during the early phase of the Yugoslav wars. The conflict is seen mostly through the eyes of the loving wife of an award-winning American photojournalist, who gets shell shocked and disappears in the Vukovar inferno. She brings him back to life with the help of a few self-sacrificial photojournalists, determined to get their colleague and the story of the Vukovar siege out. Although made when more information became available about the actual socio-political background of the conflict, the film could be seen as an illustration of what the *New York Times* described as the travails of '"irreconcilable warring tribes", incomprehensible to the civilised world' (quoted in Galt 2006: 135). A notion, expressed even more bluntly by one of its characters – 'Serb, Catholic, Croatian, Orthodox, there's no bad guys, no good guys ... They are all fuckin' insane' – and epitomised on screen by faceless soldiers-cum-callous murderers, and by a meticulously reconstructed picture of death and destruction. Framed in medium-long shots as if through journalistic photo-lens, the war remains outside of the film's Symbolic – a shocking glimpse into the messy Real, undeniably atavistic 'spectacle of a timeless cycle of passions' (Žižek quoted in ibid.).

THE *HOSTEL* CASE

The removal of the Iron Curtain made travel to the previously sealed Eastern European lands possible, thus offering yet another opportunity for construing horror, predicated mostly on the emergence of the postmodern narcissistic personality, nurtured by what Žižek calls 'injunctions to enjoy and to consume';

preoccupied with all things physical and bent on 'bio-political (self) control ... and excessive fear of harassment' (2006: 297), such a personality feels easily threatened by the impoverished Eastern Europeans, still adhering to remnants of a patriarchal, macho culture. The ensuing paranoid fear is usually that of immediate physical violation, most skilfully harnessed by the ever-escalating gruesomeness of the slasher/splatter genre, whose 'primitive language of horror' follows a similar plot: a 'group of young, urban, Western adventurers travels to a far-off land' (Badley 1995: 45) where they are eventually killed off by (or with the help of) backward locals but not before being subjected to despicable acts of torture, violating ultimate taboos of 'consuming and possessing of other bodies' (Badley 1995: 29).

There is hardly a more graphic recent example of the paradigmatic construing of Eastern Europe by the Western gaze as the site of the uncanny Other than *Hostel*, Eli Roth's versatile rendition of the slasher genre. *Hostel* (and some of its sequel, *Hostel II*) is shot on location in Český Krumlov, tucked in the heart of the more affluent 'Mittel' (or Central) European part of ex-Czechoslovakia and a favourite tourist attraction, famous for its gorgeous castle and lovingly restored medieval and baroque houses. In the film, this picture-postcard place is the hub of a unique international enterprise for the very rich, seeking to indulge their sadistic yearnings to 'consume and posses other bodies' under the protection of the ruthless local Mafia. The hapless young victims – a bunch of pleasure-seeking, somewhat arrogant, but well-meaning backpackers from Western Europe, US and Japan – are, of course, guests of the eponymous hostel, who get seduced, drugged and then delivered to the torture chambers by Mafia accomplices of Russian, Czech and Slovak origin.

Roth navigates the voyeuristic Western gaze through the stark contrast between the lovely townscapes and the creepy blandness of the post-Communist existence, contriving a phantasmic reality where the worst carnal fears seem plausible. And, by shifting the ominous fictional location further East, to Slovakia, he benefits from subtle intertextual references to Eastern Europe as a disadvantaged and dangerous place not unlike Dracula's Transylvania and the war-ravaged Balkans. Or as an eloquent exchange in *Hostel II* goes: 'Slovakia? Wasn't there some war in Slovakia? No, that's Bosnia, darling.'

Curiously enough, the source of real terror in the film does not originate with the Mafia bosses or the actual foreign perpetrators of the violations but with the locals, posing as charming promoters and receptionists, seductive female guests and burly guards. Their ruthless solidarity invests the beautiful scenery with a bloodcurdlingly realistic sensation of entrapment and irreversible damage. A sensation which cannot be dissipated even by the predictable finale where the enterprising Western 'final boy' of sorts (to paraphrase Carol J. Clover's concept of the 'final girl' [1992: 77]) succeeds in killing the most vile members of the commune on the Mafia payroll (but apparently not all, therefore the less interesting *Hostel II*).

FEAR EAST OF THE WEST

The post-Yugoslav cinema did try to come up with its own brand of 'right-wing' horror by returning the gaze and implying the West as a dangerously inefficient authority, partially implicated in the break-up of the Federation. In *Pred dozhdot/ Before the Rain* (Milcho Manchevski, 1994), the UNPROFOR troopers are construed as an incongruously decorative presence, scorned by Macedonians and Albanians alike for their inability to avert the tragic confrontation in an ethnically mixed Macedonian village.[2] *Ciganska magija/Gypsy Magic* (Stole Popov, 1997) offers a more caustic portrayal of the UN forces as a bunch of irresponsible holiday-makers who only care for drinking and sex, and occasionally pick a fight with the local thugs under the guise of 'peace-keeping'. In any case, the Western presence in these films is seen as anything but macabre. The most immediate reason for the inability or reluctance of contemporary Eastern European cinemas to construe the West as the sinister Other is arguably their ideological fatigue from decades-long, officially-endorsed demonisation of the West as the arch-enemy of Communism. Indeed, as Rosalind Galt writes in her brilliant defence of *Underground*, the relationship between East and West is 'a relationship as much of [Western] fantasy and [Eastern] desire as of history and geography' (2006: 140). Her careful search through the gaps and excesses of *Underground*'s art-cinema narration amounts to a superb reading of the ultimate Eastern European space – that of the underground tunnel – as a symbol of perennial horror and victimisation. In her view, such a 'structural articulation of abjection … prevents the Western spectator from becoming [a] privileged onlooker who has history explained to him by [the] televisual realism', sustained by the 'affective sight of ruins and bodies' as in *Harrison's Flowers* (2006: 147), thus allowing a claim to be laid 'on Balkanism from within, from the place of the primitive object of the discourse rather than its Western subject' (2006: 143).

FEAR EAST

Minotaur this is the zeitgeist, *the spirit of time.*
– Victor Pelevin, The Horror Helmet (2005: 35)

Since *Nosferatu* (F. W. Murnau, 1922) – the first screen apparition of Dracula – the 'right-wing' horror narratives have featured Eastern Europe consecutively as a breeding ground of supernatural monsters; mysterious source of annihilation (nuclear or otherwise); site of absurd ethnic strife and appalling physical atrocities. And, to quote Badley again, these narratives have invariably pointed back to the idiosyncratic 'altering of [Western] identities' from modernity to postmodernity, and to the 're-establishing of their boundaries' through the reflex of horror vis-à-vis the irrational Eastern European Other (1995: 36). Paradoxically, this process tacitly parallels the metamorphoses of horror as imagined in the East: from what Mircea Elidae calls the *illud tempus* (or the time of the mythical beginnings) of the folklore marvellous through the uncanny terror of modernity and Communism, to the abject ugliness of the post-Communist, post-modern existence (1957: 80).

The subject of this chapter is therefore Eastern European 'left-wing' horror narratives and motifs, featuring evil as primarily internal – social and individual – matter, as coming from within, or, as Galt has it, as perceived 'from the place of the primitive object' (2006: 157) of the Western phantasmic discourse. If the individual human body is the preferred site of the post-modern, 'Draculean' Western horror, then the decaying post-Communist social body – understood both as analogy of an ailing society and a fickle social contract – could be identified, quite fittingly, as the locus of 'Frankensteinian' horror, mostly psychological but also physical. Unnaturally created from incongruous bits of collectivist utopia through brutal social engineering, forcefully abolishing its private sphere for the sake of the public, this castrated Frankensteinian social body has been disintegrating for two decades now. And the ensuing attempts at killing the monster by 'restoring the psychic boundaries between the collective and the individual, the public and the private' has turned out to be 'a form of a mundane horror', plaguing the post-Communist lands (Stojanova 2004: 104).

HUNGARIAN CINEMA OF DAMNATION

Due to the traditionally uneasy relations of Eastern European cinema with genres and entertainment, and because of the specificity of its perception of horror, predicated on over-investment in Hegelian rationality – 'What is real is rational, but not everything that is rational is real' – the paradigmatic darkness, mystery and violence of the horror genre has migrated to the experimental and art cinema. First to dissident works and, after the fall of communism, to films defined by David Bordwell as a 'new tradition of bleak realism' (2006) and by others as (neo) naturalism and, not without an irony – as 'miserabilism.' Inspired by *Damnation* (1988), the second film from Béla Tarr's bleak trilogy,[3] Tony McKibbin has eloquently named this tendency 'cinema of damnation' (2005).

The proliferation of this artistic phenomenon across the region for more than two decades now could be explained with the filmmakers' apprehension in the face of the ugly social reality of the actual existing socialism and its aftermath of political corruption, organised crime, ethnic tensions and general moral degradation. The unrivalled champion of the trend so far is *Sátántangó* (Béla Tarr, 1994), encapsulating its aesthetics and conceptual essence. The plot conveys the archetypal Eastern European story of a dream-turned-nightmare for a small rural community. Anxious to leave their grim abode, site of a defunct machinery plant, the villagers fall pray to Irimiás, a smooth-talking Messiah figure, who pledges to take them to a new life on a beautiful farm. Over the course of a few rainy autumn days, he embezzles and dumps them in the middle of nowhere.

As early as 1951, the Polish thinker and poet Czeslaw Milosz envisioned the end of Communism as the aftermath of a devastating flood. Warning against naïve beliefs that its simple removal would restore normalcy, he wrote: 'a raging river ... does not merely exist; it tears up and carries away whole banks of soil, fells trees, piles up layers of mud, overturns stones until the garden of old becomes nothing more than a given number of square meters of unrecognisable land' (1990: 203). If we are to apply this dark prophecy to our discussion, then *Satantango*'s subjects are portrayed as entrapped within an uncannily similar apocalyptic *paysage*. Blinded by incessant plotting, greed and mutual suspicion, however, they are utterly isolated and their desperation is articulated by the 'constantly opening up space [of post-Communist wastelands] as Tarr shows us the enormity of malevolence' (McKibbin 2005).

Shot in black-and-white, the film takes the viewer on a voyeuristic, seven-hour-plus cinematic experience through a ghastly para-reality – as seductive as it is vile – drenched in mud and fog. And while the villagers engage in a hypnotic game of hide and seek with Irimiás, perceived both as a monster and saviour, only the youngest and the wisest remain out of his scheme. Conned by her own brother, little Estike poisons her cat and then herself in the film's emblematic sequence. Likewise, the good old Doctor, alcoholic and village chronicler, in desperation bolts himself up in his own house.

In mesmerising long takes, the camera slowly hovers around grubby characters and repetitive events – some, like the eponymous drunken dance-macabre in the local pub, are shown more than once from various points of view – until it ensnares us into the cobweb spawning on screen. This almost-enforced identification with shameful yearnings and appalling cruelty positions the viewer as both an accomplice and a victim, and points to the blind spot where the real monster is hiding – in people's collusion with their own demise, orchestrated by Irimiás. In the above mentioned discussion of *Underground*, Galt refers to Jorge Luis Borges' story *The House of Asterion* (1949), where 'the protagonist lives in a labyrinthine mansion and does not realise until the final line that he himself is the minotaur' (2006: 157). Thus 'placing oneself in the [blind space] space of monstrosity' exposes the monster within, usually obscured by self-delusional projections.

The way *Satantango* marshals decrepit Communist spaces – a symbolic articulation of the routine horror Eastern Europeans have been forced to endure – is characteristic of the 'cinema of damnation'. Concealing terrible memories and dangerous secrets in vaults and labyrinths, the featured monumental public structures – along with the desolate vistas of post-Communist wastelands – have become a formidable cinematic presence in their own right, encroaching on the humans and menacingly gaping back at us.

Hostel makes a good intertextual use of this malevolent potential of deserted Communist public spaces to further the suspenseful effect of the paradigmatic East/West face-off. Thus the reassuring 'Mittel' European beauty of Česky Krumlov looks as ominously unsettling as the crumbling Soviet-era factory, whose giant concrete basement hides a maze of torture chambers and muffles the screams of the victims, tacitly implying the complicity of indigenous bourgeois values with diabolical designs, imported from the USSR. The abandoned Stalinist edifice however harbours ghastly memories of another, much costlier human experiment – the botched attempt at creating the 'new' men and women of Socialism and Communism. The uncanny locals, lurking in the back and middle ground of *Hostel* could easily be seen as an unwarranted product of nearly five decades of relentless social engineering.

Over the last ten years or so, noteworthy specimens of 'cinema of damnation' from the post-Communist lands have foregrounded its surrealist potential in graphic representations of bodily horror-cum-social commentary. In Hungary, the traditional penchant for visual ingenuity and narrative absurdity peaked with *Taxidermia* (György Pálfy, 2006), described somewhat mockingly by *Variety's* Eddie Cockrell as an 'exercise in Central European ultra-miserabilism' (2006). The film ups its misanthropic antes by pushing *ad absurdum* the limits of abject bodily horror, and by offering a caustic socio-cultural commentary about three generations of Hungarians, whose grotesque corporeal excesses mirror the monstrosities of their *zeitgeist*. The masturbation antics of the sex-obsessed grandfather, an orderly, culminating in the iconic penis fire-shooting scene, allude to the idiocy of inter-war militarism. His gluttonous son – an *über*-obese speed-eating champion of the 1960s – pledges his allegiance to Communism by ingesting and vomiting enormous amounts of food. The grandson, a virtuoso taxidermist in present-day Budapest, embalms himself into a headless and armless replica of a Greek sculpture in a truly Frankensteinian act of paroxysmal narcissism. To quote the famous Czech master of the absurd, Jan Švankmajer, 'Surrealism is not an artistic style, but a means of investigating and exploring reality' (quoted in Hames 2001: 27).

RUSSIAN CHERNUKHA FILMS

The indigenous brand of Russian bleak cinema is called *chernukha*, a colloquial synonym for 'black', flaunting 'neo-realist depiction of bodily functions, sexuality, and often sadistic violence' in contrast to the 'more traditional Russian themes, such as emotion and compassion' (*Russian History Encyclopaedia*). Although a dominant trend in the post-*perestroika* arts and mass media throughout the 1990s, *chernukha* films have lately come to a trickle. Yet *4* (2005), the first film by young director Ilya Khrjanovsky, made quite a stir with its Tarr-like long takes and morbid narrative about the nightmarish return of three Moscow prostitutes to their native decrepit village for the funeral of the fourth one. *4* was followed by an even more explicitly macabre film about prostitutes, Yuri Moroz's *Tochka/ The Spot* (2006), featuring their graphic abuse at the social margins of a big city.

Indeed, the obstinate obsession of *chernukha* with physical exploitation can be seen as a 'naturalistic inversion' of melodrama's 'compensatory emotional expressionism', where 'concentrated emotionality is supplanted by concentrated physicality' (Graham 2000: 11). In the context of Russian philosopher Nikolay Berdyaev's influential ideas, by virtue of its physicality, *chernukha* is trapped within the 'phenomenal world of laws and material objects, alienated from personality and limiting freedom', unable (or unwilling) to offer cathartic rapport with the 'noumenal world-in-itself of spirit, personality, freedom, and creativity' (1992). Eluding emotional involvement and engagement with the social and psychological causes for the subjects' suffering, the latest crop of *chernukha* films reveals a disturbing tendency towards keenly voyeuristic exploitation of the 'new' Russian poor. Thus, by 'reversing the traditional obsession' of the Russian intelligentsia with the '"lower depths", prompted by its sense of guilt and compassion, into its diabolical double': intense fear, originating in 'purely narcissistic and neo-capitalist' anxieties about status and personal prosperity (Stojanova 2004: 102), these films all but defeat their purpose.

THE NEW RUSSIAN HORROR GENRE

Since the early 1990s, Russian cinema has been struggling to harness horror motifs and shocking imagery in a *bona fide* horror genre, which is hardly surprising given the cultural differences between the Western and the Russian sense of horror, reflected in the rich tradition of the Russian literary fantastic – more psychologically intense than scary – featuring wining and dining with the Devil (Anton Chekov's *The Shoemaker and the Devil*, 1890), playing cards with her (Alexander Pushkin's *The Queen of Spades*, 1834) and sometimes even getting a ride on her back (Nikolai Gogol's *Vyi*, 1835). Blending horror with heavy doses of supernatural mystery, or with crime thriller and science-fiction, and even lacing it with black humour, the process of trial and error continued. Until the genre graduated, so to speak, with the national and international success of the 'patriotic' blockbusters *Nochnoy dozor/Night Watch* (2004) and *Dnevnoy dozor/Day Watch* (2006) where, to make the extremely long and confused story short, the good night watchers are involved in a mystical struggle against the bad day watchers – propelling their director Timur Bekmambetov to Hollywood and *Wanted* (2008).

One of the most popular films of 2007 was the ghost story *Myortvye docheri/ Dead Daughters*, directed by the young Pavel Ruminov, a former music video director. It is based on an urban legend about six successful young professionals in present-day Moscow, who get randomly selected by the ghosts of three little girls who were murdered by their psychotic mother, and are given a 'trial period' of three days to live by the moral standards of the Ten Commandments. Those who fail are ruthlessly killed by the daughters via telekinesis. In spite of its muddled narrative and agitated camera, the film looks expensively slick with its drained-out, bluish colour palette and beautiful cast. Its semblance to famous J-horror films, like *Ringu/The Ring* (1998) and *Honogurai mizu no soko kara/ Dark Water* (2002) by Japanese director Hideo Nakata, is provocatively uncanny, but contributes little to the Russian-ness of the film. As in *Night Watch* and *Day Watch*, Moscow is rendered as a generic metropolis; outfits and behaviour are fashionably cosmopolitan, and the dialogue is heavily sprinkled with English words.

What does make the new horror films Russian is their rapport with the supernatural and over investment in the struggle of good versus evil, imagined alternatively in terms of the Manichean clash of the *phenomenal* (or material) evil with the *noumenal* (or spiritual) good, or in light of Christian Orthodox teachings and symbolism. Or as a shrewd blend of both, as in *Dead Daughters*, where *phenomenal* bodily horror is mixed with the *noumenal* psychological terror in the context of Christian orthodoxy. While the Hollywood genre cinema sees the confrontation of good and evil as a clash of wills within the rational realm of the material world, the New Russian Horror genre casts it as a holy war, helmed by a Christ-like figure, and fought on behalf of mystical spiritual forces, as illustrated by Aleksandr Melnik's multi-million dollar blockbuster *Novaya zemlya/Terra Nova* (2008).

IN LIEU OF A CONCLUSION: *CARGO 200*

The most powerful achievement of the bleak post-Communist cinema so far is the Russian film *Gruz 200/Cargo 200* (2007), arguably the most controversial film by prominent director Aleksei Balabanov. It uses shocking bodily horror-cum-painful social analysis reminiscent of *The Texas Chainsaw Massacre* (Tobe Hooper, 1974), but with a compelling psychological twist. The story about the kidnapping of Angelika, the virginal teenage daughter of a local party boss, by the sadistic police officer Zhurov, and her appalling abuse in his hands, foregrounds the dying Soviet social body on the eve of *perestroika*[4] and its vile consequences for the current state of Russian affairs. The time and spaces of this suspenseful post-mortem of the Soviet empire are inextricably linked to philosophical and moral revelations, grasped so far only by social philosophers. The year is 1984, the bleakest time of general decay, known as *zastoy*,[5] and of the futile Afghan war, fought by idealists like Angelika's fiancé, shrouds the narrative with yet another layer of gloom, encoded in the film's title, *Gruz 200*.[6] The washed-out look of the film reminds uncannily of mainstream Soviet movies, shot on the native, crude film stock produced by the long-defunct factory Svema.

Cargo 200 (Balabanov, 2007) (courtesy Intercinema Agency, Moscow)

The action alternates between a seedy town, meaningfully called Leninsk, and an isolated shack, another reminder of Tobe Hooper's classic, where Valera, a charmer and a drunk, takes Angelika to buy moonshine. And while he drinks himself into oblivion, Zhurov, who is creeping around, rapes Angelika with a bottle. Angelika is then taken as his 'bride' to the decrepit apartment in Leninsk he shares with his alcoholic mother on one of the most horrific rides in the history of cinema. In the break of the misty dawn, handcuffed to his motorbike, Angelika – petrified, bleeding and clutching her red stilettos to her chest – traverses a squalid industrial zone under the accompaniment of a chillingly blithe period tune.

Balabanov's Frankensteinian horror is effectively codified in private and public spaces, construed as ominous locations. While the public sphere has mutated into a military hierarchy, the private has become merely a transitional space or torture chamber, where regimented public rituals and roles are re-enacted: chained to her 'matrimonial' bed, next to the corpse of her Afghan hero, Angelika is raped by a convict under the barrel of Zhurov's gun. A far cry from the tormented deviants and grotesque swindlers from the 'cinema of damnation', Zhurov, like 'Bob', Leland Palmer's diabolical alter-ego from the TV mini-series *Twin Peaks* (David Lynch, 1990–92), is a rarely convincing embodiment of pure evil, who even self-proclaims by staring at the camera. Zhurov or rather, Zhurov's phenomena in all of its complexity, denotes the missing cause – past and present – of the extant misery in *chernukha* films. Fully identified with his public persona and the practically limitless power that goes with it, he is the Minotaur, the monster at the rotting heart of the Russian social body. Likewise Valera, the irresponsible draft-dodger, who abandons Angelika to her terrible lot, is a harbinger of horrors yet to come in twenty years when he and his likes would join the current Russian socio-political elite.

With *Cargo 200*, Balabanov distances himself from the self-serving muck-raking of *chernukha* and from the Draculean tropes of *Pro urodov I ljudei/Of Freaks and Men* (1998), his own brand of 'cinema of damnation' and most artistic work thus far. And certainly moves beyond the populist agenda of *Brat 1/Brother 1* (1996), hitherto his biggest commercial success, achieved by skilful adaptation of the thriller genre formula to expose the crimes of post-Soviet Mafiosi and their punishment in the hands of the vigilante hero. Here, the conventions of – or rather a set of direct references to – the horror genre serve the much greater (and nobler) task of revealing the monster within, hidden beneath the veneer of the growing Soviet nostalgia.

NOTES

1. Maria Todorova (1997) introduced the concept by delineating its differences with 'orientalism', and chronicled its evolution from the early modernity to the Yugoslav Wars.
2. United Nations Protection Force. http://www.un.org/Depts/dpko/dpko/co_mission/unprofor.htm; visited on August 1, 2008.
3. Bracketed by *Öszi almanach/Almanac of Fall* (1985) and *Sátántangó/Satantango* (1994).
4. Period of openness (*glasnost*), begun in 1985, which brought about the collapse of the USSR in 1991.
5. A period of general stagnation from the early 1970s through to the mid-1980s.
6. Gruz-200 was a code phrase for the secretive shipment of dead soldiers from Afghanistan to be buried quietly by their relatives. Any public display of grief was believed demoralising in the face of the official propaganda that the USSR was winning the war.

BIBLIOGRAPHY

Badley, L. (1995) *Film, Horror, and the Body Fantastic*. Westport, CN: Greenwood Press.
Berdyaev, N. (1992 [1946]) *The Russian Idea*. Hudson, NY: Lindisfarne Press. On-line. Available HTTP: http://www.emory.edu/INTELNET/four_thinkers.html (4 June 2007).
Bordwell, D. (2006) 'Tango Marathon'. On-line. Available HTTP: http://www.davidbordwell.net/blog/?p=31 (31 July 2008).
Clover, C. J. (1992) 'Her Body, Himself: Gender in the Slasher Film', in M. Jancovich (ed.) *Horror: The Film Reader*. London: Routledge, 77–90.
Cockrell, E. (2006) 'Taxidermia', *Variety*. On-line. Available HTTP: http://www.variety.com/index.asp?layout=features2006&content=jump&jump=review&dept=cannes&nav=RCannes&articleid=VE1117929482&cs=1&p=0 (20 July 2008).
Eliade, M. (1957) *The Sacred and the Profane*. Orlando, FA: Harcourt.
Galt, R. (2006) *Redrawing the Map: The New European Cinema*. New York: Columbia University Press.

Graham, S. (2000) 'Chernukha and Russian Film', *Studies in Slavic Cultures*, 1, 9–27.
Hames, P. (2001) 'Interview with Jan Švankmajer', *Sight and Sound*, 11: 10, 26–8.
Jones, D. (2002) *Horror: A Thematic History of Fiction and Film*. London: Hodder Arnold.
Jung, C. G. (1993) *The Collected Works of C. G. Jung*. H. Read, M. Fordham, G. Adler (eds) London: Routledge.
McKibbin, T. (2005) 'Cinema of Damnation: Negative Capabilities in Contemporary Central and Eastern European Film', *Senses of Cinema*, 34, January-March. On-line. Available HTTP: http://www.sensesofcinema.com/contents/05/34/cinema_of_damnation.html (25 July 2008).
Milosz, C. (1990 [1951]) *The Captive Mind*. London: Vintage.
Pelevin, V. (2005) *The Horror Helmet (Shlem uzhasa)*. Moscow: Otkryti Mir.
Russian History Encyclopaedia. On-line. Available HTTP: http://www.answers.com/topic/chernukha (25 July 2008).
Stojanova, C. (2004) 'Mise-en scénes of the Impossible: Soviet and Russian Horror Films', in E. Mathijs and X. Mendik (eds) *Alternative Europe: Eurotrash and Exploitation Cinema Since 1945*. London: Wallflower Press, 90–105.
____ (2005) 'Beyond Dracula and Ceausescu: Phenomenology of Romanian Cinematic Horror', in S. Scheider and T. Williams (eds) *Horror International*. Detroit, MI: Wayne State University Press, 220–35.
Todorova, M. (1997) *Imagining the Balkans*. New York: Oxford University Press.
Žižek, S. (2006) *The Parallax View*. Cambridge, MA: MIT Press.

TAXIDERMIA
A HUNGARIAN TASTE FOR HORROR

Patricia Allmer

György Pálfi's film *Taxidermia* (2006) offers a grotesque version of recent Hungarian history. The body and its horrors are used as powerful metaphors to conceptualise Hungarian history, tradition and identity. As the title of the film implies, the film is particularly interested in exploring on one level the body's boundaries and borders – 'dermia', 'skin' is the boundary between the body's inside and its outside. It is a surface which divides, holds together and covers, and is deeply engrained as a metaphor in Hungarian as well as English sayings such as 'menti a börét' ('saving one's skin') and 'nem fér a börébe' ('to jump out of one's skin'). The latter is a recurring image in this film, where bodies and their organs move outside of their borders and seem unable to contain themselves any longer. Whilst *Taxidermia* explores the fragility of bodily borders and boundaries as metaphors for political and ideological borders, it is also interested in the 'arrangement' ('taxis') and manipulation of these boundaries by political regimes.

History and political ideologies are explored through their horrific effects on the bodies of individuals. *Taxidermia*, based on two short stories by the contemporary writer Lajos Parti Nagy, is a family narrative tracing three patriarchal generations of misfits over three historical periods in Hungary. Morosgoványi, the grandfather, is a soldier during World War II, who lives with his lieutenant, his wife and two daughters in a remote area of Hungary. Kálmán, the father, is the son of Morosgoványi and the lieutenant's wife, but has been adopted by the lieutenant, and is eventually shot by him. Kálmán lives through the communist and Kádárist era, is a second-rate speed-eater, and marries Gizi, a speed-eating champion. He ends up, left by Gizi, as a grotesquely fat man unable to move, dependent on his son Lajos, who looks after him and his three overfed cats, which eventually tear Kálmán apart. Lajos, representing the third generation, lives in contemporary Hungary, and is a taxidermist who ends up gutting and preserving Kálmán and himself (by severing his own head and right arm with the help of a machine). Their preserved corpses are finally exhibited by his customer, Dr Andor Regőczy, in a museum where Lajos is lauded as an up and coming artist.

This chapter will argue that *Taxidermia* uses the codes of horror cinema to foreground the grotesque representation of the body, in order to explore political patriarchal regimes and their real as well as metaphorical penetration and manipulation of the human body. The grotesque body and its language are used to reveal the mythic nature of ideological positions which encompass such regimes, ranging from the myth of origin to the myth of hierarchies (i.e. boundaries). By revealing the fragility of the body's boundaries, the film shifts patriarchal and nationalistic categories of stable 'beings' and 'origins', anchored in any definition of national identity, to categories of 'becoming', anchored in the grotesque, marking ultimately a shift from 'being Hungarian' to 'becoming European'.

BEING

Grotesque, abject imagery and characteristics permeate *Taxidermia*. The characters consume and vomit excessively, ejaculate fire and stars, and fuck pigs' carcasses, suck breasts and lick others' underarm sweat. Piss and shit, bowels, blood, hearts and other organs are excessively on display whilst being detached from their bodies, and bodies are subjected to abnormal developments, ranging from bodily scars and birth defects to men with monstrous bellies, and oversized cats; neither reality and fiction, nor beauty and revolt can be separated in the surreal world of the film.

Taxidermia uses the grotesque to render uncomfortable any attempt to feel familiar and homely in any notion of 'Hungarianness'. According to Wolfgang Kayser, the grotesque embodies the alienated world, to which belongs 'that which was trusted and comfortable to us, which is suddenly revealed as foreign and sinister' (1957: 198). *Taxidermia* does not repress nostalgic memories, which are for example present in the familiar (and moving) depictions of typical Hungarian holidays on Lake Balaton, a traditional resort for Hungarian holiday-makers, as travel abroad was strongly restricted in the socialist era. However, whilst the film represents this comfortable resort as a space which Hungarians carved out for fond memories, these memories are immediately compromised, co-existing with and existing within horror. *Taxidermia* revisits a history of Hungary in which a consistent national identity and a 'home' cannot be found. The film's grotesque rhetoric works in the way described by Svetlana Boym: 'instead of curing alienation – which is what the imagined community of the nation proposes ... [the grotesque] use[s] alienation itself as a personal antibiotic against the ancestral disease of home in order to reimagine it' (1996: 513).

As Mikhail Bakhtin argues, images of the grotesque are dominant in the 'extra-official life of the people', so, for example, mockery and abuse are 'almost entirely bodily and grotesque. The body that figures in all the expressions of the unofficial speech of the people is the body that fecundates and is fecundated, that gives birth and is born, devours and is devoured, drinks, defecates, is sick and dying' (1984: 319). This concern for the 'language of the people', for a language more immediate, removed from official and disciplinary languages normally present in the narratives of history, resonates in one of the early speeches (a fake dialogue, monologically imposing its worldview in the process of ostensibly soliciting responses) by Morosgoványi's lieutenant:

> 'Let me ask you a direct question, in direct Hungarian speech, Morosgoványi: Is there anything better than a woman's cunt? Whatever you want to call it, it is still a cunt. Or not? Then it's not because it isn't. Or because it's ugly, the word I mean – or because it's unclean. [...] I understand that in all sorts of descriptions by poets the word is more beautiful – love's cup, dewy lily or perhaps even pussy. There's no doubt about that. [...] But that's just how people say it when they're courting someone or being polite, because really, for most people these descriptions really mean, cunt.' (Author's translation)

Or, as György Pálfi states in an interview: 'if we cut ourselves we bleed, if we eat, in the end we are also shitting' (quoted in Horeczky 2006; author´s translation). The use of the demotic Hungarian word 'pina' (cunt) enforces Hungarian colloquial speech as more expressive and more powerful than the discourses of politics and the army. However, it also momentarily locates an origin (a symbolic connection of nativity and nationhood that the film goes on to exploit) in the figure of the mother, despite the film's overt concern with paternity.

In *Taxidermia* ideology, political positions and collective memory go literally under the skin and penetrate the deepest fibres of being – the body here is political, the state of the body is also the body of the state. Bodies repeatedly fuse with and become machines – factory workers melt into the machines they are operating and the machine which operates them (be it metaphorically the state, manifest in the mechanic drills of the eating contest and the military apparatus, or literally in Lajos's case where the machine operates on him), suggesting that categories such as bodies and politics bleed into each other.

Bodies in *Taxidermia* are the very surfaces on which power struggles are acted out; they are the very objects which are deterritorialised (invaded) and reterritorialised. They represent Hungary's history as a succession of deterritorialisations and reterritorialisations. Hungary, and people's understanding of where Hungary begins and ends, have been, over the past hundred years or so, sharply shaped and reshaped. The country's borders and identity have shifted numerous times. Hungary became connected to and separated from different neighbouring nations, ranging from the connection with and separation from Austria during the Austro-Hungarian empire, and Hungary's loss of two-thirds of its pre-war territory following the Peace Treaty of Trianon in 1920, to its connection to and full embrace of Nazi Germany during Miklós Horthy's government in 1944. These developments were followed by Hungary's occupation by the Soviet Union. An attempted disconnection from the Soviets in 1956 was undermined by János Kádár, who transformed Hungary into a country which was both communist and capitalist, ruled by 'a party composed of the same reformed Communists who tried to make that system work and who finally, grudgingly, negotiated its demise' (Esbenshade 1995: 88). The country's current state, following the 1989 collapse of communism which began in Hungary, is as an independent nation, but part of the European Union.

These territorial bodies, far from being removed or being separate from the various regimes, are fuelled by them, by the food, actual and ideological, which they get fed. Food is vital to life and is also an integral part of Hungarian politics and cultural identity. One only has to recall expressions which characterise Hungarian living and politics, such as 'Salami-politics', describing political strategies which fractionalise the opposition, or 'gulyáskommunizmus' ('goulash communism'), describing the 'more capitalist' version of communism under the Kádár regime, which transformed Hungary after 1956 into the 'happiest barrack' of the socialist bloc. The close connections between Hungarian identity and food are manifest in *Taxidermia* on a number of levels. Lajos's and Kálmán's surname is Balatony, describing not only the favourite Hungarian holiday resort, but also a chocolate bar, the Balaton Szelet, which as *Taxidermia*'s website states 'is a Hungarian chocolate brand with history [which] survived all eras' (http://www.taxidermia.hu). In featuring the bar, the film once again evokes nostalgia, which however is counteracted by Kálmán swallowing hundreds of these bars without unwrapping them, metaphorically implying the swallowing of political positions, histories and traditions without questioning them.

The film's engagement with food lays bare the power structures that exist between oppressive regimes and oppressed individuals, and complicates them by engaging with the dynamics of consumption. This is exemplified in the episode where Gizi and Kálmán are giving a speed-eating demonstration to a Russian audience accompanying the celebration of the 'Russian liberation'. A dynamics of consuming and being consumed emerges in this scene – Gizi and Kálmán have agreed to this demonstration in exchange for a trip to Sochi. Whilst consuming, choking and overeating on a star-shaped bowl of red caviar, they are in turn 'consumed' as a spectacle by the Russian onlookers. The star-shaped caviar bowl symbolically draws together and signifies Russia's superiority, but also indicates Hungary's second-class status during the socialist era – red caviar is, ironically, less expensive than black. Power structures here are closely tied in with the complex to-and-fro of consuming (and the desire to consume) and being consumed (and perhaps even the desire of being consumed, as is the case with Kálmán, who is working towards being eaten up by his giant pussies).

THE NAVEL

Taxidermia is a navel-gazing at one's own history and at being in and through history. The film ends with the camera zooming in on Lajo's navel, vanishing into its darkness. This movement also returns us to the darkness at the beginning of the film, tracing Lajos's origins and the origins of contemporary Hungary. The navel is, according to Fred Botting, a 'sign, a mark of separation as well as connection [...] it speaks of loss, a certain wound, a certain severance ... a certain death' (1999: 33), marking the film's concerns with separation and connection, locating origin once again in the maternal body. Whilst the belly button is a sign of Lajos's severance, of a cut which severs all ties with the previous generations (echoing the decapitating cut of his beheading which severs him from the future), it is also the mark through which the narrative of the previous generations is re-opened, which connects Lajos to them. The belly button incorporates the film's ambiguous and complex relationship to its own history, a relationship which is embedded in the dialectics of severances and connections.

The navel button is also a scar 'forming the first mark of culture on the body' (Botting 1999: 3). This is implied in a dialogue between Lajos and Dr Regőczy, when the latter hands over a brown paper bag the contents of which he wants Lajos to stuff. Lajos enquires about the bag's content: 'Is it wild or domestic?', to which Dr Regőczy replies, 'Domestic, I suppose'. The bag's content turns out to be an embryo – whilst stuffing it, Lajos carefully manipulates its navel cord, examining the thread which marks origin, but is also the mark of enculturation, of the beginning of being penetrated by ideologies and political positions.

However, Lajos not only severs himself from the previous generation (reminiscent of the violent severance of Bev Mantel from his twin brother Ellie in David Cronenberg's *Dead Ringers* [1988]), his story (his-story) also becomes the narrative of his severance from blood ties, the genealogical narratives penetrating personal, historical and religious discourses and perpetuating hierarchies as credible and objective. This process reveals the conventional, traditional and patriarchal approach to origins and genealogy and its claims of objectivity as fraught, and questions conventional notions of 'inheritance'. The film portrays a grotesque family saga, where the progress from underclass (Morosgoványi is a soldier of the lowest rank) to middle class (Lajos owns his own taxidermy business) is questionable, mocking other narratives of this genre which conventionally celebrate the law of inheritance. Its actors are failures, disempowered and bullied – Morosgoványi is bullied by his lieutenant, Kálmán remains a second-class speed-eater who is constantly over-eating and nostalgically dreaming of the good old times, unable to change. Lajos, himself a socially isolated figure, is bullied by Kálmán, his father, for being too thin.

Myths of origin and creation are reversed. Kálmán is not the lieutenant's child, but the son of Morosgoványi. This is also signified by the lieutenant's severing of Kálmán's pig-tail, a birth defect which is a mark connecting him to Morosgoványi and which serves as a 'reversed' or 'perverse' navel cord. Kálmán's fatherhood is also questionable, since his wife Gizi had intercourse with his speed-eating competitor on the night of his wedding. The third generation, Lajos, in turn, performs a symbolic self-castration by beheading himself, erasing any possibility of reproduction and therefore of passing on tradition and inheritance; this final cut signifies the terminus of the family line.

Lajos himself undermines myths of origin in a number of ways. He literally stuffs his father, thereby 'recreating' him, reversing causality and transforming himself into the creator of his father. He not only becomes his own creator (by stuffing himself he re-creates himself as an art-work), but also destroys his own status as creator, destroying himself in the act of his creation. Even the machine,

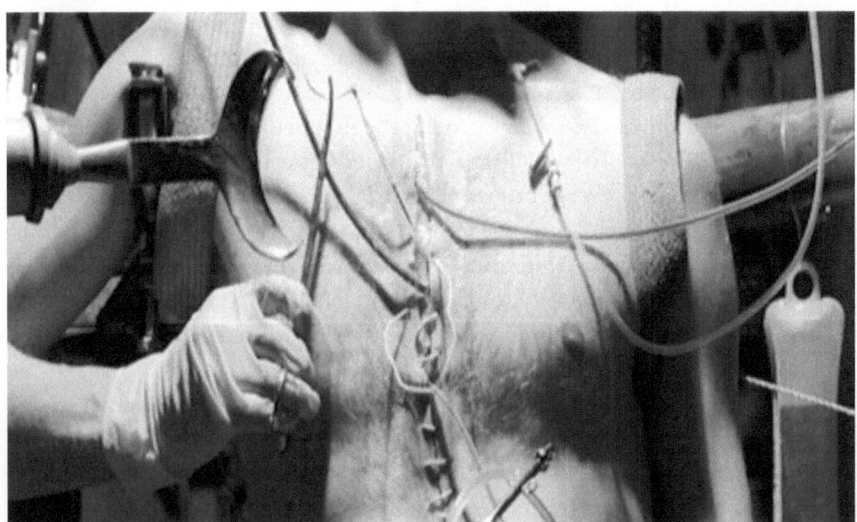

Lajos stuffing himself (*Taxidermia*, 2006)

which is created by Lajos and is ultimately his executor, destroys its own creator. Old fashioned company labels on the different machine parts reveal other creators, which once again undermine notions of origin and unique creation by signifying factory production. Far from providing a stable basis for the construction of origins, heritage here is 'an unstable assemblage of faults, fissures, and heterogeneous layers that threaten the fragile inheritor from within or from underneath' (Esbenshade 1995: 87).

Taxidermia itself symbolically cuts itself off from its originator, Lajos Parti Nagy, on whose short stories the film is based and who shares his name with the film's 'anti-hero', by giving him a cameo role as a corpse in a funeral scene. The self-consciousness of the filmic apparatus also becomes clear when the machine which dissembles Lajos winds up his intestines onto a reel, reminiscent of film reels. Film here is represented as an instrument winding up the past, but also having the potential to dismember and behead conventional ideological beliefs and positions, whilst the filmic cut and splice resembles the navel button's dialectic of severance and connection.

BECOMING

Whilst *Taxidermia* mocks the stability of notions such as origin and being, it offers instead visions of becoming as alternatives to beings tainted by the ideological stasis offered by communism and Nazism. Being here is characterised in the excessively overweight figure of Kálmán, suggesting the over-determination of the patriarchal body-state. The rejection of this stasis is expressed in Lajos's final row with his father where he explains why his mother left: 'She didn't want to get stuck in your huge arse and rot along with you. Cause everything rots here. Everything. Well I won't.' Becoming, instead, signifies the self-determination present in Lajos, who stuffs a bear (a symbol of Russian national identity) and then continues to stuff his father's corpse (a symbol of patriarchal origin) and finally himself (a symbol of the continuation of patriarchal relations).

The ending of the film shows Lajos's stuffed corpse exhibited as an art-work admired by visitors, marking the shift from being to a state of becoming and transformation anchored in art. Lajos's corpse draws together two philosophical concepts of becoming and fluidity mapped out in bodily metaphors: the 'Acephal' theorised by George Bataille, and the 'body-without-organs' discussed by Gilles Deleuze and Félix Guattari. Bataille's Acephal is incorporated in a drawing by André Masson showing a beheaded man carrying his blazing heart in his right hand. Lajos resembles the Acephal, not only through his own beheading, but also in an earlier scene where he holds his own heart in his right hand. The Acephal carries the double meaning of having no 'head or chief'. It projects a social community in which 'possible structures are not based on individualism, totalitarianism, or the feeble cohesion of democracies' (Bataille 1995: 12) and in which 'man can set aside the thought that it is he or God who keeps the rest of things from being absurd' (ibid.).

The Acephal has left thought and rationality behind, marking, in Alastair Brotchie's words, a 'headless organisation, one abjuring hierarchy' (Brotchie quoted in ibid.). The acephalic structure of 'headless organisation' counters hierarchy and stability, both of which are leading domains of fascism. The importance of 'disorganisation' is stressed by Lajos's torso being literally a body-without-organs, corresponding to Deleuze and Guattari's concept of the body-without-organs which is 'opposed not to the organs but to that organization of the organs called organism' (2002: 158). The body-without-organs opens the body to 'connections that presuppose an entire assemblage, circuits, conjunctions, levels and thresholds, passages and distributions of intensity, and territories and deterritorializations measured with the craft of a surveyor' (2002: 160). In *Taxidermia* history and being in history consist of 'connections of desires, conjunctions of flows, [a] continuum of intensities' (2002: 161) where everything is only always in becoming, destroying any notional master-discourse. This is expressed in a scene where Morosgoványi is shown fucking a being which is permanently transforming and becoming 'other', and with whom he gurgles and chants entranced: 'Let's scream together! Let's laugh together! Let's grunt together because life's too short! Get it in! Get it in as hard as you can!'

Taxidermia repeatedly subverts the coherence of 'being' and 'containment', instead presenting bodies which cannot contain themselves, but open up onto and spill into the world, marking a breakdown of boundaries and oppositions, between subjectivity and objectivity, between personal story and history, between outside and inside, opening orifices and revealing crevices through which a history, marked by boundaries, borders and restrictions, can seep out and interpenetrate. As Bakhtin comments, 'All these convexities and orifices have a common characteristic; it is within them that the confines between bodies and between the body and the world are overcome [...]. Thus the artistic logic of the grotesque image ignores the closed, smooth, and impenetrable surface of the body and retains only its excrescences (sprouts, buds) and orifices, only that which leads beyond the body's limited space or into the body's depth' (1984: 317). These filmic transgressions also revolt against the restrictive ideological boundaries imposed on Hungarian freedom by various regimes (without victimising Hungary *per se*) which were manifest in the historically real restrictions imposed on the crossing of real borders, ranging from strict border controls and harassment to people's economic inability to travel. These restrictions on the crossing of borders stood in crass contrast to the ruling classes' overstepping of the boundaries of peoples' personal freedoms, and to the hypocritical permissions granted for the exporting of valuable trading goods whilst restricting people's travel and additionally leaving them with second-rate goods. This is clear from Kálmán's narrative about rum-cherries: 'They were very rare then. We didn't even see them at Christmas, they all went into export.'

The bodily transgressions of boundaries are imitated by the film's generic transgressions, which comprise interpenetrating narratives ranging from historical film, family saga, fairy-tale, comedy/satire, pornography and particularly horror. These generic transgressions undermine any attempt to establish a 'coherent', 'objective' or dominant discourse of history, instead representing history as something which cannot be objective and which cannot be separated from myths and individual stories and perspectives. Through this, the 'history' presented here becomes an anti-history, as Pálfi states: 'history is always written by the winners. This is not a family of winners' (quoted in Horeczky 2006).

Perhaps what is 'coming to an end' in *Taxidermia* is the very notion of 'being Hungarian', its demise instead marking the inception of the new moment of 'becoming European'. Fluidity and the overstepping of boundaries between countries and traditions are present at a number of levels. The film was produced by five different production companies located in three different countries, Hungary, Austria and France. The final scene is recognisably 'displaced' from the previous Hungarian settings onto Vienna's Museum of Modern Art, where Lajos and his father's preserved bodies are exhibited. The different connections and links, which counteract any possibility for a master discourse to emerge, go still further into the multitude of European traditions from which *Taxidermia* emerges. The grotesque itself emerges out of a European tradition; as noted by Bakhtin, it not only predominates 'the art of European peoples, but also in their folklore' (1984: 319). The film connects to a number of past and contemporary European filmic traditions. It relates back to Hungary's own central position in European horror narratives – Hungary is a significant place in Stoker's *Dracula* (1897); the 'foreign language' spoken in F. W. Murnau's *Nosferatu* (1922) is Hungarian whilst the narrative of *Dracula* (a narrative which maps the whole of Europe) was influenced by the historic figure of the blood-thirsty Hungarian aristocrat Countess Elizabeth Báthory.

Whilst there are few contemporary Hungarian horror films, early Hungarian cinema was interested in the genre and produced a number of cult films such as Károly Lajthay's *Drakula Halála* (1921), the first filmic adaptation of Stoker's *Dracula*, and Michael Curtiz and Edmund Fritz's *Alraune* (1918). *Taxidermia* also relates to recent German horror films such as Stefan Ruzowitzky's *Anatomy* (2000) and *Anatomy II* (2003), and Robert Schwentke's *Tattoo* (2003). The main focus of these films is on the idea of preserving the body or skin, pointing to an artistic tradition, strongly present in *Taxidermia*, that includes Leonardo da Vinci's anatomical drawings and the work of contemporary international artists like Günter von Hagens and Géza Szöllösi, as well as the body art of Viennese Actionism. It is therefore no coincidence that the final scenes of *Taxidermia* play in Vienna's Museum of Modern Art, as its basement is dedicated to the display of the permanent collection of Viennese Actionist art.

The final scene of *Taxidermia* (leading back to its beginning) is accompanied by Dr Regőczy's voice presenting the exhibition in Hungarian with a simultaneous English translation, mingling the sound of the two languages together, stating that the narrative of Lajos's family is maybe 'only important, because this is the end of something, and if something comes to an end, also its beginning becomes important.' Perhaps the 'end of something' here is Pálfi's grotesque reconfiguration of horror and other filmic conventions in order to imagine a potential severance from myths of a stable Hungarian identity, and the subsequent beginning of a transnational 'becoming European'.

BIBLIOGRAPHY

Bakhtin, M. (1984) *Rabelais and His World*. Trans. H. Iswolsky. Bloomington, IN: Indiana University Press.

Bataille, G. et. al. (1995) *Encylcopædia Acephalica*. R. Lebel and I. Waldberg (eds) London: Atlas Press.

Botting F. (1999) *Sex, Machines and Navels: Fiction, Fantasy and History in the Future Present*. Manchester: Manchester University Press.

Boym, S. (1996) 'Estrangement as a Lifestyle: Shklovsky and Brodsky', *Poetics Today*, 17: 4, 511–30.

Deleuze, G. and F. Guattari (2002) *A Thousand Plateaus: Capitalism & Schizophrenia*. Trans. B. Massumi. London and New York: Continuum.

Esbenshade, R. S. (1995) 'Remembering to Forget: Memory, History, National Identity in Postwar East-Central Europe', *Representations*, 49, Winter, 72–96.

Horeczky, K. (2006) *Interview - Pálfi György: Taxidermia*. On-line. Available HTTP: http://www.magyar.film.hu/object.0746c3c0-8a28-43a4-997b-96e7a3265289.ivy (25 January 2006).

Kayser, W. (1957) *The Grotesque in Art and Literature*. Trans. U. Weisstein. Bloomington, IN: Indiana University Press.

Taxidermia, undated. On-line. Available HTTP: http://www.taxidermia.hu/ (27 January 2006).

HORROR FILMS IN TURKISH CINEMA:
TO USE OR NOT TO USE LOCAL CULTURAL MOTIFS, THAT IS NOT THE QUESTION

Kaya Özkaracalar

Until the mid-2000s, horror movies had been very rare in Turkish cinema. Any discussion of this subject had to start with facing the challenging question of why it was the case that the vibrant popular cinema of Turkey had largely avoided horror while at the same time engaging in, for instance, genres as 'alien' as the western. However, in 2004, the Turkish film industry gave birth to a mini-boom of horror with the number of Turkish horror movies produced within a span of a few years surpassing that of all such movies made throughout the entire history of Turkish cinema.

The insider's answer as to why the Turkish cinema had largely stayed away from horror productions was offered by Bülent Oran (2001), a prolific scriptwriter who in his youth had also acted in an early Turkish horror movie, *Drakula Istanbul'da/ Dracula in Istanbul* (Mehmet Muhtar, 1953). Oran argued that Turkish audiences like to identify strongly with the characters on the screen and that horror movies do not offer grounds for such a strong level of identification. While horror movies might indeed entail more complex identification mechanisms than clear-cut melodramas or heroic movies, such an explanation seems insufficient in the face of the fact that foreign horror films had always existed in the Turkish market.

It is clear that Turkish audiences were not culturally or psychologically allergic to horror cinema, but Turkish filmmakers did not have the confidence that they themselves could make commercially viable horror movies. The insufficient technical assets of the Turkish film industry in such areas as special effects, make-up and set design come to mind in this regard (see Scognamillo and Demirhan 1999: 69). While it is true that several highly acclaimed masterpieces of Western horror cinema were low-budget efforts, most of those were the works of maverick auteurs. The lack of competent technical assets and know-how at the disposal of Turkish commercial filmmakers might understandably have acted as a deterrent to indulging in a genre where they felt such elements were necessary and they would not take risks until one or the other 'chance event' encouraged them and showed the way forward. And, as will be recounted, the one or two initial experiments in horror filmmaking apparently did not turn out to be such 'chance events'. On the contrary, the reverse happened decades later. However, as will be clear from the developments discussed on the section on the mini-boom of the 2000s below, 'chance events' themselves occur when a suitable environment has slowly matured.

Another issue which needs to be addressed is the absence of certain motifs frequently utilised in conventional Western horror movies in the Turkish cultural setting, such as vampires, werewolves, gothic castles or serial killers. At first sight, it might indeed be tempting to explain away the absence of a fully-fledged Turkish horror cinema with these cultural omissions. Such essentialist lines of thought actually fall flat in the face of the facts that cowboys were in principle as alien to Turkish audiences as vampires, or that the folk belief in vampires originated in Orthodox lands and was originally pretty much alien to, for instance, Western and Protestant populations – until being appropriated by popular cultures there.

Nevertheless, what has been shown as a recipe for the prospects of horror movie production in Turkey is the option of utilising the 'neglected' original horror motifs from the cultural heritage of Turkey itself (see Evren 2005: 165–7). This option is found not only in conventional wisdom expressed by commentators, but has also been appropriated by most of the filmmakers involved in the mini-boom of horror films in the 2000s. This chapter will problematise this rhetoric and strategy by showing the complexities at work through revealing the domestic behind the alien and the alien behind the domestic.

ISOLATED CASES OF HORROR FILMS IN THE HISTORY OF TURKISH CINEMA

The first Turkish horror film *Çığlık/Scream* (Aydın Arakon, 1949) is considered a lost movie.[1] The oldest Turkish horror film currently available for viewing is *Dracula in Istanbul*, directed by Mehmet Muhtar for the US-educated producer

Turgut Demirağ, who was one of the new generation of film producers in Turkey in the post-war era when the Turkish cinema industry was in its 'take-off' years. Demirağ was not particularly interested in horror cinema, but has explained his decision to commission a horror movie as part of his policy of trying his hand in all genres (see Scognamillo and Demirhan 1999: 70).

Contrary to what one might assume at first, this film is not a remake of Hollywood's *Dracula* (Tod Browning, 1931) within a Turkish setting. Instead, it is a screen adaptation of *Kazıklı Voyvoda* (*The Voivode with the Stakes*) (1928), a retitled, abridged and altered translation of *Dracula*, Bram Stoker's original novel, into Turkish. Furthermore, despite featuring 'Turkified' protagonists, *Dracula in Istanbul* is actually more faithful to Stoker's work in several ways than the earlier American movie.[2] For instance, many situations depicted by Stoker, such as the Count sporting canine fangs, were brought to the screen for the first time in this movie.

In addition, the link between Count Dracula and the historical Dracula, a Romanian warlord from the fifteenth century notorious for impaling his enemies *en masse*, is firmly present in *Dracula in Istanbul*. In Stoker's novel, Count Dracula describes himself in passing as a 'Voivode' who had fought the Turks in the past (Stoker 2002: 53). This vague reference must have initially seemed obscure and trivial and hence negligible to Western screenwriters adapting the novel. However, 'the Voivode with the Stakes', as he is known to the Turks, is an integral part of official medieval Turkish history as a convenient embodiment of the cruelty of the Turks' enemies. Hence, neither the Turkish abridged translation of *Dracula* nor the Turkish movie based on it could have failed to underline this connection.

One consequence of the Turkification of the protagonists in *Dracula in Istanbul* is that some of the most familiar elements in the iconography of vampire movies are missing. Since Turks are a predominantly Muslim people, no rosaries or holy wafers are to be seen in *Dracula in Istanbul*, where it is only garlic which repels the vampires. It should be noted that these Christian motifs have not been replaced by any Islamic counterparts, as they would be in two Turkish horror movies in the 1970s, which will be covered below. The abstinence from the implantation of Islamic iconography in this case is understandable in light of the fact *Dracula* was translated into Turkish at a time when Turkey was undergoing a full-swing secularisation drive at the hands of the new Republican regime.

Beyond being a curiosity item, *Dracula in Istanbul* is an average horror outing considered on its own merits, within the genre's terms. For instance, despite sophisticated black-and-white cinematography, the irrelevant stock library music indicates a lack of grasp of the genre on the part of the filmmakers. The box office performance of *Dracula in Istanbul* is not known,[3] but it does not appear to have been successful enough to spawn other horror movies in its immediate aftermath. It remained an isolated attempt in Turkish cinema and, even though horror figures such as vampires occasionally appeared in other genres such as historical epics, it was not followed by another Turkish horror movie for almost two decades.

The next Turkish horror movie came only in 1970 with *Ölüler Konuşmazki/ The Dead Don't Talk*, a black-and-white film produced and directed by prolific Z-grade filmmaker Yavuz Yalınkılıç. The largely incoherent plot involves an undead man who has risen from the grave to haunt a mysterious mansion. In the end, the zombie is destroyed by a *hoja* or Islamic priest reciting from the Quran, while his accomplices hold up copies of the holy book. Hence, *The Dead Don't Talk* implants Islamic motifs into a narrative frequently seen in the West and becomes the first example of this practice in Turkish horror cinema, which would be repeated in several other Turkish horror films in the future.

The second Turkish horror film from the decade, *Şeytan/Satan* (1974), is even more remarkable in this regard. It is a Turkish remake of *The Exorcist* (William Friedkin, 1973) in which the plot is set in Turkey. This unauthorised remake was commissioned by mainstream producer Hulki Saner obviously to cash in on the public interest aroused by media coverage of *The Exorcist* and helmed by well-known director Metin Erksan. *Satan* follows the plot structure of *The Exorcist* fairly closely, replicating all of the possession and exorcism scenes with less convincing special effects, even utilising the music score of the American movie.[4] The main difference between the two films is that the lead male protagonist, a priest in *The Exorcist*, is here a medical doctor who has chosen to devote himself to researching the 'belief and practice' of exorcism. However, in a not-dissimilar fashion to the way that the priest in *The Exorcist* is portrayed as having doubts about his faith, but eventually faces a confirmation of what the Catholic doctrine preaches, the protagonist of *Satan* is portrayed as a positivist and an implied atheist who eventually undergoes a similar ordeal within Islamicised rhetoric.[5]

Hence, the main theme of *Satan* is clearly the reconfirmation of Islam's power and validity within the conflict between modernisation and tradition in general and between materialism and religion in particular. Even after the plot has reached its conclusion, the finale of the movie reinforces this notion once again. At the end of *Satan*, the de-possessed girl piously visits a mosque where she feels an impulse to kiss the hand of a *hoja* who happens to be the key figure in helping the protagonists to contact an exorcist in the first place. The movie ends with the camera panning across the interiors of the mosque as Islamic music plays on the soundtrack.

The next time Turkish filmmakers would remake another American horror film would be more than twenty years later when veteran producer and occasional director Mehmet Alemdar turned out *Kader Diyelim/Let's Say It's Fate* (1995). This unreleased ultra-low budget, 16mm movie is a Turkish version of *Psycho* (1960). Its narrative, which follows Hitchcock's movie fairly closely, especially in the first act, even though the 'mother' angle is absent, is punctured by extra-diegetic singing sequences as in many Indian movies. Hence it is an example of the degree to which national filmmakers could bend and break generic conventions if they wanted to blend foreign sources with local traditions.

The last of the horror movies was from the Turkish art-house film circuit: *Karanlık Sular/Dark Waters* (1993), produced and directed by the US-educated young filmmaker Kutluğ Ataman as his debut feature. Far surpassing all of the earlier Turkish horror films in terms of craftsmanship in creating an atmosphere reminiscent of Alain Robbe-Grillet's *L'Immortale* (1963), and making best use of Istanbul locales to create a mood, *Dark Waters* has a deliberately multi-layered narrative with some too-obvious metaphors. At the heart of the plot is the quest of separate individuals and groups for a lost ancient manuscript, and there is a parallel storyline about the pressures on an elderly woman from an aristocratic background to dispose of her grand mansion for insurance money. Each character appears to stand for parts of Turkish identity or forces shaping this identity. For instance, the old woman with her mansion symbolises the Ottoman heritage which was the target of the bourgeois Republican regime intent on burning bridges with the past to integrate with the Western world. Consequently, her businessman family friend symbolises the Turkish bourgeoisie and Republican regime, his American colleague symbolises the US imperialism, and so on. And the main protagonist, the old woman's ghostly son, can be said to reflect the trials and tribulations of the tortured Turkish psyche under stress from all these forces pulling it in different directions.

Even though *Dark Waters*, which was also screened in several festivals abroad under the title *Serpent's Tale*, received very good reviews upon its theatrical release in Turkey, it fared miserably at the box office and failed to generate any interest in horror, remaining yet another isolated case in the history of Turkish cinema. In any case, by the time *Dark Waters* was made and released, the Turkish cinema was at the last stage of a chronic crisis, initiated by the proliferation of television in the 1970s and exacerbated by home video in the 1980s. The industry was about to give out its last breath with theatrical distribution of Turkish films and their attendance approaching zero level (see Öz and Özkaracalar 2007). However, this low point for Turkish cinema turned out to be the eve of a new revival, which would subsequently include a mini-boom of horror movies in its repertoire.

THE MINI-BOOM OF TURKISH HORROR FILMS IN THE 2000s

The first ground test for introducing horror into the repertoire of the flourishing new (post-crisis) Turkish cinema came with a horror-comedy hybrid, *Okul/ The School* (2004). This movie was the brainchild of Doğu Yücel, a young author of *fantastique* literature, who proposed the idea of adapting one of his novels for cinema to young directors Durul and Cem Taylan (see Yücel 2004: 37). The Taylan

Brothers were a natural choice for such a project, as they had earlier directed the television mini-series *Sır Dosyası/Mystery File* (1998), a Turkish version of *The X-Files*. *Mystery File* had not lasted very long due to insufficient ratings, but it had nevertheless caught the attention of Turkey's newly emerging horror fandom circles as a well-crafted and effective work.

Indeed, a fandom was slowly but noticeably emerging since the late 1990s, manifested as well as facilitated by such diverse factors as young lecturers educated abroad introducing contemporary horror film analysis into the curriculum of film studies in universities, young cinema journalists giving special attention to horror films, a new independent periodical titled *Geceyarısı Sineması* (*Midnight Cinema*) specialising in *cine-fantastique*, specialty stores selling bootleg copies of imported videos and the like, and a parallel growth of heavy metal music fandom which also took an interest in horror. It should also be added that the spread of Internet access was providing prospective fans with greater exposure to information and consolidating their interests. By the early 2000s, horror shorts by young, prospective filmmakers were being seen with increasing frequency in national film festivals. Hence, it appeared that the ground was set for new Turkish horror movies.

The Taylan Brothers immediately introduced Yücel to producer Sinan Çetin, one of the major figures of new Turkish cinema, who happened to be already toying with the idea of commissioning a horror movie from the Brothers. Without hesitation, Çetin bought the project Yücel was proposing (Yücel 2004: 37). The budget was not restricted, and *The School* became the first Turkish feature shot on Super 35 film stock as well as utilising chroma key special effects. Kevin Moore of Dream Theater was commissioned to write an original music score and Turkey's cult *fantastique* comics artist Galip Tekin to design the monster figures (even though they eventually took up very little screen-time). The cast was largely made up of television celebrities.

Çetin seemed uncertain how to market the movie as initial television spots and the theatrical teaser featured only the horrific scenes but the eventual theatrical trailer with the 'horribly funny' tagline gave the impression that it was basically a comedy with a ghost story plot. The finished product is actually a mild horror movie about a haunted high school with large doses of comedy which sometimes function as 'comic relief' but quite often stand on their own. Çetin was apparently cautious about the box office prospects of *The School* and issued only 65 prints for distribution, a number somewhat less than the average for major releases of mainstream Turkish movies. At the time of release, Durul Taylan expressed his opinion that 'maybe it will create less of an impact than we expect, but it will definitely have a place in the history of Turkish cinema' (2004: 14). Box office results proved him wrong as *The School* eventually drew 837,000 spectators, becoming the sixth most successful movie of 2004.

In retrospect, Yücel would comment that *The School* 'was a transition movie which would open the firmly locked gates of the industry to horror and it succeeded in this mission' (2006: 42). *The School* had opened in January 2004 and the tail end of the same year saw the release of Turkey's first straight horror movie in many years, *Büyü/Spell*, which had been commissioned by Faruk Aksoy, another major Turkish producer, for veteran director Orhan Oğuz; 140 prints of *Spell* were issued for distribution in a very strong release push. A large fire broke out during its premiere, threatening the lives of hundreds of people, including several celebrities, who were trapped in the theatre. Live news coverage of the rescue operation during evening prime time served as publicity for the movie. But despite being a very gory and occasionally atmospheric supernatural horror movie, *Spell* suffers from incompetent acting by some of the major cast, not to mention some of their lines being badly written, which caused unintentional bursts of laughter from audiences and unanimous critical snubbing from reviewers. Nevertheless the film was a major box office success with 551,000 spectators, coming close to the top ten grossing films of 2005.

Consequently, 2006 saw the unprecedented release of three new Turkish horror movies as well as one police thriller and one psychological thriller, both of which also tread firmly on horror territory. While *The School* and *Spell* had both been distributed by long-standing Turkish distributors Özen Film, the two US-based distributors working in Turkey, UIP and WB, also jumped onto the bandwagon this time, the former distributing the police thriller *Beyza'nın Kadınları/The Women of Beyza* (Mustafa Altıoklar, 2006) and the latter the insane asylum horror *Gen/Gene* (Togan Gökbakar, 2006). Özen Film itself naturally also continued with horror, feeling confident enough to distribute independent production *D@bbe* (2006), the first feature of a little-known young director-producer, Hasan Karacadag. The remaining two titles, *Araf/Limbo* (Biray Dalkıran, 2006) and *Küçük Kıyamet/Little Apocalypse* (Durul and Cem Taylan, 2006), were picked up by smaller-scale Turkish distributors which obviously saw their chances to carve a larger slice for themselves in the market. On the production side, these movies also showed variability. *The Women of Beyza* was directed and produced by Mustafa Altıoklar, one of the names responsible for the revival of Turkish cinema since mid-1990s. *Gene* was the first feature of a young director, but it was a commissioned work produced by a DVD distribution company which opted to make its first incursion into film production with a horror movie. *D@bbe* and *Limbo* were the self-produced first features of young horror-buff directors. Finally, the psychological thriller was the second collaborative effort of the Taylan Brothers with Yücel, this time financed by a lesser-known production company. As this brief overview shows, thanks to the box office successes of *The School* and *Spell*, the Turkish film industry's long-time historical neglect of horror was definitely overcome by 2006 and, on the contrary, horror had quickly come to be seen as a bankable asset by producers and distributors who were even giving chances to newcomers.

The outcome of this rush of production was mixed. *D@bbe*, the first to reach screens accompanied by an aggressive promotion campaign highlighted by extensive television spots, was once again a commercial success story with 539,000 spectators despite press reviews hitting on, above all, the performances of an amateurish cast. On the other hand, *Gene* became the first Turkish horror movie to open to favourable reviews and even win some awards at national festivals, but sold only 173,000 tickets, which was nevertheless around the average level for all Turkish movies released that year. *Limbo* fared worst, both in reviews and at the box office with 127,000 attendances, but it might not have been a big money-loser due to its very low budget. Meanwhile, *The Women of Beyza* and *Little Apocalypse* sold 272,000 and 382,000 tickets respectively.

The number of Turkish horror movies decreased to two in 2007. Of these, *Gomeda* (Tan Tolga Demirci, 2007) was yet another low-budget first feature of a young director which was picked up by a small-scale distributor. It failed to generate much interest and disappeared quickly from screens after gaining only 47,000 attendances. Nevertheless, Özen Film itself continued to give chances to horror by distributing *Musallat/Pestering* (Tan Tolga Demirci, 2007). It can be said that while the law of diminishing returns had started to show its effects on Turkish horrors by 2007, the marginal benefits of the genre have not apparently been depleted completely, as manifested by the release of yet another horror title, *Semum* (Hasan Karacadağ), in 2008.

FILMS OF THE MINI-BOOM

Most of the Turkish horror movies from this mini-boom utilise Islamic motifs. *Spell*'s trailer and posters had featured a verse from the Quran which warned that those who practice magic shall not be admitted to the heavens. The plot of the movie revolves around a group of archaeologists studying an ancient Turkish-Islamic civilisation becoming stranded in an excavation site and falling victim to a curse. *Gomeda* features a very similar narrative; this time, the victims stranded at an ancient site in the countryside are vacationing teenagers, and the ancient civilisation in question is a fictional one without Islamic trappings.

Spell director Oğuz has said that he 'was very glad to sign his name' to this movie because it was 'a thriller[6] which belongs to us, which comes from these lands' and actress Dilek Serbest was even more outspoken in calling it 'something never done before in Turkey, a horror movie about us, about our religion, not an imitation of the works of the foreigners' (*Spell* DVD extra features). And yet, both *Spell* and *Gomeda* display stereotypical stories very familiar from many Western horror movies. Furthermore, *Spell* also peculiarly sports what might justifiably be called an Orientalist attitude, again very familiar in some Western horror movies, with regards to the Kurdish population of 'eastern' Turkey.

D@bbe takes its title from the name of a mysterious being mentioned in the

Quran which will emerge from the earth to challenge those who broke their covenant with God and is interpreted as a sign of the apocalypse. The plot of the movie concerns the *dabbe* emerging from the Internet, and a small Turkish town being one of the sites of the apparent start of the apocalypse. At the time of its release in a review published in an Islamist fundamentalist newspaper film critic Ali Murat Güven (2006) wrote that, unlike previous Turkish horror films which were strongly informed by 'Western mythologies', *D@bbe* 'was carrying an Islamic discourse to the screens'. *D@bbe*, directed by a Japan-educated Turkish director assisted by a Japanese art director, is actually an unauthorised remake of the Japanese horror movie *Kairo* (Kiyoshi Kurosawa, 2001)[7] which has not been released in Turkey. The Turkish version, especially in its first and second acts, features over-the-top grossly scary visuals as well as some very gory scenes in contrast to the slow-moving and moody *Kairo* and yet the stories are identical until the source of the mayhem, the Internet, is revealed halfway in *D@bbe* to be of Quranic origin, whereas it remains not fully explained in the Japanese movie. (It should be noted that the tendency to fully explain everything to the audiences is a trademark of conventional Western-style film narration). In any case, *D@bbe* may indeed have an 'Islamic discourse', but through similar means to those employed in *Satan*.

Limbo, detailing the trials and tribulations of a young woman haunted by the ghost of her aborted child, was another horror movie upheld by the Islamist fundamentalist media. In a programme on an Islamist television channel broadcast on the day of its commercial release, a turbaned anchor-woman said the film was 'under a lynch threat from leftist film critics' and her guest, Islamist critic Güven continued in the same vein by claiming that while secularist media editors had refused to promote *D@bbe*, 'this time, certain circles were trying to undermine *Limbo* due to its conservative messages' and added that those same critics 'gladly praise movies like *The Exorcist, The Omen* (Richard Donner, 1976) and *Stigmata* (Rupert Wainwright, 1999) which nourish from Christian sources' (*Limbo* DVD extra features). Actually, *Limbo* avoids taking a clear-cut anti-abortion stand in principle because the abortion in the story is carried out after the pregnancy has progressed beyond the legal limits of abortion. On the other hand, what is far more problematic in the movie is that the aborted pregnancy was the result of an extra-marital relationship between a married man and a girl much younger than himself, and yet it is the female who gets the 'hellish punishments', referred to in the quotes from the Quran featured in the trailer and the poster of the movie.

Gene represents the opposite tendency, both to these titles and the possession movies *Pestering* and *Semum*, all of which strive to gain 'nourishment' from Turkey's own cultural depository. *Gene* director Togan Günbakar openly says that the movie's 'role models' were American and that the movie 'was made in such a way that it would look like an American production'. To this end, the production team 'preferred not to use any local motifs' (2006).

Distinct from these two opposing tendencies is the approach of the Yücel and Taylan Brothers team. At the time of *The School*'s release, Durul Taylan had stated that they 'cannot compete with the Americans on the technical level, but we believe we will cover this deficit thanks to our story where we have something to say' (2004: 14). *The School* is a 'teens in peril' movie where the graduating class of a high school is being haunted by the ghost of a fellow student who had committed suicide after being publicly ridiculed for his platonic love for the most beautiful girl on the campus. To make matters worse, the haunting had started when the graduation class was already under stress cramming for the impending university entrance examinations. The girl at the centre of the controversy is especially vulnerable psychologically since she is on the verge of a career decision which will shape her whole life as she decides whether she should apply for music conservatory where her natural talents seem to lie or for business management faculties with better material prospects. As even this much of a plot summary implies, the movie is a light-hearted critique of the Turkish education system and furthermore, the twist ending reveals a sentimental morality lesson, that one should follow the path where her heart leads. One critic especially touched upon the real ingenuity of *The School* by writing that 'despite its flaws, knowing that such a movie was made gives a hope ... that Turkish cinema can also begin to do what the humour magazines in Turkey are doing for years, that is visualising the daily life in Turkey by deforming it in humorous caricature and blending this with other genres' (Köstepen 2004: 83).

The Yücel-Taylan team continued in this vein in *Little Apocalypse*, but this time without any hint of humour, as that aspect of contemporary reality in Turkey which they visualised by 'deforming' was deadly serious. One unforgettable night in 1999, the entire population of Istanbul was woken by tremors in a neighbouring city which killed close to 20,000 residents there. Subsequently, seismologists announced the findings that a major earthquake hitting Istanbul itself was inevitable sometime in the coming decades, and unanimously warned that this impending quake will be an unprecedented disaster given the low quality of constructions in Istanbul unless the government immediately starts a major rejuvenation push. Yücel has explicitly stated that in *Little Apocalpyse*, they intended to 'underline that the necessary precautions are not being taken against the impending Istanbul quake' (2006: 43). The movie, set in an undetermined post-1999 year, starts with a bourgeois family in Istanbul feeling tremors. They manage to rush out of the city for a resort house only to encounter many uncanny happenings there, leading to a twist ending. The story has to do with the consequences of refusing to bow down to 'fate'.[8]

In brief, Yücel and the Taylans' movies provide an alternative avenue for making movies of a genuinely domestic nature by treading on socially relevant territories, rather than the easier way of utilising recognisable cultural motifs which lead, at best, into mazes or, at worse, dead ends of cultural essentialism.

Still from *Little Apocalypse* (2006)

NOTES

1   Little is known about it other than that the story takes place in a 'mysterious mansion' (Özgüç 1998: 55), but its recently surfaced theatrical poster (published in Evren 2005: 103), featuring illustrations of a green-faced man with blazing red eyes and a 'damsel in distress', indicates that it was indeed a horror movie.
2   For a detailed comparison of *Dracula in Istanbul* with *Dracula* as well as with Stoker's novel and its Turkish translation, see Özkaracalar 2003: 206–9.
3   Reliable and comprehensive box office returns began to be compiled in Turkey only in the late 1980s.
4   Pete Tombs and Giovanni Scognamillo call *Satan* 'more or less a scene-by-scene Turkish "version" of the original, much like the 1931 Spanish version of Tod Browning's *Dracula*' (1997: 113). In similar vein, Peter Blumenstock, in perhaps the first-ever English-language review of a Turkish horror film, says *Satan* 'follows William Blatty's *Exorcist* screen-play page by page' (1993: 29).
5   It is a moot point whether this Islamicisation of *The Exorcist*'s Catholic motifs in *Satan* is strictly valid in terms of the orthodox Islamic canon. While the practice of exorcism is not institutionalised in Islam to the degree it is in the Catholic Church, and the idea of possession by Satan himself (as in *Satan*) is indeed out-of-place, the Quran sanctions belief in malign metaphysical entities named *djins* which, by extension, are endowed with possession capabilities according to folk belief (and exorcising them was a very familiar folk practice in Turkey).
6   *Spell* is strictly a horror movie, but Oğuz's reference to it as a 'thriller' is typical of the attitude of filmmakers worldwide coming from outside horror cinema traditions, who have great difficulty in acknowledging that they themselves have made horror movies.

7   *Kairo* has also been officially remade in Hollywood as *Pulse* (Jim Sonzero, 2006) the same year as *D@bbe*.
8   At the movie's climactic moment, the caretaker of the resort, the ever-absent landlord's employee, who is terrorising the family, says to the mother of the tenant family: 'Do not resist, sister; it's in vain. This is my duty; I take away those whose turn has come. There is nothing to be afraid of, the time is up. First, you; then, the children, but you first. Come on, sister; let's not make the landlord wait.' However, the mother will not bow down, but struggles on in order to protect her children.

BIBLIOGRAPHY

Blumenstock, P. (1993) 'Turkey', *Video Watchdog*, 20, 27–31.
Evren, B. (2005) *Türk Sineması – Turkish Cinema*. 42nd Altın Portakal Film Festivali.
Günbakar, T. (2006) Interview with author, 15 June.
Güven, A.M. (2006) 'Türk Korku Sineması'nda İlk "İslami Bakış"', *Yeni Şafak* [daily newspaper New Horizon] 10 February.
Köstepen, E. (2004) 'Gerilimi Gizemsizleştiren Bir Anlatının İçindeki Yeni Diyaloglar', *Altyazı*, 26, 82–3.
Oran, B. (2001) Interview with author, 15 June.
Öz, Ö. and K. Özkaracalar (2007) 'Path Dependencies, Lock-In and the Emergence of Clusters: Historical Geographies of Istanbul's Film Cluster', Paper presented at the 23rd EGOS Colloquim, Vienna University.
Özgüç, A. (ed.) (1998) *Türk Filmleri Sözlüğü 1: 1914–1973 [Dictionary of Turkish Films 1: 1914–1973]*. Istanbul: SESAM.
Özkaracalar, K. (2003) 'Between Appropriation and Innovation: Turkish Horror Cinema', in S. J. Schneider (ed.) *Fear Without Frontiers*. Surrey: FAB Press, 205–17.
Scognamillo, G. and M. Demirhan (1999) *Fantastik Türk Sineması* [Turkish Cine-Fantastique]. Istanbul: Kabalcı.
Stoker, B. (2002) *Dracula*. Boston: Bedford St Martins.
Taylan, D. (2004) 'Taylan Biraderler Ne Diyor?', *Altyazı*, 25, 14.
Tombs, P. and G. Scognamillo (1997) 'Turkey: Dracula In Istanbul', in P. Tombs (ed.) *Mondo Macabro: Weird & Wonderful Cinema Around the World*. London: Titan Books, 103–15.
Yücel, D. (2004) 'Bir Filmin Hikayesi: *Okul*', *Altyazı*, 25, 37–9.
____ (2006) 'Bir Filmin Hikayesi: *Küçük Kıyamet*', *Altyazı*, 57, 42–4.

FILMOGRAPHY

4 (Ilya Khrjanovsky, Russia 2005)
12 Monkeys (Terry Gilliam, USA 1995)
28 Days Later (Danny Boyle, UK 2002)
71 Fragmente einer Chronologie des Zufalls/71 Fragments of a Chronology of Chance (Michael Haneke, Austria 1989)
2001 – A Space Odyssey (Stanley Kubrick, USA 1969)
Abandoned, The (Nacho Cerdá, Spain/UK/Bulgaria 2006)
Abominable Dr Phibes, The (Robert Fuest, UK/USA 1971)
Accused, The (Jonathan Kaplan, USA/Canada 1988)
Africa Addio (Gualtiero Jacopetti and Franco Prosperi, Italy 1965)
Al lado del Atlas (Guillermo Fernández Groizard, Spain 1994)
Alien (Ridley Scott, UK/USA 1979)
Allanamiento de morada/Nobody Knows Anybody, on DVD *Nadie conoce a nadie* (Mateo Gil, Spain 1999)
Alraune (Michael Curtiz and Edmund Fritz, Hungary 1918)
American Werewolf in London, An (John Landis, UK/USA 1981)
Anatomie/Anatomy (Stefan Ruzowitzky, Germany 2000)
Anatomie II/Anatomy II (Stefan Ruzowitzky, Germany 2003)
Ansiktet/Magician, The (Ingmar Bergman, Sweden 1958)
Antwerp Killer, The (Luc Veldeman, Belgium 1983)
A Propos de Nice (Jean Vigo, France 1930)
Araf /Limbo (Biray Dalkıran, Turkey 2006)
Assassin, The/Point of No Return (John Badham, USA 1993)
Au service du diable/Devil's Nightmare, The (Jean Brismée, Belgium/Italy 1972)
Aus dem Leben der Marionetten/From the Life of the Marionettes (Ingmar Bergman, Germany 1981)
AVP: Alien versus Predator (Paul W. S. Anderson UK/USA/Canada/Germany/Czech Republic 2004)

Baise-moi (Virginie Despentes, Coralie Trinh Thi, France 2000)
Barbe-bleue/Bluebeard (Georges Méliès, France 1901)
Basic Instinct (Paul Verhoeven, USA 1992)
Bathory (Juraj Jakubisko, Slovakia/Czech Republic/ UK/ Hungary/USA 2008)
Battle Royale II: Chinkonka (Kenta Fukasaku, Kinji Fukasaku, Japan 2003)
Bedtime with Rosie (Wolf Rilla, UK 1974)
Belve Feroci/Wild Beasts (Franco Prosperi, Italy 1984)
Benny's Video (Michael Haneke, Germany 1992)
Beröringen/Touch, The (Ingmar Bergman, Sweden 1970)
Beyza'nın Kadınları/Beyza's Women (Mustafa Altıoklar, Turkey 2006)
Big Heat, The (Fritz Lang, USA 1953)
Bila jednom jedna zemlja/Underground (Emir Kusturica, Yugoslavia/France/Germany/Hungary 1995)
Birds, The (Alfred Hitchcock, USA 1963)
Blade (Stephen Norrington, USA 1998)
Blade 2 (Guillermo del Toro, USA/Germany 2002)
Brat 1/Brother 1 (Aleksei Balabanov, Russia 1996)
Bride of Frankenstein (James Whale, USA 1935)
Bride Wore Black, The (François Truffaut, France 1968)
Brides of Dracula (Terence Fisher, UK 1960)
Britannia Hospital (Lindsay Anderson, UK 1982)
Bunker, The (Rob Green, UK 2001)
Burnt Offerings (Dan Curtis, USA/Italy 1976)
Büyü/Spell (Orhan Oğuz, Turkey 2004)
Caché/Hidden (Michael Haneke, Germany 2005)
Calvaire/Ordeal, The (Fabrice Du Welz, Belgium/France/Luxembourg 2004)
Cannibal Holocaust (Ruggero Deodato, Italy 1980)
Cat People (Jacques Tourneur, USA 1942)
C'est arrivé près de chez vous/Man Bites Dog (Rémy Belvaux, André Bonzel, Benoît Poelvoorde, Belgium 1992)
Children of the Corn (Fritz Kiersch, USA 1984)
Children of the Damned (Anton Leader, UK 1963)
Child's Play III (Jack Bender, UK/USA 1991)
Christmas Holiday (Robert Siodmak, USA 1944)
Ciganska magija/Gypsy Magic (Stole Popov, Republic of Macedonia 1997)
Çığlık/Scream (Aydın Arakon, Turkey 1949)
Cinque tombe per un medium/Terror Creatures from the Grave (Massimo Pupillo, Italy 1965)
Cobra Woman (Robert Siodmak, USA 1944)
Cradle of Fear (Alex Chandon, UK 2000)
Creep (Christopher Smith, UK/Germany 2005)
Criss Cross (Robert Siodmak, USA 1949)

Cry of the City (Robert Siodmak, USA 1948)
Curse of Frankenstein, The (Terence Fisher, UK 1957)
Custer of the West (Robert Siodmak, France/UK/USA 1967)
D@bbe (Hasan Karacadağ, Turkey 2006)
Danza macabra/Castle of Blood (Antonio Margheriti, Italy 1963)
Dark Mirror, The (Robert Siodmak, USA 1946)
Darkness (Jaume Balagueró, USA/Spain 2002)
Das Kabinett des Dr Caligari/Cabinet of Dr Caligari, The (Robert Wiene, Germany 1920)
Das Schlangenei/Serpent's Egg, The (Ingmar Bergman, USA/West Germany 1977)
Das Testament des Dr. Mabuse/The Testament of Dr. Mabuse (Fritz Lang, Germany 1933)
Dawn of the Dead (George A Romero Italy/USA 1978)
Dawn of the Dead (Zack Snyder, USA 2004)
Day of the Dead (George Romero, USA 1985)
Day of the Triffids, The (Steve Sekely, UK 1962)
Day the Earth Caught Fire, The (Val Guest, UK 1961)
De man die zijn haar kort liet kippen/Man Who had his Hair Cut Short, The (Andre Delvaux, Belgium 1968)
Dead Ringers (David Cronenberg, Canada/USA 1988)
Death Line (Gary Sherman, UK 1972)
Deathwatch (Michael J. Bassett, UK/Germany 2002)
Deer Hunter, The (Michael Cimino, UK/USA 1978)
Deliverance (John Boorman, USA 1972)
Dellamorte Dellamore/Cemetery Man (Michele Soavi, Italy/France/Germany 1994)
Dèmoni/Demons (Lamberto Bava, Italy 1985)
Dèmoni 2: L'incubo ritorna/Demons 2 (Lamberto Bava, Italy 1986)
Der Frosch mit der Maske/Fellowship of the Frog (Harald Reinl, Denmark/West Germany 1959)
Der Siebente Kontinent/The Seventh Continent (Michael Haneke, Austria 1989)
Descent, The (Neil Marshall, UK 2005)
Det Sjunde Inseglet/Seventh Seal, The (Ingmar Bergman, Sweden 1958)
Devil's Rejects, The (Rob Zombie, USA/Germany 2005)
Die Schlangengrube und das Pendel/The Blood Demon (Harald Reinl, West Germany 1967)
Die 1,000 Augen des Dr. Mabuse/1,000 Eyes of Dr. Mabuse, The (Fritz Lang, Germany 1960)
Dirty Weekend (Michael Winner, UK 1993)
Dnevnoy dozor/Day Watch (Timur Bekmambetov, Russia 2006)
Dog Soldiers (Neil Marshall, UK/Luxembourg 2002)
Double Indemnity (Billy Wilder, USA 1944)
Dracula (Tod Browning, USA 1931)

Dracula/Horror of Dracula (Terence Fisher, UK 1958)
Dracula: Prince of Darkness (Terence Fisher, UK 1966)
Drakula Halála/Death of Dracula, The (Károly Lajthay, Hungary/Austria/France 1921)
Drakula Istanbul'da/Dracula in Istanbul (Mehmet Muhtar, Turkey 1953)
Duel (Steven Spielberg, USA 1971)
Ein Toter Hing im Netz/Horrors of Spider Island (Fritz Böttger, West Germany/Yugoslavia 1959)
E tu vivrai nel terrore - L'aldilà/Beyond, The (Lucio Fulci, Italy 1981)
En Passion/Passion of Anna, The (Ingmar Bergman, Sweden 1968)
Eraserhead (David Lynch, USA 1977)
El buque maldito/Zombie Flesh Eater (Amando de Ossorio, Spain 1974)
El espinazo del diablo/The Devil's Backbone (Guillermo del Toro, Spain, Mexico 2001)
El laberinto del fauno/Pan's Labyrinth (Guillermo del Toro, Mexico/Spain/USA 2006)
El orfanato/The Orphanage (Juan Antonio Bayona, Mexico/Spain 2007)
El Segundo nombre/Second Name (Paco Plaza, Spain 2002)
El vampiro de la autopista/Horrible Sexy Vampire, The (Jim Delavena/José Luis Madrid, Spain 1970)
Et mourir de plasir/Blood and Roses (Roger Vadim, Belgium 1960)
Event Horizon (Paul W. S. Anderson, UK/USA 1997)
Evil Dead, The (Sam Raimi, USA 1981)
Evil Dead 2 (Sam Raimi, USA 1987)
Exorcismo (Juan Bosch, Spain 1974)
Exorcist, The (William Friedkin, USA 1973)
Fanny och Alexander/Fanny and Alexander (Ingmar Bergman, Sweden/France/West Germany 1982)
Fantastic Four (Tim Story, USA/Germany 2005)
Fantastic Four: Rise of the Silver Surfer (Tim Story, USA/Germany/UK 2007)
Fatal Attraction (Adrian Lyne, USA 1987)
Fausto 5.0 (Isidro Ortiz, Alex Ollé and Carlos Padrissa, Spain 2001)
Femme Fatale (Brain De Palma, USA 1991)
Fight Club (David Fincher, USA 1999)
File on Thelma Jordon, The (Robert Siodmak, USA 1950)
Fly, The (David Cronenberg, USA 1986)
Frágiles/Fragile (Jaume Balagueró, Spain/UK 2005)
Frankenstein Must Be Destroyed (Terence Fisher, UK 1969)
Freaks (Tod Browning, USA 1932)
Freeze Me (Takashi Ishii, Japan 2000)
Friday the 13th (Sean Cunningham, USA 1980)
Frisson des vampires/Shiver of the Vampire (Jean Rollin, France 1970)
From Dusk Till Dawn (Robert Rodriguez, USA 1996)
Funny Games (Michael Haneke, Austria 1997)

FILMOGRAPHY

Funny Games U.S. (Michael Haneke, USA, France, UK, Austria, Germany, Italy 2007)
Gen/Gene (Togan Gökbakar, Turkey 2006)
Golem, The (Paul Wegener and Henrik Galeen, Germany 1915)
Gomeda (Tan Tolga Demirci, Turkey 2007)
Gothic (Ken Russell, UK 1986)
Gritos en la noche/Awful Dr. Orloff, The (Jesus Franco, Spain/France 1962)
Grudge, The (Takashi Shimizu, Japan 2003)
Gruz 200/Cargo 200 (Aleksei Balabanov, Russia 2007)
Halloween (John Carpenter, USA 1978)
Hands of the Ripper (Peter Sasdy, UK 1971)
Hangmen Also Die! (Fritz Lang, USA 1943)
Hangover Square (John Brahm, USA 1945)
Haunting, The (Robert Wise, USA 1963)
Haunted Curiosity Shop, The (Walter R. Booth, UK 1901)
Haute tension/Switchblade Romance (Alexandre Aja, France 2003)
Hellraiser (Clive Barker, UK 1987)
Henry: Portrait of a Serial Killer (John McNaughton, USA 1990)
Hills Have Eyes, The (Wes Craven, USA 1977)
Hills Have Eyes, The (Alexandre Aja, USA 2006)
'Himenóptero' on DVD *Tesis* [1996] (Alejandro Amenábar, Spain 2002)
Hitcher, The (Robert Harmon, USA 1986)
Honogurai mizu no soko kara/Dark Water (Hideo Nakata, Japan 2002)
House of Dark Shadows/Dark Shadows (Dan Curtis USA 1970)
House of the Dead (Uwe Boll, Germany/Canada/USA 2003)
House of 1000 Corpses (Rob Zombie, USA 2003)
Hostel (Eli Roth, USA 2005)
Hostel II (Eli Roth, USA 2007)
Hotel Rwanda (Terry George, UK/USA/Italy/South Africa 2004)
I Know What You Did Last Summer (Jim Gillespie, USA 1997)
I lunghi capelli della morte/The Long Hair of Death (Antonio Margheriti, Italy 1964)
I Spit on Your Grave (Meir Zarchi, USA 1978)
I vampiri/The Vampires (Riccardo Freda, Italy 1957)
Il conde Dracula/Count Dracula (Jesus Franco, Spain/West Germany/Italy/Lichtenstein 1969)
Il mulino delle donne di pietra/Mill of the Stone Women (Giorgio Ferroni, Italy/France 1960)
Il pleut dans la maison/It Rains in my House (Pierre Laroche, Belgium/France 1968).
Incubo sulla città contaminata/City of the Walking Dead/Invasion By The Atomic Zombies/Nightmare City (Umberto Lenzi, Italy/Mexico/Spain 1980)
Inferno (Dario Argento, Italy 1980)
Inferno dei morti viventi/Zombie Creeping Flesh (Bruno Mattei, Italy/Spain 1982)
In Love with Dead (Guy J. Nijs, Belgium 1970)

Inquisición/Inquisition (Paul Naschy, Spain 1976)
Intacto/Intact (Juan Carlos Fresnadillo, Spain 2001)
Invasion of the Body Snatchers (Don Siegel, USA 1957)
Irréversible/Irreversible (Gaspar Noé, France 2002)
Jaws (Steven Spielberg, USA 1975)
Jungfrukällan/Virgin Spring, The (Ingmar Bergman, Sweden 1960)
Karanlık Sular/Dark Waters (Kutluğ Ataman, Turkey 1995)
Kader Diyelim/Let's Say It's Fate (Mehmet Alemdar, Turkey 1995)
Kairo (Kiyoshi Kurosawa, Japan 2001)
Kárhozat/Damnation (Béla Tarr, Hungary 1988)
King Kong (Merian C. Cooper and Ernest B. Schoedsack, USA 1933)
Killers, The (Robert Siodmak, USA 1946)
Kiss of the Vampire (Don Sharp, UK 1962)
Küçük Kıyamet/Little Apocalypse (Durul and Cem Taylan, Turkey 2006)
La Belle et la bête/Beauty and the Beast (Jean Cocteau, France 1946)
L'anneé dernière à Marienbad/Last Year at Marienbad (Alain Resnais, France 1961)
L'Immortelle (Alain Robbe-Grillet, France 1963)
La Haine (Mathieu Kassovitz, France 1995)
La lengua de las mariposas/Butterfly Tongue (José Luis Cuerda, Spain 1999)
La marca del hombre lobo/Mark of the Werewolf (Enrique López Eguiluz, Spain 1968)
La maschera del demonio/Black Sunday/Mask of the Demon/The Mask of Satan (Mario Bava, Italy 1960)
La maudite/Damned, The (De Meyst, Benoit, Jauniaux, Belgium 1949)
La noche de las gaviotas/Night of the Seagulls (Amando de Ossorio, Spain 1975)
La noche de Walpurgis/The Werewolf's Shadow (León Klimovsky, Spain 1970)
La noche del terror ciego/Tombs of the Blind Dead/Night of the Blind Terror Dead (Amando de Ossorio, Spain 1971)
La ragazza che sapeva troppo/Evil Eye, The (Mario Bava, Italy 1963)
La terza madre/The Mother of Tears (Dario Argento, Italy/USA 2007)
La torre de los siete jorobados/The Tower of the Seven Hunchbacks (Edgar Neville, Spain 1944)
Ladies Club (Janet Greek, USA 1986)
Land of the Dead (George Romero, USA 2005)
Laura (Otto Preminger, USA 1944)
Las garras de Lorelei/Grasp of the Lorelei (Amando de Ossario, Spain 1973)
Last House on the Left (Wes Craven USA, 1972)
Last of England, The (Derek Jarman, UK/West Germany 1987)
Last Seduction, The (John Dahl, USA, 1994)
League of Gentlemen (Basil Dearden, UK 1960)
Le corbeau/Raven, The (Henri-Georges Clouzot, France 1943)
Le locataire/The Tenant (Roman Polanski, France 1976)
Le manoir du diable/The Devil's Castle (Georges Méliès, France 1896)

Le Nosferat/ Nosferatu (Maurice Rabinowicz, Belgium 1974)
Les diaboliques/Fiends, The (Henri-Georges Clouzot, France 1955)
Les fleurs d'Harrison/Harrison's Flowers (Elie Chouraqui, France 2000)
Les lêvres rouges/Daughters of Darkness (Harry Kümel, Belgium/France/West Germany 1971)
Les mémés cannibales/Rabid Grannies (Emmanuel Kervyn, Belgium/France/Netherlands 1988)
Les quatre cents farces du diable/400 Tricks of the Devil, The (Georges Méliès, France 1906)
Les revenants/They Came Back (Robin Campillo, France 2004)
Les tueurs fous/Lonely Killers, The (Boris Szulzinger, Belgium 1972)
Les yeux sans visage/Eyes without a Face (Georges Franju, France/Italy 1960)
Le Temps Du Loup/Time of the Wolf (Michael Haneke, France 2001)
Lodger, The (Alfred Hitchcock, UK 1926)
Long Time Dead (Marcus Adams, UK/France 2001)
Los otros/The Others (Alejandro Amenábar, USA/Spain/France/Italy 2001)
Lost Highway (David Lynch, USA/France 1996)
Lost Weekend, The (Billy Wilder, USA 1945)
Lucker (Johan Vandewoestijne, Belgium 1986)
Lust for a Vampire (Jimmy Sangster, UK 1971)
'Luna', on DVD *Abre los ojos/Open Your Eyes* (Alejandro Amenábar, Spain 1997)
M (Fritz Lang, Germany 1931)
Macunaíma (Joaquim Pedro de Andrade, Brazil 1969)
Magic Sword, The (Walter R. Booth, UK 1901)
Magnificent Obsession (Douglas Sirk, USA 1954)
Malpertuis (Harry Kümel, Belgium/France/West Germany 1973)
Mangiati vivi!/Eaten Alive (Umberto Lenzi, Italy 1980)
Mama Dracula (Boris Szulzinger, France/Belgium 1980)
Mar adentro/The Sea Inside (Alejandro Amenábar, Spain/France/Italy 2004)
Matrix, The (The Wachowski Brothers, Australia/USA 1999)
Ministry of Fear (Fritz Lang, USA 1944)
Mira, of de teleurgang van de Waterhoek/Mira (Fons Rademakers, Netherlands/Belgium 1971)
Mondo Cane (Gualtiero Jacopetti, Franco Prosperi, Paulo Cavara, Italy 1962)
Monsieur Hawarden (Harry Kümel, Netherlands/Belgium 1968)
Mummy, The (Stephen Sommers, USA 1999)
Mummy Returns, The (Stephen Sommers, USA 2001)
Musallat/Pestering (Tan Tolga Demirci, Turkey 2007)
My Beautiful Laundrette (Stephen Frears, UK 1985)
Myortvye docheri/Dead Daughters (Pavel Ruminov, Russia 2007)
Natura contro/Cannibal Holocaust 2 (Antonio Climati, Italy 1988)
Nekromantik (Jörg Buttgereit, West Germany 1987)

Nightbreed (Clive Barker, USA 1990)
Night of the Demon (Jacques Tourneur, UK 1957)
Night of the Living Dead, The (George Romero, USA 1968)
Nikita (Luc Besson, France 1990)
Nochnoy dozor/Night Watch (Timur Bekmambetov, Russia 2004)
Nosferatu, Eine Symphonie des Grauens (F. W. Murnau, Germany, 1922)
Novaya zemlya/Terra Nova (Aleksandr Melnik, Russia 2008)
Nuova Guinea del Isola dei Cannibali/Guinea Ama (Akira Ide, Italy/Japan 1974)
Okul/The School (Durul and Cem Taylan, Turkey 2004)
Ôdishon/Audition (Takashi Miike, Japan 1999)
Ölüler Konuşmazki/The Dead Don't Talk (Yavuz Yalınkılıç, Turkey 1970)
Omega Man, The (Boris Sagal, USA 1971)
Omen, The (Richard Donner, USA 1976)
Orphée (Jean Cocteau, France 1950)
Öszi almanach/Almanac Of Fall (Béla Tarr, Hungary 1985)
Paradine Case, The (Alfred Hitchcock, USA 1947)
Patriot, The (Roland Emmerich, Germany/USA 2000)
Paura nella città dei morti viventi/City of the Living Dead/Gates of Hell, The (Lucio Fulci, Italy 1980)
Peeping Tom, (Michael Powell, UK 1960)
Persona (Ingmar Bergman, Sweden 1966)
Phantom Lady (Robert Siodmak, USA 1944)
Phantom of the Opera (Dario Argento, Italy 1998)
Porcile/Pigsty (Pier Paolo Pasolini, Italy 1969)
Pred dozhdot/Before the Rain (Milcho Manchevski, Republic of Macedonia/France/UK 1994)
Pro urodov I ljudei/Of Freaks and Men (Aleksei Balabanov, Russia 1998)
Promenons-nous dans les bois/Deep in the Woods (Lionel Delplanque, France 2002)
Psycho (Alfred Hitchcock, USA 1960)
Pulse (Jim Sonzero, USA 2006)
Quatermass and the Pit (Roy Ward Baker, UK 1967)
Quella villa accanto al cimitero/The House by the Cemetery (Lucio Fulci, Italy 1981)
¿Quién puede matar a un niño?/Who Can Kill a Child? (Narciso Ibáñez Serrador, Spain 1976)
Reazione a catena/Bay of Blood (Mario Bava, Italy 1971)
Rec (Paco Plaza, Spain 2002)
Reign of Fire (Rob Bowman, UK/Ireland/USA 2002)
Repulsion (Roman Polanski, UK 1965)
Resident Evil (Paul W. S. Anderson, UK/USA/Germany/France 2002)
Ringu/Ring, The (Hideo Nakata, Japan 1998)
Riten/Ritual, The (Ingmar Bergman, Sweden 1967)
Romasanta (Paco Plaza, Spain 2002)

S. (Guido Henderickx, Belgium 1998)
Sammy and Rosie Get Laid (Stephen Frears, UK 1987)
Såsom i en spegel/Through a Glass Darkly (Ingmar Bergman, Sweden 1960)
Sátántangó/Satantango (Béla Tarr, Hungary 1994)
Schock/Shock (Mario Bava, Italy 1977)
Scream (Wes Craven, USA 1996)
Secrets of a Door to Door Salesman (Wolf Rilla, UK 1973)
Semum (Hasan Karacadağ, Turkey 2008)
Sesso Perverso, Mondo Violento/Libidomania 2 (Bruno Mattei, Italy 1980)
Sesso Perverso/Sexual Aberration (Bruno Mattei, Italy 1981)
Seul contre tous/I Stand Alone (Gasper Noé, France 1998)
Severence (Christopher Smith, UK/Germany 2006)
Şeytan/Satan (Metin Erksan, Turkey 1974)
Shaun of the Dead (Edgar Wright, UK/France 2004)
Shining, The (Stanley Kubrick, USA 1980)
Silence of the Lambs, The (Jonathan Demme, USA 1992)
Sisters (Brian de Palma, USA 1973)
Sleeping with the Enemy (Joseph Ruben, USA 1991)
Soldier (Paul W. S. Anderson, UK/USA 1998)
Son of Dracula (Robert Siodmak, USA 1943)
Species (Roger Donaldson, USA 1995)
Spiral Staircase, The (Robert Siodmak, USA 1945)
Stepford Wives, The (Brian Forbes, USA 1974)
Stigmata (Rupert Wainwright, USA 1999)
Strange Affair of Uncle Harry, The (Robert Siodmak, USA 1945)
Straw Dogs (Sam Peckinpah, USA 1971)
Suspect, The (Robert Siodmak, USA 1944)
Suspiria (Dario Argento, Italy 1977)
Sweeney Todd: The Demon Barber of Fleet Street (George King, UK 1936)
Tattoo (Robert Schwentke, Germany 2003)
Taxidermia (György Pálfi, Hungary/Austria/France 2006)
Tenebrae (Dario Argento, Italy 1982)
Terror at the Opera/Opera (Dario Argento, Italy 1987)
Terrore nello spazio/Planet of the Vampires (Mario Bava, Italy 1965)
Tetsuo (Shinya Tsukamoto, Japan 1989)
Texas Chainsaw Massacre, The (Tobe Hooper, USA 1974)
Texas Chainsaw Massacre, The (Marcus Nispel, USA 2003)
Thelma and Louise (Ridley Scott, USA 1991)
Thing, The (John Carpenter, USA 1982)
Thing from Another World, The/The Thing (Christian Nyby, USA 1951)
Time Out of Mind (Robert Siodmak, USA 1947)
Tochka/Spot, The (Yuri Moroz, Russia 2006)

Twins of Evil (John Hough, UK 1971)
Tystnaden/Silence, The (Ingmar Bergman, Sweden 1962)
Un chien Andalou/The Andalusian Dog (Luis Buñuel, France 1929)
Una notte alla cimitero/Graveyard Disturbance (Lamberto Bava, Italy 1987)
Underworld (Len Wiseman, USA/Germany/Hungary/UK 2003)
Underworld: Evolution (Len Wiseman, USA 2006)
Urban Legend (Jamie Blanks, USA 1998)
Vampire Lovers, The (Roy Ward Baker, UK 1970)
Vampyr (Carl Theodor Dreyer, Germany 1932)
Van Helsing (Stephen Sommers, USA/Czech Republic 2004)
Vanilla Sky (Cameron Crowe, USA 2001)
Vargtimmen/Hour of the Wolf (Ingmar Bergman, Sweden 1968)
Vierges et vampires/Virgins and Vampires (Jean Rollin, France 1971)
Village of the Damned (Wolf Rilla, UK 1960)
Village of the Damned (John Carpenter, USA 1995)
Violent Shit (Andreas Schnaas, West Germany 1989)
Wanted (Timur Bekmambetov, USA/Germany 2008)
West Side Story (Robert Wise, USA 1961)
Wicker Man, The (Robin Hardy, UK 1973)
Witchfinder General (Michael Reeves, UK 1968)
Wolf Creek (Greg Mclean, Australia 2005)
Woman in the Window, The (Fritz Lang, USA 1944)
Wrong Turn (Rob Schmidt, USA 2003)
X (Luis Marías, Spain 2002)
Zombi/Dawn of the Dead (George A. Romero, Italy/USA 1978)
Zombie Chronicles, The (Brad Sykes, USA 2001)
Zombi 2/Zombie Flesh Eaters/Island of the Living Dead (Lucio Fulci, Italy 1979)
Zombie 3/Zombie Flesh Eaters 2 (Lucio Fulci, Italy 1988)
Zombie Holocaust (Marino Girolami, Italy 1980)

TELEVISION SERIES AND PROGRAMMES

A for Andromeda, (BBC, 1961)
Black Books, (Channel 4, 1999–2001)
Dr Who, (BBC, 1996 –89. relaunched 2005–present)
Het Eenzame Harten Buro/The Lonely Hearts Bureau, (VRT, 1990–92)
Jambers, (VTM, 1989–2000)
Little Britain, (BBC, 2003–05)
NV De Wereld/The World Inc. (VRT, 1989–93)
Office, The (2001–03)
Quatermass Experiment, The (BBC, 1953)

Quatermass II, (BBC, 1955)
Quatermass and the Pit, (BBC, 1959)
Spaced, (Channel 4, 1999–2001)
Striptease (RTBF, 1990–)
Teletubbies (BBC, 1997–2001)
Tribe, (BBC2, 2007)
Twin Peaks (ABC, 1990–92)

INDEX

absence 9–10, 27, 67, 70–1, 99–100, 118, 160, 221–2, 250
Acconci, Vito 138
Adams, Marcus 80
Agee, James 187, 189–91
Aguilar, Carlos 121
Aja, Alexandre 92, 99, 104–9, 111, 113, 208
alien 14, 33, 65–6, 72–3, 106, 225, 249–50
Allmer, Patricia 1, 9, 61–3, 91, 117, 155, 181, 221–2, 239
Amenábar, Alejandro 118–19, 141
Anderson, Paul 9, 14, 78
Aranda, Vicente 117, 122
Argento, Dario 2, 9, 14–15, 18–19, 25–32, 155–6, 159, 161, 167–77
art-horror 208–9
audiences 2, 9, 11, 15, 22, 35, 61–2, 80, 125–7, 137, 188, 191, 216, 222, 249–50

Baker, Roy Ward 46
Bakhtin, Mikhail 241, 246–7
Barker, Clive 31, 62, 70
Bava, Lamberto 137–9
Bava, Mario 11, 15, 18, 26, 29, 31, 51, 54, 56, 118, 155–6, 159
Bayona, Antonio 118, 150
BBC 66, 165
BBFC (British Board of Film Censors) 50–1, 61–2

Belvaux, Rene 36
Benjamin, Walter 133, 137, 196, 204
Bergman, Ingmar 3–4, 94, 183, 195–200
Blair, Tony 79, 85
bodies 97, 100, 132, 149, 158, 169, 175–6, 228–9, 239–42, 246–7
Boll, Uwe 139, 182
Bordwell, David 36, 45, 230
boundaries of horror 4, 65, 67, 93
Boyle, Danny 1, 63, 80, 83, 138
Brick, Emily 1, 9, 61, 91–3, 117, 155, 181, 221
Brismee, Jean 36, 41
British Horror 21, 33, 51, 61–3, 77, 85
Brophy, Philip 111
Browning, Tod 1, 44, 155, 251, 259
Burch, Noel 99–100
Butler, Ivan 53, 91, 112

cannibalism 156–7, 159, 222
Carpenter, John 31, 33, 66, 105, 214, 225
Catholicism 4, 39, 125–6
censorship 3, 9–10, 16, 50–1, 57, 61–3, 96, 100–1, 118, 124, 182, 189
Cherry, Brigid 2, 10, 16, 25, 31–2, 34
children 37, 49, 57, 62, 65–6, 68–74, 79, 84–5, 149–50, 204, 260
church 70–1, 125–8, 138, 215, 259
cinema history 135
cinema of damnation 230–2, 235–7

INDEX

cinematic discourses 104, 158
cinematic sensorium 167–76
Clarens, Carlos 53, 155
Clouzot, Henri-Georges 91
Clover, Carol 4, 93–6, 98, 107, 109, 228
Cocteau, Jean 91
communism 2, 20, 222, 226, 229–32, 242, 245
contemporary horror cinema 53, 56, 100, 107, 111, 114, 254
Corman, Roger 50, 52, 56
Craven, Wes 93, 105, 107, 208
Creed, Barbara 95, 108, 168
critics 10, 13–17, 35–9, 41–5, 51–2, 54, 92, 95, 105, 158, 163, 185, 187, 191, 195–6, 257
Cronenberg, David 70, 243
Curtis, Dan 32, 214
Cushing, Peter 56, 61–2

Deleuze, Giles 5, 156, 167–77, 245–6, 248
Del Toro, Guillermo 118, 149–50
Demons 29, 80, 131–9
Despentes, Virginie 92–3, 96
Devil 1, 36, 39–41, 91, 100, 118, 128, 149, 159, 233
devil worship 128
Dracula 1, 3, 6, 21, 34, 41, 43, 50–2, 54, 57–8, 118, 186, 189, 221–2, 225–9, 223–7, 247, 250–1
Dreyer, Carl-Theodor 42, 167

Eurogore 26–9, 31–2
European Union 2, 62, 242
evil 9–10, 13–21, 46, 99–100, 105–7, 126–7, 156, 192, 196, 211, 225–7, 230, 234

FAB Press 19
fan canon 10, 25–34
fan cultures 16, 22, 25
film noir 100, 147, 185, 187, 192
films
    anti-Nazi 196, 198
    cannibal 161
    chernukha 232–7

cult 41, 158, 247
gore 27, 32, 182
proto-horror 182
slasher 4, 93–4, 99, 101, 105, 108–9, 236
vampire 21, 92
zombie 139, 156–65
Fisher, Terence 52, 54
Franco, Jess 2, 41, 92, 122
Franco regime 117–18, 122–3, 128, 142
Franju, Georges 32, 91, 118
Frankenstein 21, 51–3, 189, 225, 230, 232, 235
Freeland, Cynthia 32, 108, 208–10, 215
French horror cinema 91–2
Freud, Sigmund 103, 106, 112
Friedkin, William 70, 123–4, 252
Fulci, Lucio 18–19, 25, 28, 135–8, 155–6, 164

Galt, Rosalind 226–7, 229–31
gang rape 99
gaze
    male 107, 110, 113
gender 4, 10, 28, 31, 77–80, 83–5, 95, 107–9, 111, 143, 146, 160, 191
genre cinema 149, 158, 164, 225, 234
German horror cinema 182
Goebbels, Josef 196–8
gothic 32, 52, 56, 61–2, 74, 118, 138–9, 149–50, 175, 182, 250
grotesque 56, 160, 188, 198–9, 222, 232, 235, 239–41, 246–8
Hammer films 33, 50–1, 62, 92, 118
Haneke, Michael 182–3, 207–19
Harper, Jessica 14, 32, 170
Hawkins, Joan 16, 122
Hebdige, Dick 50, 56
Hill, Derek 53, 91
Hills, Jennifer 98
Hitchcock, Alfred 4, 30, 32, 37, 61, 91, 106, 118, 138, 143, 186, 189, 208, 252
Hitler, Adolf 188, 196–201
Hollywood 3–4, 14–15, 19, 33, 94, 100, 141, 157, 181, 186–92, 226, 233–4, 251

273

horror
  bodily 232, 234
  contemporary 53, 56, 100, 107, 114, 254
  modern 1, 4–5, 44, 105, 111–14, 158
horror aesthetics 29, 31
horror cinema traditions 259
horror consumption 10
horror cycles 26
horror fans 9, 13, 19, 29, 31
horror fiction 106–8, 112
horror film production 1, 51, 181
horror films
  contemporary Hungarian 247
  early British 61
  early Spanish 117
  explicit 38
  pretentious 186
  psychological 104, 187
  realist 208–10, 215
  tasteless 52
  true 113
horror genre 4, 10, 41, 68, 108, 111, 122, 155, 190, 192, 233–6
horror motifs 69, 72, 222, 233
horror production 2, 21, 92, 181–2, 249
horror tradition 9, 17, 91, 142, 162, 164
Hutchings, Peter 2, 4, 9, 13–14, 51–2, 62
Huxley, David 1, 9–10, 49, 61, 91, 117, 155, 181, 221

Ishii, Takashi 94
Italian horror cinema 16, 26, 33, 155

j-horror films 33, 234
Jancovich, Mark 4, 27, 121, 183, 185–93
Japanese horror 33, 94, 257
Jones, Alan 19, 92
Jovovich, Milla 14

Kermode, Mark 62
Kervyn, Emmanuel 39, 46
killers 108–9, 175, 210, 150

Kinder, Marsha 117
Kneale, Nigel 66
Kubrick, Stanley 70, 74, 143–4, 214
Kumel, Harry 35, 37–8, 41–2

Landis, John 82
Lang, Fritz 181, 183, 188, 195–6, 200, 204
Lee, Christopher 3, 54, 56, 62, 118, 182

McLean, Greg 100
McGillivray, David 54
Madness 104, 111–12, 149, 167
Margheriti, Antonio 50, 56, 118
Marshall, Neil 33, 63, 80, 111
Masculinity 66, 68, 79–80, 83, 85
Mattei, Bruno 156–8, 161–5
Melies, Georges 1, 91
Miike, Takashi 94
Modernity 70–1, 132, 204, 229–30
Modleski, Tania 111
mondo films 155, 161–5
monsters 20, 34, 54, 79–80, 105–6, 108, 133, 137, 208–9, 212, 216, 227
Mulvey, Laura 107, 109, 171
Murders 32, 43, 128, 146, 156, 171, 175, 199–201
Murnau, Friedrich Wilhelm 1, 3, 37, 42, 181–2, 229, 247
Myths 3, 66, 87, 183, 221–2, 244, 247–8

Nakata, Hideo 33, 208, 234
Naschy, Paul 41, 117–18, 121–9
Nazi Germany 189, 197, 199, 242
Newman, Kim 20, 135, 138, 158
Nispel, Marcus 82, 106
Noe, Gaspar 92–3, 100

Ossario, Amando de 118
Otherness 3, 74

panics, moral 10
Polanski, Roman 26, 33, 42, 51, 70, 96, 104

INDEX

Politics 36, 63, 67, 78, 94, 97–8, 106, 127, 139, 157–66, 241–2
Powell, Michael 62, 106, 145, 208
Price, Vincent 57
priests 39, 126
Pupillo, Massimo 51

Rabinowicz, Maurice 43
Rape 35, 43–6, 84, 92–3, 132, 201, 235
rape-revenge films 92–102
Ray, Jean 37
Realism 37–8, 40, 43, 78, 166, 230
Reeves, Michael 56, 62
religion 35, 39, 117, 122, 125, 128, 148, 222, 252, 256
Resnais, Alain 42
Rice, Anne 21
Rilla, Wolf 63, 65–75
Rodriguez, Robert 100
Romero, George 13, 82, 131–8, 156, 165
Rosenberg, Abel 200, 202
Roth, Eli 1, 70, 100, 106, 208, 222, 228

Sangster, Jimmy 46, 50, 54
Satan 15, 31, 123–4, 252, 257, 259
Schmidt, Rob 106
Schneider, Steven 2, 4, 17, 29, 37, 91, 168
Scott, Ridley 33, 93, 96, 146
Sekely, Steve 83
serial killers 108, 175
sex 10, 38–46, 53–4, 65, 92, 96–100, 107, 110, 122, 139, 147, 167, 188, 202, 229, 232
sexualised violence 40, 45, 99
Seyrig, Delphine 41–2
Sharp, Don 54
Siodmak, Robert 181, 185–93
Smith, Christopher 80, 222
Snyder, Stephen 214
Snyder, Zack 138
Soavi, Michelle 28–9
Sommers, Stephen 20
Sontag, Susan 30, 65

Spanish horror cinema 117–23
Stam, Robert 157, 159, 164–5
Steele, Barbara 32, 56
Stevenson, Robert Louis 105
Stojanova, Christina 221–2, 225–6, 230, 233
surrealism 17, 38, 42, 44, 232
survival 11, 84, 140, 143
suspense 31, 53, 68, 143–4, 147–8, 189–90, 213, 232, 234
Szulzinger, Boris 43

terror 14, 17, 30, 51, 56, 65, 85, 104, 109, 114, 123, 162, 167, 171, 173–4, 188–92, 200–1, 208, 226, 228, 230, 234, 260
textuality 111
Thatcher, Margaret 77–9
Third Reich 197–8
Third World 158–60, 165
thriller 13, 91, 142, 144, 146–51, 156, 182–5, 190–2, 213, 226, 233, 236, 255–6, 259
Thrower, Stephen 18–19
Tohill, Cathal 2, 17–18
Tombs, Pete 2, 17–18
Trevelyan, John 50–1, 57
Truffaut, Francois 99
Tsukamoto, Shinya 29
Turkish horror cinema 4, 222, 249–60

Umland, Samuel 183, 195
Universal horror films 181
US horror films 20

Vadim, Roger 42, 91
Vampires 21, 51, 56–7, 92, 155, 183, 209, 214, 221, 250–1
Vergerus, Hans 199–204
Vietnam war 53, 215
viewers 28, 34, 213
violence 10, 14, 36, 38–45, 56, 72, 79, 83–4, 94, 96–100, 105, 107, 111–12, 117, 124, 146–8, 156, 164, 167, 182–3, 207–18, 222, 230, 232

Wegener, Paul 181
Wertham, Frederik 49, 53
western horror cinema 221
Whale, James 21
Wilder, Billy 96, 185
Willis, Andy 118, 121–2
Wise, Robert 82
Wiseman, Len 19–20

Wood, Robin 40, 208, 212
world cinema 33
Wright, Edgar 63, 80
Wyndham, John 68

Zarchi, Meir 92, 94
Zombie, Rob 100, 106
zombies 80–2, 132–40, 161, 165, 214

GPSR Authorized Representative: Easy Access System Europe, Mustamäe tee
50, 10621 Tallinn, Estonia, gpsr.requests@easproject.com

www.ingramcontent.com/pod-product-compliance
Lightning Source LLC
Chambersburg PA
CBHW050900300426
44111CB00010B/1309